Judaism:
Myth, Legend, History, and Custom, from the Religious to the Secular

Other fine books from the same publisher:

The Traitor and The Jew, by Esther Delisle
Zen & the Art of Post-Modern Canada, by Stephen Schecter
The Last Cod Fish, by Pol Chantraine
Seven Fateful Challenges for Canada, by Deborah Coyne
*A Canadian Myth: Quebec, between Canada and the
Illusion of Utopia*, by William Johnson
Economics in Crisis, by Louis-Philippe Rochon
Dead-End Democracy, by Yves Leclerc
Voltaire's Man in America, by Jean-Paul de Lagrave
Moral Panic: Biopolitics Rising, by John Fekete

Canadian Cataloguing in Publication Data

Arnold, Abraham J.
  Judaism: Myth, Legend, History, and Custom, from the Religious to
  the Secular.
  Includes bibliographical references and index

  ISBN 1-895854-26-1

  1. Judaism.   2. Judaism - Customs and practices.   3. Jews - Social life
and customs.   4. Antisemitism   5. Fasts and feasts - Judaism.   6. Israel.
I. Title.
  BM 155.2.A76 1995   296   C95-940268-3

Cover art: detail of mosaic from the synagogue of Hamat (4th century).

To receive our current catalogue and be kept on our mailing list for
announcements of new titles, send your name and address to:

Robert Davies Publishing,
P.O. Box 702, Outremont, Quebec, Canada H2V 4N6

Abraham J. Arnold

Judaism:

Myth, Legend, History, and Custom,
from the Religious to the Secular

edited by Käthe Roth

ROBERT DAVIES PUBLISHING
MONTREAL—TORONTO

This book may be ordered in Canada from

General Distribution Services,
☎1-800-387-0141 / 1-800-387-0172 FAX 1-416-445-5967;
in the U.S.A., dial toll-free 1-800-805-1083;

or call the publisher, toll-free throughout North America:
1-800-481-2440, FAX (514)481-9973.

The publisher takes this opportunity to thank the
Canada Council and the *Ministère de la Culture du Québec*
for their continuing support.

Part of chapter two first appeared in *Outlook* (April and May, 1990)
and in *The Jewish Post* (Winnipeg, 4 April 1990).
Part of chapter three appeared in the *Jewish Western Bulletin* (Vancouver)
as an article entitled "Literature, Language and Jewish Culture"
(14 and 21 Jan. 1955).
Parts of chapter four appeared in the *Canadian Jewish News* (Toronto, 16 Sept.
1977, 27 Apr. 1978, 25 Nov. 1979) and *Western Jewish News*
(Winnipeg, 30 Apr. 1978, 29 Nov. 1979).
Parts of chapters six, seven and eight appeared in the *Canadian Jewish News* (5
Sept. 1975, 24 Sept. 1976) and in *Western Jewish News* (12 Sept. 1974, 4 Sept.
1975, and 16 Sept. 1976). An article entitled "The High Holidays, from the Re-
ligious to the Secular" first appeared in *Outlook* (Vancouver, Sept.-Oct. 1987)
and in the *Jewish Post* (7 Sept. 1988). An article entitled "Reinterpreting Chanu-
kah—from Zadok to *Apikoros*" appeared in *Outlook* (Dec. 1992).
Part of chapter ten appeared in an article entitled
"Human Rights and Civil Liberties" in Outlook (July-Aug. 1985).
Parts of chapter eleven appeared in *Western Jewish News* and
Canadian Jewish News in the 1970s.

For my Grandchildren

Vanessa and Jonah
Manya, Jennifer, Bryon
and
Jeremiah

Table of Contents

PART ONE:
FROM THE BIBLICAL ERA
TO JEWISH SECULAR HUMANISM

(Notes are at the end of each chapter)

Acknowledgments

This book is one of several retirement projects that I have undertaken since 1988, all of them based on plans I had long wanted to fulfil. This is the second project to come to fruition. The first one was carried out during 1991-92, when over twenty linear feet of my manuscripts, published works, and other papers were placed with the Provincial Archives of Manitoba (PAM). These were primarily acquired during more than forty years working as a journalist and editor in four cities.

My spouse, Bertha Arnold, served as an Archives volunteer to sort and organize the papers in preparation for the development of a database and a Finding Aid. Without Bertha this project could not have been carried out.

I extend thanks to the Provincial Archives for accepting my papers. My appreciation also goes to the Manitoba Heritage Federation and the Jewish Foundation of Manitoba for their grants in support of the development of a computerized database.

My special thanks go to members of the Archives staff, and especially to Barry Hyman, who advised and assisted in the preparation of the Finding Aid. I also thank the archivists for their help whenever I came in to do research for the book for which my own papers were the first source.

In the writing of the manuscript, my mentor has been Sybil Shack, who read and critiqued every chapter in its initial draft; I am deeply grateful to her. Yvonne Petrie assisted me with my research for the book. Earlier, she also worked in preparing the database for my Finding Aid. Special thanks are due as well to R.B. Chochinov, my computer programmer, for his ongoing help.

I wish to thank Nina Thompson, librarian at the Winnipeg Jewish Public Library, for responding to many requests, and Shirley Pinsky, the former librarian. My thanks also go to Bonnie Tregebov and Esther Slater at the Jewish Historical Society of Western Canada, for their help, to Esther Leven for translations from Yiddish, and Sally Chochinov for typing assistance.

Carol Rose was kind enough to loan me several important books from her library and to read and comment on the chapter on women. Thanks are also due to librarians at the University of Manitoba, the University of Winnipeg, and the Winnipeg Centennial Library.

Finally I must express my great appreciation to Robert Davies for undertaking to publish this book, and to Käthe Roth, the editor.

Background:
A Personal Memoir

I was born in 1922 into a nominally Orthodox Jewish family; my mother kept a kosher kitchen until the early 1940s; she also lit the Sabbath candles. My father attended synagogue on the High Holidays (Rosh Hashonah and Yom Kippur) and sometimes on Sukkot, Simchat Torah, Passover, and Shavuot, if he didn't have to work on those days. The only Sabbath proscription we observed for a while was not to write on Saturday.

When I was six, my maternal grandmother enrolled me in Hebrew school, which was held in a converted house. A little later, around 1929, this school became part of the United Talmud Torah in a new building at St. Joseph and Jeanne Mance, where I attended two hours a day, after elementary school, Monday to Thursday, and Sunday morning, until I was thirteen. Though she started me on a traditional Jewish education, I never thought of my grandmother as *frum*, strictly pious, but rather as *orentlach*, honest in her approach to life and to Jewishness. She lit the Sabbath candles, but she did not strictly observe the Sabbath rules. In fact, we often visited Grandma's house on Friday evening to listen to radio programs since we didn't have our own radio.

My own active interest in Jewish culture began at age ten, when my Aunt Ethel enrolled me as a juvenile member in the YMHA, then on Mount Royal Avenue at Jeanne Mance. In 1932, I joined the B'nai David club. We read Bible stories in

English, learned public speaking, and I began to write for the *Junior Beacon*. In the fall of 1933, our group became the Balfour Club, reflecting an interest in the developing Jewish homeland in Palestine. (Sir Arthur Balfour was the British Foreign Secretary, in World War I, who made the formal promise of a Jewish homeland that became known as the Balfour Declaration.) In 1934, the club name was changed again, to the Lord Reading Club, after Sir Rufus Isaacs, an English Jew who became the Marquess of Reading and served as viceroy of India in the 1920s. This change reflected an expanded interest in Jewish and world affairs. The Lord Reading Club continued to be active until 1942, when its members began to enlist in the armed forces and work in support of the war effort.

Our home celebrations for Passover, Chanukah, and Purim were very important, as were the festive meals at the High Holidays. At Chanukah, we lit the candles even when we had no Menorah; we ate *zudik haise*, sizzling hot *latkes* (potato pancakes), received Chanukah *gelt*, and spun the *dreidel* (Chanukah top). I remember with nostalgia the "Y" holiday programs and my first experience in theatre in the Chanukah and Purim plays. I don't remember ever wishing for a Christmas tree. Our winter holiday was the feast of the "miracle" of the lights, no other. And at Purim we ate *hamentashen*, cookies filled with prunes and nuts or poppy seeds, modelled on the three-cornered hat of Haman (the villain of the Purim story, whose name we drowned out when the Book of Esther megillah was read aloud).

The Passover seder, a month after Purim, was our biggest celebration. I remember bringing home wine from a relative to supplement my mother's wine, and above all, watching my grandfather making the *charoses* (symbolizing the mortar used by the Jewish slaves in Egypt), a confection of nuts, apples, and wine, in his brass *shteisel* (mortar and pestle). Out on the street during Passover week, we played with filbert nuts instead of marbles.

For several years, I attended synagogue on the High Holidays, and one year I sang in a synagogue choir; I also attended on Sukkot and Simchat Torah. We ate *boxer* (carob fruit) on Tu b'Shevat, the New Year for Trees, and cheese blintzes on Shavuot.

In, 1933 I joined the "Y" Junior Congregation and attended services faithfully every Saturday morning. I returned to the "Y" every Saturday afternoon for Havdallah, the end-of-Sabbath ceremony, and I sang in the Havdallah choir. This ceremony had an added attraction: it was followed by a movie program for children, who were barred from attending regular movies under the age of sixteen.

At age twelve, I became a cantor (prayer leader) at the "Y" junior congregation, where I had my Bar Mitzvah when I was thirteen. By that time, I was an officer of the congregation; when I was fourteen I served as congregation president. I also began learning to be a Baal Koreh, a Torah reader. By age fifteen, however, I was disenchanted and gave up on religious practice.

Unlike most other Jewish children of that era, my mother tongue was not Yiddish but English. My Polish-born maternal grandmother had been brought up in England and was fluently bilingual in English and Yiddish. My mother and her siblings spoke English as their first language, and my mother did not learn Yiddish until she got married. My Yiddish-speaking father, an orphan, was brought to Canada from Rumania in 1904, at the age of fourteen, by an aunt and uncle who had come to Montreal a few years earlier. My maternal grandfather, from Belorus, also Yiddish-speaking, migrated to England as a young adult and married my grandmother in the mid-1890s. They came to Canada with five children in 1909. The social and cultural milieu of my father and grandfather did not extend beyond the *landsmanshaft* benefit societies to which they belonged. With regard to language and culture, female influence was predominant in our family. Apart from Hebrew school and the stress placed on speaking good English, I was free to choose my own cultural direction.

When I was fourteen, I was invited to a meeting of Young Judea, a Zionist youth group; I went only once. Some of my friends joined the Hashomer Hatzair, a left-wing Labour Zionist youth group, but I was not attracted to that group either. At the "Y" we did discuss questions relating to the Jews in Palestine, but, since I understood Zionism to mean dedication to the idea of settling in Palestine, I was not drawn to it. I believed that Jews who lived in countries where they were persecuted should be able to settle in Palestine if they chose to do so, but I did not see the "Homeland" idea as the solution to the "Jewish problem" for all Jews. I always felt strongly Canadian, and of course I still do.

Growing up in Montreal in the Great Depression, I felt the pangs of poverty but not the sting of anti-Semitism. I learned about the special threat that fascism presented to the Jews and I knew that anti-Semitism existed, even in Quebec. Yet I felt the warmth of Jewish life in my family and at the YMHA, even though we moved to a new flat every May Day from 1928 to 1934, which meant that I attended three different public schools until I became part of the larger flock of Jewish students at Baron Byng High School (now a food bank). In addition to regular studies, there was the school choir and its annual operatic concert–Carmen, Faust, Martha–and even the Christmas concert, for which each class competed with its own song. And on the street, we learned that French Canadians could be good neighbours.

All of these things contributed to making me a secular humanistic Jew with an abiding interest in and concern for Canada and for the Jews. When I did become politically aware, in my late teens, I was attracted by socialist internationalism, but this did not diminish my interest in Jewishness–Yid-dishkeit. In fact, my Jewish cultural interest deepened. After I graduated from high school, I worked in an office and re-mained active at the "Y." I joined the Journalism Club and learned the elements of the craft that led me to become a full-fledged journalist. Rejected for military service on medical grounds, I served on the "Y" War Efforts Committee, and represented the organization on the Youth Council of Cana-dian Jewish Congress, which launched a war-effort program for blood donors and salvage.

My family moved to Toronto in 1942. In 1945, I began working as a journalist, and in the summer of 1946 I became editor of an Anglo-Jewish news service. A year later I became the English editor of the Yiddish-language newspaper *Vochen-blat*, the *Canadian Jewish Weekly*, a position I held for eighteen months. In Toronto's left-wing secular Jewish movement, I began to broaden my appreciation of Jewish history, literature, language, and culture.

Early in 1949, I began my tenure as publisher-editor of the *Jewish Western Bulletin* in Vancouver, a position I held until 1960, when I returned to Montreal to become public-relations director for the Jewish Federation. Late in 1965 I became western regional director with Canadian Jewish Congress in Winnipeg and served until early 1973; during this period I was the founding staff member of the Jewish Historical Society of Western Canada.

As a secular Jew, I never gave up my active association with the Jewish community; I have served as a volunteer with various Jewish groups, as well as participating in human-rights and inter-cultural programs, some of which also involved inter-faith activities that were, nevertheless, secular and humanistic in nature.

My major work over the years has been as a journalist, writing on Jewish and related themes. My own articles on Jewish festivals and customs, culture, and history, have been the primary source for this book. As I began to reconsider my earlier work, in the summer of 1993, I found it necessary to review sources previously used, right back to the Jewish Holy Scriptures. I have also explored many new and old works on Jewish history, religion, literature, and philosophy. These works have become part of my renewed voyage of discovery leading me to more varied sources of Jewish culture in my quest for a deeper understanding of why I am a secular Jew.

Why I Wrote This Book

I wanted to explain to my own children and grandchildren how I see my Jewishness and give them an opportunity to think about their own identity as Jews in a reasonable way, without necessarily becoming associated with a synagogue. I also wanted to explain myself as a Jew to the larger Jewish community in which I have worked for most of my adult life as a journalist and editor, as a staff member of several organizations, and as a volunteer. And, of course, I hope that friends and colleagues in human-rights, ethno-cultural, and inter-faith organizations will also appreciate the approach I am taking to the heritage of Judaism.

Since the 1940s, most, though not all, of my writing has been on subjects that might be described as Jewish issues, and I have been involved in activities in which I believe I have acted out of a Jewish impulse for peace, justice, and equality for all people. In the religious tradition pioneered by the ancient Pharisees, every Jew may personally commune with God without an intermediary. As a consciously secular Jew, I have sought out the elements of Jewish culture and traditions that make it possible for me to remain a practising Jew without following the belief in a supernatural god.

Among Jews, many of those who break with the synagogue do not know what to replace it with, and some believe that they are no longer "good Jews." I hope that this book will help such people to find a broader understanding of what it is to be a Jew and possibly to become associated with elements of Judaism with which they may personally identify, whether through history or literature or with new types of non-theistic observance.

I also hope that this book will help illuminate the development of secularist views and tendencies in Jewish life going back to the time of the Hasmonean Maccabees. Since the onset of the Haskalah (Jewish Enlightenment), some two hundred years ago, people who rejected traditional Jewish religious practices have made creative contributions to Jewish culture. Contemporary Jewish secular humanists and their organizations are among the heirs of the Haskalah; they offer another path by which Jews may be creatively Jewish without necessarily being religious in the traditional sense.

In this book, I have tried to bring to light aspects of the Jewish experience that fall between biblical memory and lachrymose history. It has also been my objective to show that the ultimate inhumanity of the Holocaust makes it necessary to chart a secular path to the future, through Jewish history. The rise of the modern state of Israel, though a break with the belief in the coming of a "Messiah," should be seen as part of a continuum on the broad path of Jewish history and as a movement toward a messianic age of peace and equality for all people brought about through human endeavour.

CHAPTER 1

What is Judaism?
Myth, Legend,
History, and Heresy

It is still widely believed that Judaism means only the monotheistic religion of the Jews, based primarily on the Old Testament Bible, and that the practice of Judaism can be
manifested only by synagogue attendance. This view prevails
even though the concept and practice of Judaism have under-
gone tremendous changes since the era of emancipation began
in the late eighteenth century.

In fact, the word "Judaism" does not appear in the Bible. It
was created by Hellenistic Jews from the Greek *Judaismos* to
describe their unusual way of serving God. It is first mentioned
in the book of Maccabees II, 2:21,[1] one of the books the early
rabbis refused to include in the Bible. The rabbis themselves
first used the term in *Esther Rabbah*, a midrashic commentary
on the Book of Esther. [2]

In the late 1980s, contemporary Jewish scholars disagreed
radically on the nature of Judaism, and even on whether the
term should be used. It was pointed out that current interpretations of Judaism range from "steadfast traditionalism to radical universalism."[3] *The New Catholic Encyclopedia* has
recognized that Judaism "admits of various meanings," including the "manifold expression of Jewish history and culture" as
well as the "sum total of commandments, rites, traditions and
beliefs that make up the Jewish religion. . . . Even in its

religious signification the term is not univocal."[4] Yosef Hayim Yerushalmi, a contemporary Jewish historian, has agreed that Judaism cannot be limited as to meaning. It cannot be seen "as something absolutely given and subject to *a priori* definition. Judaism is inseparable from its evolution through time, from its concrete manifestation at any point in history."[5]

Gershom Scholem (1897—1982), the world-famous expositor of the history and doctrine of Jewish mysticism,[6] also made profound comments on the nature of Judaism. He opposed those who viewed the events of Jewish history from a fixed, dogmatic standpoint and disagreed with the assumption that there is "a well defined and unvarying 'essence' of Judaism."[7] Later, he added that Judaism, because it "has no essence . . . cannot therefore be regarded as a closed historical phenomenon. . . . Judaism is rather a living entity."[8]

Avowed secular humanists, of course, and some other religionists have also interpreted Judaism in terms going beyond religion. Mordecai M. Kaplan, for example, who founded the Reconstructionist movement, defined Judaism as an "ethnic civilization" and carried on a vigorous polemic against Jewish supernaturalism.[9] *The Encyclopedia of Judaism* takes the definition of Judaism beyond the monotheistic faith of the Jews and also recognizes secular humanistic Judaism: "In fact, 'Judaism' is an all-embracing concept, incorporating not only the ritual aspects, and has been described as an entire 'way of life,' or 'civilization.' Judaism sanctifies all aspects of life . . . even what today is called the 'secular.' . . . . Judaism's fundamental orientation is practical and this-worldly. There is no officially recognized body of dogma."[10]

Since the eighteenth-century emancipation, it has been possible for Jews to express their Jewish identification while not accepting a religious belief. Zionism and the European prewar Jewish socialist Bund are now recognized as manifestations of Judaism. In addition to the Reform, Conservative, and

Reconstructionist movements that arose beyond Orthodoxy, there is the recent "small movement for Humanistic Judaism [that] has developed a non-theistic Judaism." [11]

The Encyclopedia of Judaism defines agnosticism and atheism as "terms denoting separate positions on the existence or nonexistence of God." [12] While some Jews do call themselves agnostics, the concept of agnosticism does not appear in Jewish religious literature. Atheism is also a concept for which there is no equivalent in Hebrew, "since ancient Israel was part of a world where no one doubted the existence of supernatural forces," [13] and rabbinic sources give no evidence of atheism among Jews. The Nazi Holocaust during the Second World War gave rise to religious doubt and loss of faith. However, many Jews who now define themselves as agnostic and are "estranged" from ancestral faith and practices have remained Jews, "since Jewish identity is not only a matter of religious belief but . . . involves other commitments . . . including the Jewish people, a cultural tradition and a Jewish homeland." [14]

Secular humanistic Judaism has been defined as "a tendency that sees in Judaism the civilization of the Jewish people rather than a solely or mainly religious concept." Jewish secularists claim that the theocentric foundations of Judaism were questioned even in ancient times, citing the case of Elisha Ben Abuya, who declared, "There is no law and no Judge." The belief in "an omnipotent and omnipresent God" presents insuperable problems for secular humanistic Judaism today. Moreover, many Jews in Israel and the Diaspora have no contact with organized religion. In the United States, the proportion of "religiously non-affiliated" Jews is estimated at over 50 per cent; in Israel, it is said to be lower [15]–although the latter claim is open to question. In fact, it is reported elsewhere that a majority of Jews in Israel, identifying themselves and recognized as Jews under Jewish law, are not brought up with the strictures of the Torah and receive no traditional education.[16]

Modern Zionism emerged "mainly as a secular movement" in Judaism.[17] The socialist Bund in Eastern Europe supported "a non-religious, Yiddish-language Jewish autonomous culture in a framework of a progressive gentile environment." The International Federation of Secular Humanistic Jews was founded in 1985, and the U.S. Society of Humanistic Jews, the Congress of Secular Jewish Organizations, in the U.S. and Canada, and similar groups in Brussels and in Israel are International Federation affiliates.[18]

Recognizing the contemporary pluralism of Judaism and the varied ways in which one may give expression to being Jewish is key to the survival of the Jewish people, whether as a nation in Israel or as significant cultural groups in other countries. The primary significance of Judaism may be seen as devotion to the traditional ideals of *sholem* and *tzedaka*–peace and justice for all people–based on the millennial history and culture of the Jews.

Jewish Myth and Legend

In suggesting that Judaism is based on myth and legend as well as history and custom, ranging from the religious to the secular, I have drawn a distinction between myth and legend, on the one hand, and history and custom, on the other. A myth is a traditional story of people in a preliterate society, dealing with supernatural beings or ancestors who were originators of a primitive view of the world. A legend is an unverifiable popular story, handed down from earlier times, and may in fact be developed out of ancient myth. In Jewish history, the distinction between myth and legend may be explained, I believe, by comparing the story of Passover, universally recognized as a major festival, with the story of Chanukah, generally considered a minor festival.

The exodus from Egypt, on which Passover is based, is drawn from unverifiable myths, which grew into legends, about the ancient Israelites being led by Moses, with the help of numerous "miracles of God," out of slavery in Egypt to become a nation and a "chosen people." Nevertheless, Passover has become very important in Jewish history because of the recorded events overlaying the myths and legends from which it was conceived. The story of the Maccabees, from which the celebration of Chanukah is extracted, comprises part of the confirmed record of the history and culture of the Jewish people in the Hellenistic era, during the rise and fall of the Syrian-Greek empire and the growth of Roman power. Chanukah is a lesser festival because the Pharisaic rabbis made it so, basing it on the legendary miracle of the one-day vial of sacred oil that burned for eight days. However, the full account of the Maccabees is more important to Jewish history than is the part credited in the story of Chanukah.

The biblical era is that period of Jewish history in which the idea of one God was developed out of the mythology of primitive peoples. The people who became the Jews formed a new concept of religion from these early myths. For instance, "Genesis I-II, often called the 'primeval history,' makes use of ancient near eastern mythological material as reinterpreted by Israelite monotheism."[19] As well, the folklore of the Old Testament includes major elements of "myth and story, inherited by Israel from her pagan ancestors or adopted from her neighbors."[20]

Thus, "Creation," whether fashioned by one or more gods, as well as Adam, Eve, Lilith, Cain, Abel, Seth, and Noah and his sons, are all based on myths. The first Jews, or Hebrews, took the myths of other primitive peoples and fashioned them into new legends, then probably said, "Our legends are better than the old myths." The Jewish Holy Scriptures, created over a millennium from these legends, were eventually declared the "words of God," said to have been received by Moses directly from God on Mount Sinai. This is how the first five books of the Bible, the Pentateuch, came into being.

The other books, eventually accepted into the Bible by the early rabbis, were based on real events and on legends about how the earlier "words of God" were applied by the Hebrews-Israelites-Jews as they fashioned their new nation. After the Bible was closed, the rabbis began to elaborate on the biblical stories with new legends and commentaries that became part of the Mishnah, or "Oral Law," and the Aggada (*Aggada,* or *Haggada,* is a generic term for post-biblical commentaries; the Passover Haggada is one example). Eventually, all of these works were recorded in what became the Talmud. Scholars have been writing, rewriting, and compiling Jewish legends ever since.

In the twentieth century, the great compiler has been Louis Ginzberg, who produced a seven-volume work, *The Legends of the Jews.* Ginzberg gathered from original sources all legends referring to biblical personalities and events. His sources were not limited to rabbinic literature, but he considered the Talmudic-Midrashic works to be of primary importance because they contain the major part of Jewish legendary material covering the period from the second to the fourteenth century, C.E.

Ginzberg was critical of scholars who considered rabbinic literature "purely a learned product," because he believed the popular character of rabbinic literature to be its most prominent feature: "Folklore, fairy tales, legends, and all forms of story telling akin to these are comprehended, in the terminology of the post-Biblical literature of the Jews, under the inclusive description Haggada."[21] A more recent writer explains Haggada as "a communication, a telling," the form introduced by the Pharisees in place of historical narrative for their laws, lore, and doctrine. Haggada might be "an anecdote, a description of a historical event or a paradigm for the righteous life." [22]

Ginzberg described the Jews as "the great disseminators of folklore," with legends originating in Egypt or Babylonia "appropriated by the European peoples" and European fairy tales finding their way to Asia "through the medium of the Jews, who on their long wanderings" from east to west and back again "brought the products of oriental fancies to occidental nations and the creations of occidental imagination to oriental peoples." [23] He also pointed out that some legends and myths have several variants. [24] Perhaps the earliest example of Jewish myth variant occurs in the two versions in the Bible of the creation of man and woman (Genesis 1:27 and 2:20—13). Another example is in the story of Abram in the idol shop, of which I have found four or five versions.

Development of Jewish History

The Bible commands Jews to remember (*zakhor*) "no less than 169 times." It is common among all people, not only Jews, that "what is remembered is not always recorded and . . . what has been recorded is not necessarily remembered." Concern with history "is not an innate human endowment." [25] There is dramatic evidence of the dominant place of history in ancient Israel, since "even God is known only insofar as he reveals himself 'historically.'" Moses spoke to the Hebrew slaves in the name not of the Creator but of the "'God of the fathers,' that is to say of the 'God of history.'" [26] Biblical history abounds in recitals of "acts of God," but the actions of men and women and the deeds of Israel and the nations are predominant. Historical writing in ancient Israel was rooted in the belief in history as divine manifestation, and the result was "not theology, but history on an unprecedented scale." The biblical record is not "factual" in the modern sense, yet its poetic and legendary elements are not "fictions" in the modern sense.[27] Beyond the biblical period, the books of the Maccabees are the most important works of Jewish history in ancient times, for they contain "the prototype of the literature of martyrology." They are also described as "a final burst of ancient Jewish historiography." [28]

The Jerusalem and Babylonian Talmuds and the Midrash, preserved in anecdotal or legendary form, comprise much of traditional Jewish knowledge of post-biblical history, including the Hasmonean (Maccabee) and Herodian kingdoms, the late period of the Second Temple, the revolts against the Romans, and the rise of the Pharisee sages and rabbis. However, the Pharisees themselves had no interest in history. They used historical personalities and events only to help further their "crucial concern" with personal salvation. Thus they were not concerned with the distinction between "fact and non-fact" or with whether an event had or had not occurred. [29]

After the close of the biblical canon at Yavneh, about 100 C.E., the Jews virtually stopped writing history.[30] The history of the Talmudic period itself cannot be elicited from its own literature. Major historical events either are not recorded or are mentioned in a legendary and fragmentary way, which often precludes their retrieval. [31]

For several centuries, no new Jewish history was written. Renewed writing was motivated by the desire to commemorate Jewish martyrs of the First Crusade in the Rhineland (1096—99). However, liturgy and ritual took primacy over historical narrative as the vehicle for Jewish memory in the Middle Ages. Only in the sixteenth century was there a rebirth of Jewish historiography comparable to that of the Hellenistic era.[32] The catastrophe that befell Jewish life in the Iberian Peninsula was the impetus for ten major Jewish historical works in the span of one hundred years. Their authors ranged from Solomon Ibn Verga (Spanish, born in the fifteenth century) to David Gans (Westphalian, born 1541).[33]

The most important historian of this period was Azariah de' Rossi (Italian born, 1511—78), the only one who truly absorbed the spirit of Renaissance historical writing. De' Rossi's book, *Meor Enayim* ("Light for the Eyes"), included essays on Hellenistic Jewish literature and the first historical scrutiny of classical rabbinic aggadah and the Jewish calendar.[34] He was the first to apply the critical principles of the Renaissance to Jewish records, and his sources included the Bible, Greek and Roman classics, medieval Talmudists, and church priests and humanists, along with Jewish writers of every age.[35] The book aroused a storm of criticism for its "unrestricted critical spirit,"[36] but it has also been called "the real beginning of historical criticism . . . [and] the most audacious Jewish historical work of the 16th century."[37] Concerned that his book would be seen as a denigration of Talmudic sages, de' Rossi tried to make excuses for some of the contradictions he found in the Talmud.[38] He defended that which by tradition came from Moses on Sinai, but he declared it necessary to deal differently with "matters which by their very nature could not have been announced . . . on Sinai."[39]

In the sixteenth century, historical works were still held in relatively low esteem by most Jews. History had not yet recovered from its failure to achieve recognition and legitimacy in medieval Judaism.[40] Maimonides, in *Guide to the Perplexed,* had suggested that the reading of history books was at best a diversion for one's leisure hours,[41] and introductions to most sixteenth-century works presented apologies for dealing with history.[42] Thus, after Jewish history had a brief flowering in this period, it withered again, and interest in Kabbalah mysticism was renewed. (The Kabbalah was first adopted by Jewish mystics in the twelfth century.)

In the late eighteenth century, the Haskalah movement for secular enlightenment led to the beginning of a consensus that knowledge of history was somehow desirable for Jews. A 1782 proposal for a new Jewish school curriculum included the study of history and other secular subjects.[43] In 1783, a Haskalah group started a monthly journal, *Ha-Measseph* (The Gatherer) and decided to publish biographies of famous Jews. Concerned that such material might be considered trivial, the journal first published an article on the utility of history.[44]

Over the following forty years, the attitude toward history changed yet again. In 1817, Leopold Zunz (1794—1886), who was later called the greatest Jewish scholar of the nineteenth century, published a booklet calling for the historical study of Jewish civilization. Two years later, Zunz and several others founded the *Verein fur Cultur und Wissenschaft der Juden* (Society for Culture and Scientific Study of the Jews). In the first issue of its journal, the society published an essay by Immanuel Wolf, "On the Concept of the Science of Judaism," drawing attention to how earlier Jewish scholars had neglected to study history.[45]

History had now achieved a recognized status, and Judaism had to prove its validity to history, rather than the reverse.[46] The critical approach of modern scholarship posed problems for the Jewish religion (and other religions). It called into question the historical authenticity of crucial events and key personalities, challenged scripture, and disclosed data that contradicted "received tradition."[47]

Between 1820 and 1828, Isaac Marcus Jost (Germany, 1793—1860) published a nine-volume work entitled *History of the Israelites,* which marked the beginning of modern Jewish historiography. Jost's work was soon superseded by that of Heinrich Graetz and others, but he is still recognized as a founder and pioneer of modern Jewish history.[48]

Graetz (1817—91) is considered the great Jewish historian of the nineteenth century, despite critical views expressed about his multi-volume *History of the Jews,* first published in German between 1853 and 1876.[49] His views on religion contributed to the development of Conservative Judaism.[50] A six-volume English-language version of Graetz's original German work was published as *History of the Jews* by the Jewish Publication Society of America between 1891 and 1896. Simon Dubnow (1860—1941) inherited Graetz's mantle as the "national Jewish historian."[51] Dubnow's work achieved distinction in both the nineteenth and twentieth centuries, and he was recently ranked with Graetz and Salo Baron as one of the "three giants of modern Jewish historiography."[52] East European and self-educated, Dubnow emphasized social factors and the role of the Jews in Eastern Europe, both of which Graetz had overlooked. Dubnow's major work, begun in 1910, is *World History of the Jewish People.* It is regarded as the first secular and purely scholarly synthesis of all of Jewish history with no dogmatic or theological trappings.[53] Salo Baron is, by all accounts, the greatest Jewish historian of the twentieth century, in that he "synthesized the intellectual-religious history of Graetz and the communal social history of Dubnow."[54]

Seltzer cites the vastness and complexity in the development of Jewish history and questions whether it will ever be possible to formulate a few "clear and simple truths" that all may learn from Jewish history to "enable us to reforge Jewish identity in its future travails." He adds the hope that history may offer a perspective "on being Jewish and on the human condition."[55]

If history can indeed offer a perspective on being Jewish, Dubnow's view of the use of Jewish history is worth examining. His theory of Jewish cultural nationalism failed in the context of nineteenth-century Europe, but the theory of cultural pluralism originally advocated by Horace Kallen[56] can be seen, in an American context, as a reinterpretation of Dubnow's concept. As well, the Canadian notion of multiculturalism, which has been accepted in some other countries, brings another perspective to cultural pluralism. In this context, Jews in Canada and elsewhere are exercising a new kind of cultural autonomy as an ethnic group that cannot be based solely on traditional religion or theology.

This presents a problem for Jews who see history as a reflection of Jewish memory, reinforced in the synagogue by the constant repetition of Jewish scriptures–Torah and Tanach–and prayers from rabbinic writings. For those who defect from the synagogue, without a rational replacement for the Torah and the prayer liturgy, their only memory after biblical history may be of the seemingly endless story of Jewish martyrology. Thus, many Jews today are in search of a past, but they clearly do not want the past that is offered by earlier historians.[57] Indeed, historians should confront "contemporary Jewish reality" and get away from the view that Jewish history involves little more than "how Jews died and the books they wrote." [58]

Yerushalmi is a follower of Baron, who was his teacher, but the latter did more than write and speak to and for other historians. In 1947, for example, as a guest speaker at the Seventh Plenary Assembly of the Canadian Jewish Congress in Montreal, Baron stressed the need to re-interpret Jewish history to make it "significant and vital" for today. Saying that he was a Zionist, a year before the establishment of the State of Israel, he spoke against the "old doctrine of the negation of the *galus*," or Diaspora. It is no use to go into "eulogies" about the life in the Polish or Russian ghettoes he said; Jewish youth in Canada and the United States were now interested in the history of Jews in their own countries. He criticized the Jewish communities of both countries for the failure to preserve "our historic records of past generations."[59]

Generations have grown to adulthood since Baron made those comments, and documentary records are now being saved. It has also been demonstrated that Jews can be reintroduced to Jewish history through their experience in the country in which they live. For Jewish secularists who seek to invoke Jewish history beyond the Bible and the Talmud, it is appropriate to turn to Yerushalmi, who said that the modern effort to reconstruct the Jewish past witnessed a "sharp break in the continuity of Jewish living." This perception has certainly been true since the emancipation that gave rise to the Jewish Reform movement and other religious trends and ideologies, as well as the secular trends of Zionism and the socialist Bund, which led to "an ever-growing decay of Jewish group memory." In this sense, history became what it never was before–"the faith of fallen Jews." Thus, for the first time, history, rather than a sacred text, became "the arbiter of Judaism,"[60] especially for Jews who came to believe in the new ideologies. By the late twentieth century, however, many Jews had lost their ideologies, and thus their concern with history. Jews, as individuals or in groups, may find renewed interest in Jewish history by discovering the experiences of their own forebears on a pedlar's route in Quebec, Ontario, or Ohio, on a prairie farm, in a city factory or a small-town store, in a trade union, a workmen's circle, or a *landmanschaft* (self-help group based on place of origin), or even the Klondike gold rush. For most Jews, the path of forebears leads back to Europe and thousands of years of Jewish history on that continent.

Turning to European history, it should be recalled that the economic changes effected by capitalism also touched Jewish life in the nineteenth century. These changes led most Jews to the urban working class in the early twentieth century, but by mid-century they were forsaking the working class for entrepreneurial pursuits, the sciences, and learned professions. This development had a profound effect on their attachments to religion, ideology, history, and culture.

Jewish Heretics

In eastern Europe, from the eighteenth to the early twentieth century, many Jewish centres had organized *kehillas*, or councils, which looked after the community's needs. Baron, writing about the influence of rabbinic learning in an essay on Jews in the modern age, related the following episode: "A Polish Jewish labor leader once voted in favor of a large appropriation for a local *yeshiva*, explaining to an amazed inquirer that out of that *yeshiva* would come the future leaders of the Socialist Bund." The Bund was a secular organization, and all of its members were non-believers, or *apikorsim*. Baron also pointed out that most of the Hebrew and Yiddish writers and scholars, and a great many Zionist and socialist leaders, received their early training in one or another field of rabbinics.[61]

By the early 1900s, when the Bund began to support national minority rights for the Jews, the non-religious were able to co-operate with the religious through the *kehilla* in support of Jewish rights. Such co-operation among Jews, and recognition of those who consciously follow the secular humanist approach, comprise an important element in fostering Jewish survival against the negative aspects of assimilation. There are still obstacles in the way of such co-operation, which may be traced back to the treatment of skeptics and "heretics" in ancient and medieval history.

Apikoros is the best known of several ancient terms for "heretic," terms that at times were used interchangeably. But the *apikoros* became better known as a skeptic and non-believer who challenged the Torah and the rabbis' views, while heretics who turned to another faith were called *minim*.[62] The latter word, however, has fallen into disuse except in scholarly and religious circles; thus, both skeptics and "heretics" may be called *apikorsim*.

Christians were originally considered heretics against the Jewish faith, as were some other ancient and medieval Jewish sects, including the Sadducees, the Karaites, and the Sabbateans. Before the Jewish Enlightenment and the modern era, heretics were rare and, except for Spinoza, left no body of writing; they are known only from what their opponents said about them. Beginning in early Christian times, there was a concerted effort to wipe out all traces of their doctrines. The name of Hiwi al-Balkhi,[63] a late-ninth-century Jewish heretic, turns up only in the works of a critic, Saadiah Gaon (882—942), a famed rabbinic scholar in Egypt and Babylonia. Al-Balkhi wrote a Bible commentary with two hundred queries, which has been lost; he sought to explain biblical miracles naturally and detected later additions in the biblical text. Surviving quotations show him to have been "a daring and free-thinking scholar."[64]

In the late Middle Ages, Jewish orthodoxy was threatened by philosophical and religious radicalism when Jews in southern France and Spain began to study Greek and Arab philosophy and natural sciences. Some even denied the divine authority of the Bible. A conflict arose between the Orthodox and the liberals; Moses Maimonides, long recognized as the greatest Jewish scholar of that era, was in the centre of the struggle. Maimonides was concerned that some people could not withstand tendencies that might lead to heretical beliefs. Thus he cautioned against raising "the slightest thought which might cause a person to reject any principles of the Torah."[65]

Yet Maimonides' own writings, particularly *Guide for the Perplexed* and *Book of Knowledge*, were considered heretical by the Orthodox.[66] Maimonides knew that a fine educational system was not enough to preserve the faith. At the same time, he was the chief scholar to emphasize the need for capable people to study the secular subjects of philosophy and medicine.[67] The controversy over Maimonides' position led to a ban against philosophical study, first introduced by Rabbi Solomon ibn Adret (1235—1310) of Barcelona in 1305 for his own community. This ban was gradually accepted in other cities and other lands. Rabbi Adret had decreed that, for the next fifty years, no man under twenty-five "shall study, either in the original language, or in translation, the books which the Greeks have written on religious philosophy or the natural sciences."[68] Reading of original Jewish works, however, "even those of Maimonides," was permitted at any age. Despite the criticism of some of his contemporaries, Maimonides was a strong defender of the Jewish faith, although some of his views have given encouragement to later secularists.

Throughout the Middle Ages, any Jews who did rise against the faith did not have the option of turning to a secular way of life. Only with the onset of Protestantism in the sixteenth century and the Enlightenment in the eighteenth century did secular values begin to compete with religion. Large numbers of Jews, who still identified themselves as Jews, sought to be free from the commandments of religious tradition. This development gave rise to Reform, and eventually to organized Jewish secular movements.

A century ago, Rabbi Emanuel Schreiber said, "The heretics of 50 years ago are the saints of today."[69] Jewish heretics and *apikorsim* need not be acclaimed saints, but their alleged heresies should be reconsidered for the significant thinking they brought to light.

Who is a Jew?

In the first decade following the establishment of the State of Israel, the question "Who is a Jew?" became a subject of world-wide debate among Jewish scholars and religious leaders. The debate began when David Ben Gurion, Israel's first prime minister, wrote to Jewish scholars for their opinion on the question of "how to register under the headings of *religion* and *nationality* children born of mixed marriages, when the father is a Jew and the mother is not a Jew and has not become converted but both of them agree that the children should be registered as Jews." The controversy arose because of the Orthodox view, based on Jewish religious (Halakhic) law, that only a child born to a woman who is Jewish by birth or by Orthodox conversion may be considered a Jew. The Orthodox rabbinate in Israel has exercised jurisdiction on religious matters going back to the days of Turkish rule over Palestine. Nevertheless, Ben Gurion said, "All religious or anti-religious coercion is forbidden in Israel and a Jew is entitled to be either religious or non-religious." This statement has never been fulfilled in practice, and freedom of religion for Jews in Israel remains a problem to this day: in 1988, Orthodox authorities in Israel and in the Diaspora began a campaign to impose their definition of Jewish identity on all Jews, and in Israel they tried to have the Law of Return amended to recognize only orthodox conversions. The Conservative and Reform movements mounted a strong counter-campaign in their own self-interest.

The responses of the scholars who were asked for their views on this question were summarized by Rabbi W. Gunther Plaut, who reported that the respondents were far from unanimous, but they tended to agree on several propositions, probably the most important of which was, "Being a Jew is, for the Jew, determined by his own tradition."[70] The other points of agreement were that in cases of no religious marriage, "ascription of Jewishness" should be through the mother; being a Jew has to do with parental descent, except in cases of conversion; gentiles who convert to the Jewish faith are considered as though they are descended from Abraham and as though their forefathers stood at Sinai; Jews who convert to another faith and consider themselves faithful practitioners of that faith are no longer Jews. The Reform movement now recognizes as a Jew anyone who has either a Jewish father or a Jewish mother. The most open approach to the definition of who is a Jew is taken by the Jewish Secular Humanist movement. In the United States, certified Jewish secular representatives have been granted the right to perform marriages in some states, and humanism has been granted religious status.

In 1988, the International Federation of Secular Humanistic Jews adopted a resolution affirming "that a Jew is a person of Jewish descent or any person who declares himself or herself to be a Jew and who identifies with the history, ethical values, culture, civilization, community and fate of the Jewish people." The preamble to this resolution asserts that millions of Jews do not find their Jewish identity in religious belief or practice, but in the historic experience of the Jewish people. Thousands of men and women in Israel and other countries want to be Jewish but find themselves rejected by the "narrow legalism of traditional religious authorities." The Secular Humanist Federation challenges the assumption that Jews are primarily or exclusively a religious community and that "religious convictions or behavior are essential to full membership in the Jewish people." The Federation describes the Jews as "a world people with a pluralistic culture and civilization all its own." Judaism is called "the culture of the Jews [which] is more than a theological commitment." Judaism encompasses many languages, a vast body of literature, historical memories, and ethical values. Moreover, the Holocaust and the State of Israel have become "a central part of Jewish consciousness." The Secular Humanist movement also opposes the Orthodox policy that children and spouses of intermarriage who wish to be part of the Jewish people must be excluded from the Jewish community if they do not have Jewish mothers and do not wish to undergo religious conversion.[71]

Is there a way out of this impasse? Emmanuel Rackman, a noted rabbi and modern Orthodox scholar, has said that there is a small group in Orthodox ranks who recognize "the inviolability of the persons of all human beings, including Jewish dissenters. . . . Thus they encourage dialogue with all Jews, solutions to painful problems in Jewish family law [and other sensitive issues]."[72] Gerson D. Cohen, Chancellor of the Jewish Theological Seminary of America, has declared that the Conservative movement tolerates diversity within its camp and outside it ranks and "has always insisted on the solidarity of the Jewish people as a whole, in all its myriad forms and orientations. From the Conservative perspective the secular Jew is as much a Jew as the observant Jew."[73]

Rackman's view is a minority position among the "modern" Orthodox, and not all of Cohen's Conservative colleagues accept his attitude toward the secular Jew. Yet, if Orthodox and Conservative representatives of their calibre could meet with like-minded leaders of Reform, Reconstructionist, and Secular Humanist Jews, perhaps a path toward mutual recognition of the definition of a Jew could be found, taking as a starting point Plaut's statement, "Being a Jew is, for the Jew, determined by his own tradition." Of course, this means considering Jewish tradition in its broadest perspective.

In Canada a new way of defining "Who is a Jew" has resulted from the Canadian census, which asks two questions every ten years: "To which ethnic or cultural group(s) did your ancestors belong?" and "To which religion or denomination do you belong?" Respondents to the census are permitted to choose only one religion and up to four ethnic affiliations. Based on the census findings, the Consortium for Ethnicity and Strategic Social Planning at McGill University has developed the following definition: "A Jew is someone who identifies him/herself as being 'Jewish by religion' or 'Jewish by religion and Jewish by ethnic origin' or 'Jewish by ethnic origin with no religion.'"

There is one more interpretation of who is a Jew to be considered, because it takes into account the Reform view as well as the secular humanist resolution. After a historical assessment of the question, Salo Baron proposed that it would be practical to recognize as a Jew everyone who "is born of Jewish parents and has not been converted to another faith; is born of mixed parentage but declares himself [herself] a Jew and is so considered by the majority of neighbours; and one who by conscious will has adopted Judaism and joined the membership of the Jewish community."[74] "Conscious will" may include formal "conversion" to any one of the Jewish religious denominations or acceptance into community membership on the basis outlined in the Secular Humanist resolution.

The main denominations of the organized Jewish religion are, in fact, experiencing a considerable decline in the numbers of their adherents. This decline in religious practice is not limited to Jews. Recent reports show a sharp drop in church attendance among established Christian denominations. In Sweden, for example, in the late eighties, 99.6 per cent of the population were registered Lutherans, but church attendance was only 4 per cent.[75] In Canada, a survey in 1994 showed that just 44 per cent of Canadians thought it important to belong to a religious group, while 59 per cent agreed with the statement: "I am not a religious person, but I am a spiritual person." This study, *A Survey Regarding the Spiritual Dimension in the Canadian Public,* conducted by Environics Research for Vision TV, the English multi-faith cable-TV channel, also found that 46 per cent of Canadians do not believe in traditional religions; 83 per cent said that belief in God is a personal matter and church attendance is not necessary to prove one's faith; 70 per cent have constructed their "own personal religions"; and 60 per cent believe that "all religions are equally valid." Also in 1994, Statistics Canada reported that 80 per cent of Canadians considered religion an important part of their lives, but membership in the largest denominations is declining dramatically. In the 1991 census, a record 3.4 million people listed themselves as having "no religion."

The search for new forms of religious expression is leading some people to fundamentalism, which is on the rise among Jews, Christians, and Muslims. These movements do not offset the overall decline in attendance at houses of worship, but they do have negative implications for society–for example, the tendency of some fundamentalists to become involved in terrorism.

In Israel a sharp struggle is going on for freedom of religion between the Orthodox rabbinate, other religious groups, and the growing secular movement; the judiciary and the politicians are also active players (see chapter on Israel). The resolution of the question of who is a Jew is therefore tied to the larger question of freedom of religion.

Notes

1. Baron, *Treasury of Jewish Quotations*, p. 247.
2. *Encyclopedia of Judaism*, p. 397.
3. E. Borowitz, "Judaism, an Overview" in *Encyclopedia of Religion*, vol. 8, p. 127.
4. J.M. Ostereicher, "On Judaism" in *New Catholic Encyclopedia*, vol. 8, p. 3.
5. Yerushalmi, *Zakhor*, pp. 91—92.
6. Cohen and Mendes-Flohr, *Contemporary Jewish Religious Thought*, p. 1111.
7. Scholem, *Sabbetai Sevi*, p. xi.
8. Scholem, in Cohen and Mendes-Flohr, *Contemporary Jewish Religious Thought*, pp. 505—08.
9. Kaplan, *Judaism Without Supernaturalism*.
10. Wigoder, *Encyclopedia of Judaism*, pp 397—98.
11. Ibid., pp. 399—400.
12. Ibid., pp. 37—38.
13. Ibid.
14. Ibid.
15. Ibid., p. 357.
16. Cohen and Mendes-Flohr, *Contemporary Jewish Religious Thought*, p. 350.
17. Kaplan, *Judaism Without Supernaturalism*, pp. 17—18.

18. Wigoder, *Encyclopedia of Judaism*, p. 357.

19. Robert M. Seltzer, "History, Jewish Views," in *Encyclopedia of Religion*, vol. 6, p. 391.

20. Gaster, *Myth, Legend and Custom*, p. xxv.

21. Ginzberg, *Legends*, vol. 1, pp. viii—xi.

22. Rivkin, *Shaping of Jewish History* p. 60. See also Cohen and Mendes-Flohr, *Contemporary Jewish Religious Thought*,pp. 7—12.

23. Ginzberg, *Legends*, vol. 5, p. vii.

24. Ibid., p. ix.

25. Yerushalmi, *Zakhor*, pp. 5—6.

26. Ibid., p. 9.

27. Ibid., p. 13.

28. Robert M. Seltzer, "History: Jewish Views," in *Encyclopedia of Religion*, vol. 6, p. 392.

29. Ibid.; Rivkin, *Shaping of Jewish History*, p. 61.

30. Yerushalmi, *Zakhor* pp. 15—16.

31. Ibid., p. 18.

32. Robert M. Seltzer, "History: Jewish Views, in *Encyclopedia of Religion*, vol. 6, p. 393; Yerushalmi, *Zakhor*, pp. 39—40.

33. Yerushalmi, *Zakhor*, pp. 57—58.

34. Ibid.

35. Roth, *History of the Jews of Italy*, pp. 218—19.

36. Ibid.

37. Yerushalmi, *Zakhor*, p. 69.

38. Ibid., p. 71.

39. Baron, *History and Jewish Historians*, p. 171.

40. Yerushalmi, *Zakhor*, p. 66.

41. Robert M. Seltzer, "History: Jewish Views, in *Encyclopedia of Religion*, vol. 6, p. 393.

42. Yerushalmi, *Zakhor*, p. 67.

43. Roth and Wigoder, *New Standard Jewish Encyclopedia*, p. 1954; Yerushalmi, *Zakhor*, p. 82.

44. Yerushalmi, *Zakhor*, p. 83.

45. Plaut, *Rise of Reform Judaism*, pp. 16—17, 107—08; Yerushalmi, *Zakhor*, p. 83.

46. Yerushalmi, *Zakhor*, p. 83.

47. Robert M. Seltzer, "History: Jewish Views, in *Encyclopedia of Religion*, vol. 6, p. 393.

48. Baron, *History and Jewish Historians*, pp. 241—47; Plaut, *Rise of Reform Judaism*, pp. 110—11.

49. Baron, *History and Jewish Historians*, pp. 266—67.

50. Roth and Wigoder, *New Standard Jewish Encyclopedia*, pp. 475—76.

51. Pinson, "Introduction," in Dubnow, *Nationalism and History*, p. 3.

52. Seltzer, "Graetz, Dubnow, Baron," p. 169.

53. Pinson, "Introduction," in Dubnow, *Nationalism and History*, p. 30.

54. Seltzer, "Graetz, Dubnow, Baron," p. 181.

55. Ibid., pp. 181—82.

56. See Roth and Wigoder, *Encyclopedia Judaica*, vol. 10, pp. 712—13.

57. Yerushalmi, *Zakhor*, p. 97.

58. Ibid., p. 100.

59. Baron, "Work among Our Youth," pp. 62—64.

60. Yerushalmi, *Zakhor*, p. 86.

61. Baron, *Great Ages*, p. 372.

62. Ze'ev Gries, "Heresy," in Cohen and Mendes-Flohr, *Contemporary Jewish Religious Thought*, pp. 339—41.

63. Ibid., p. 343.

64. Roth and Wigoder, *New Standard Jewish Encyclopedia*, p. 918.

65. Ze'ev Gries, "Heresy," in Cohen and Mendes-Flohr, *Contemporary Jewish Religious Thought*, pp. 343—44.

66. Marcus, *Jews in the Medieval World*, p. 189.

67. Ze'ev Gries, "Heresy," in Cohen and Mendes-Flohr, *Contemporary Jewish Religious Thought*, pp. 345—46.

68. Marcus, *Jews in the Medieval World*, pp. 190—91.

69. E. Schreiber, "Reformed Judaism," in Baron, *Treasury of Jewish Quotations*, p. 179.

70. Plaut, *Your Neighbour*, pp. 3—4.

71. "Preamble to Resolution: Who Is a Jew?" *Humanistic Judaism* (Spring 1989): 5.

72. Rackman, "Orthodox Judaism," in Cohen and Mendes-Flohr, *Contemporary Jewish Religious Thought*, p. 683.

73. Cohen, "Conservative Judaism," in Cohen and Mendes-Flohr, *Contemporary Jewish Religious Thought*, p. 98.

74. Bauer, "Who is a Jew?" p. 6.

75. S.W. Baron, History and Jewish Historians, pp. 21-22.

For additional source material see Bibliography.

Part One

FROM THE BIBLICAL ERA TO JEWISH SECULAR HUMANISM

CHAPTER TWO

Jews and the Idea of God
Since Abram in the Idol Shop

My Jewish family Bible defines God as "the Supreme Being, the Creator and Sovereign of the Universe, and Ruler over the destinies of man and the world and everything in it." [1]This is not a view of God that I accept for myself. In this chapter I present various Jewish ideas about God in relation to my own and other views.

The earliest Jewish idea about God as an invisible, supernatural being is said to have started with Abram, as he was first known, the "father" of the Jews. When I was a boy in Montreal, I took part in a play called "Abram in the Idol Shop." This play was set in ancient times, when people worshipped stone idols as gods. It was based on a story from the Talmud, the books by the ancient rabbis interpreting and enlarging on Jewish law and customs.

Abram's father, Terah, owned an idol shop and was himself an idol worshiper. One day, Terah had to go into town to do some business. He asked his son, Abram, to look after the shop while he was away. Soon after Terah left a man came in to buy an idol to protect his home from thieves.

"Don't you have one?" Abram asked in surprise.

"We did have one," the man replied, "but it was stolen!"

"How can you expect an idol to protect your family against thieves," Abram asked, "when it can't even protect itself?"

"But we must have something to worship," the man insisted.

"How old are you?" Abram asked.

"Fifty," the man answered.

"What!" Abram exclaimed. "A man your age wants to buy an idol and bow down to a stone image that isn't more than a week old!"

The man walked out without buying. A seed of truth was planted.

A little later, a woman entered the shop and offered Abram a bowl of flour as a sacrificial offering to the idols. When she left Abram picked up a stick and broke all the idols, except the biggest one. He then placed the stick in the hand of the big idol.

When Terah came home and found the idols broken into little pieces, he got very angry and cried out, "Who did this?"

"What happened, Father," Abram replied, "is that a woman came in with a bowl of flour as an offering for the idols and I placed the bowl before them. Immediately they began to argue and fight among themselves. Each idol said the flour was meant for him. While they were arguing, the biggest idol picked up a stick and . . . As you can see, he killed them all!"

"You no-good-nik," cried Terah. "How can you say the idols argued when they can neither move, speak, nor understand?"

"Father," Abram responded, "You have just spoken true words about the idols. What good are they to anyone?"[2]

In an older version of the story, Abram, at the age of twenty, goes peddling the idols on the street. His encounters with the idol-worshipers are similar to those in the idol shop, but Abram is presented in a more activist role, promoting the idea of one supreme, invisible god.[3]

In fact, according to the Bible, God did not make Himself known to Abram until he was seventy-five years old,[4] when God is said to have told him to go to the land of Canaan. When Abram was ninety, God told him to change his name to Abraham. These are the first steps by which Abraham is said to have been introduced to the belief in one God–the concept of monotheism–that became the central belief of the Jewish religion about a thousand years later.

The religion of the "Patriarchs" (Abraham, Isaac, and Jacob) has been described as a family-type of worship that was at most "monolatric," addressing itself to a single God but not ruling out the existence of other gods. References to the "one God" belief in Genesis are said to be "anachronistic" and more appropriate to the Exodus story in the time of Moses.[5]

After the "miracle" of the parting of the Red Sea to help the Israelites escape the pursuing Egyptians, Moses sang to the children of Israel about the glory of God: "Who is like unto thee, O Lord, among the mighty?"[6] Moses was setting the stage to have Yahveh recognized by the Israelites above all other gods. And, of course, the Ten Commandments begin, "Thou shalt have no other gods before me."[7] God warns the Israelites at that moment, and again later, against bowing down to any other god or making any graven image or "molten god,"[8] and calls on them to "overthrow" other gods and "break in pieces their pillars."[9] There are more warnings against idolatry in the Holy Scriptures. Joshua warned the Israelites, "If ye forsake the Lord, and serve strange gods, then he will turn and do you evil. . . . Now therefore put away the strange Gods which are among you."[10]

Solomon, who built the first Jerusalem Temple, said, "Great is our God above all gods."[11] Later, he had troubles, which are explained as punishment for "allowing idolatrous cults to penetrate the court" when he was diverted by his "alien wives."[12]

Before the time of the Prophet Isaiah (740—701 B.C.E.), Jews seldom thought of Yahveh as the one God, even of all the Hebrews.[13] The concept of "only one God" was not fully accepted until the Torah was canonized after the return from exile in Babylonia (538 B.C.E.). It was thus more than a millennium after Abraham and several centuries after Moses' legendary meeting with God on Mount Sinai before the Jews embraced Yahveh as the one and only God and accepted monotheism.

Some authorities claim that the Jews were the first to introduce the concept of monotheism. It is known, however, that a form of monotheism was introduced in Egypt by Akhenaton around 1370 B.C.E., about 150 years before Moses, and by Zoroaster in Persia in the sixth century B.C.E.[14] One commentator suggests, however, that "even in the Yahvistic stage the Hebraic religion came closer to monotheism than any other pre-Prophetic faith except the ephemeral sun-worship of Ikhnaton . . . [and] Judaism was immensely superior to the other religions . . . in philosophic unity and grasp, in moral fervor and influence."[15] In other words,

> Very few ideas in the history of human progress have had as decisive an effect on the course of civilization as Jewish *ethical* monotheism. . . . The true significance of the Jewish contribution was that, after having reached the conclusion that there was only one God, the Jews had gone on to universalize and spiritualize their conception of him in socially idealistic and ethical terms.[16]

Monotheism was considered an advance over idolatry and paganism; the story of Abram in the idol shop shows that primitive peoples were dismissed as worshipers of "dumb idols." This view oversimplifies paganism as the worship of wood and stone. In fact, the current definition of a pagan is one who is neither a Christian, a Muslim, or a Jew; a heathen; or a person with no religion.[17] The prevailing tendency after more than two millennia is still to dismiss the significance of the religions that were widespread before the advent of Judaism, Christianity, and Islam.

Paganism must not be mistaken for fetishism, which involves, in a religious sense, the ascribing of magical powers to a material object.[18] "The basis of the pagan religion is the deification of natural phenomena." All manifestations of nature are said to be "divine powers [and] aspects of a mysterious supernatural vitality." Thus heaven and earth, the sea, the sun, the moon and stars, the wind, mountains, and rivers are all divine beings. This concept gave rise to the worship of "natural gods." Out of nature's phenomena–lightning, thunder, the changing seasons, and so on–pagans created stories about the life of the gods, which were formalized into a mythology. Just as every modern religion has its theology, the study of the nature of God, "every pagan religion has its theogony, an account of the birth of the Gods." The essence of paganism is that the gods are not ultimately sovereign. "The deification of nature [imposes] natural or supernatural compulsion on the gods." Nor do the pagan gods enjoy "ultimate freedom." They are subject to the same impulses as people to eat, drink, and have sex. Human experiences are mythologized in the lives of gods. The pagan cult also has a magical character.[19]

The idols that people worshipped usually represented mythological pagan gods. Thus the Bible, "the arch-antagonist of idolatry . . . misconceives pagan religion as the worship of wood and stone" and never really comes to grips with the essence of paganism, "the belief in mythological gods."[20] The God of Israel is held to stand above pagan mythology, to be the creator of nature, rather than subject to nature's control, and to have neither pagan nor human attributes. God is referred to as "He," but is said to have no sexual attributes.[21]

Biblical tradition implies that the first men, Adam, Cain, and Abel, and the generations until Noah, were worshipers of the "one God," because idolatry is not mentioned in Genesis 1—11. There is no credible evidence to support the existence of monotheism among primitive man, nor, on the other hand, that "the empirical history of monotheism does not antedate the rise of Israel."[22]

There is no clear answer to the question of how Abraham (c. 2000 B.C.E.), designated by tradition as "the first Jew," could have come to the concept of one God at a time when the Mesopotamian world was "sunk in . . . abysmal demon and fetish worship." However, anthropologists have found evidence about the existence of "one God" among some Australian food-gathering peoples and among North American natives at a time when a vast majority of those peoples "were sunk in animistic beliefs and practices." Therefore, Abraham's belief in "one God" may not be an anomaly.[23]

The Jewish God may have stood above paganism, but it took the ancient Israelites a long time to overcome fetish and idol worship. There is biblical evidence that the ancient patriarchs worshipped sacred stones (*matsevot* in Hebrew), which were akin to totems. The setting up of such "holy" stones on "high places" was common among Israel's neighbours, the Canaanites, Moabites, and Philistines, and among the more advanced Greeks and Romans in the Hellenistic era.

Prior to the Babylonian conquest, in 586 B.C.E., only a small minority of Jews followed the Prophets in the practice of spiritual and ethical monotheism. In the First Temple era, many Israelites and Judeans, from King Solomon down, did not care for the nonsexual character of Yahveh; they were entranced by Baal and his consort, Ashtoreth (Astarte), the fertility gods of the Canaanites. A campaign was started to purge the Israelites by force of their many "fetishistic and polytheistic [pagan] aberrations."[24]

By the time Greek Hellenism came on the scene, the Jewish religion had matured into full-scale Torah Judaism, with "one God" at its core. A struggle began between two highly developed religious philosophies: polytheistic Hellenism and monotheistic Judaism. Many Jews did adopt Hellenistic ways, but monotheism was never completely undermined. The monolithic character of Torah-Judaism was ended, however, and there arose different Jewish sects, including the Pharisees, the Saducees, the Essenes, and others. In modern terms, this development might be described as the first manifestation of Jewish denominationalism.

Many Jews were captivated by the style of Hellenism; some were also impressed by its philosophy. But Zeus could never replace Yahveh in Jerusalem, except by an invading force. Some Jews, who were attracted by the secularist, anti-theist views of Epicurus, later earned the epithet of *apikoros* from the rabbis, although no Jew was named an *apikoros* during the Second Temple period. In the late first century C.E., however, Rabbi Eleazar Ben Arach advised his disciples to be prepared with answers for the *apikoros*.[25]

The First Apikoros

The first recorded case of a Jewish personality who was an *apikoros* is that of Elisha ben Abuya, in the early second century C.E. Ben Abuya is described as having adopted "heretical" opinions and expressing doubts about the unity of God, reward and punishment, and the resurrection of the dead. While the Jews endured Roman persecution, ben Abuya profaned the Sabbath and incited others to do the same and to neglect Torah study in favour of heretical literature. When he wished to repent, it is said, a "Divine voice" rejected him. Several compositions were written about him in the Haskalah period (the nineteenth-century Jewish enlightenment), and he has been the subject of a novel.[26] He was called an apostate, one who gives up his own faith for another, and a gnostic, one who believed God was a dual being.[27]

Several nineteenth- and twentieth-century writers have commented on ben Abuya's career, as it is reflected in the Talmud. Graetz believed he "despised the Jewish Law," and adopted the "evil Gnostic morality."[28] He was given the name "Acher" (another) by his contemporaries "as a mark of his apostasy."[29] Gerson Cohen, writing on the relationship of Jews to God in the Talmudic Age, states, "The average Jew . . . was little concerned over belief in God." A "renegade" like ben Abuya, "who left the fold despondent and shouting, 'There is neither Judge nor justice,'" would have earned "a perfunctory note of condemnation." However, "one senses in the Talmudic account of him a deep feeling of pity and horror for a man who has lost all hope and has sunk to the last depth of despair." Cohen implies that ben Abuya openly denied God, which "was a rare phenomenon in the ancient world."[30] Ausubel cites ben Abuya as a "classic example" of Jewish seekers after chachmah, or wisdom who "ended their quest in apostasy," and describes him as "the brilliant heretic" who was the teacher of Rabbi Meir, a "pious traditionalist," and a member of the Sanhedrin, the Jewish supreme council in Roman times.[31]

One may wonder whether ben Abuya had really declared himself an atheist or became an apostate in the manner recognized since the advent of Christianity. The Talmud says of him, "[He] joined the pagan philosophic camp, disputed with Jewish scholars, and ridiculed the Jewish religion." Yet the Talmud description of him has "a certain grandeur and [he] is accorded grudging respect." [32]

Historian Simon Dubnow believed that a Jew cannot abandon the religion of Judaism and remain a Jew. Yet Dubnow, who turned his back on formal religious practice, modeled himself as a "free thinker" after Elisha ben Abuya.[33] Explaining ben Abuya's loss of faith in Torah Judaism, Dubnow wrote that he stood "apart and alone in this austere world of spiritual discipline." [34]

There were rumours that ben Abuya collaborated with the Romans during the time of Emperor Hadrian's persecution of the Jews.[35] Nevertheless, Rabbi Meir defended his continued friendship with the heretic: "I found a pomegranate so I ate the fruit and discarded the husk."[36] According to Dubnow, Rabbi Meir said that ben Abuya "died with the thought of repentance." Ben Abuya and Rabbi Meir shared such mutual respect that once, according to the Talmud, when the former rode horseback on a Sabbath, the latter followed on foot listening to his wisdom.[37] It has been written that their friendship would have been "impossible" had ben Abuya been a true apostate.[38]

Elisha ben Abuya certainly qualifies as a historic example of an *apikoros*. His relationship with Rabbi Meir shows that it is possible for people with different beliefs about God to respect each other's views and even to remain friends.

The Jewish claim to have originated the "one God" belief arises from the fact that the other two major monotheistic religions, Christianity and Islam, were founded several centuries after Judaism was fully established. Christianity clearly grew out of Judaism; to this day, some theologians speak of a Judaeo-Christian heritage. Islam has also been considered a "daughter religion" of Judaism, since Abraham, traditionally the father of the Arabs as well as the Jews, is just one of the Biblical figures accepted in the pantheon of Islamic prophets.[39]

Another belief developed in the Jewish religion was the coming of the Messiah, a God-appointed saviour, who would lead the Jews and all other people to an era of peace and brotherhood. The Jews believed that the Messiah would come some time in the future, but no one could say exactly when that would be.

In the century after the destruction of the Second Temple, a number of individuals stepped forward claiming to be the Messiah. With the exception of Jesus of Nazareth, all Messiah claimants served as rallying points for Jewish resistance to Roman rule. They were usually leaders of the zealot wing of the Pharisees, while Jesus was an Essene pacifist. The earlier would-be Messiahs were leaders of uprisings that caused severe losses of manpower and damaged the prestige of the Roman legions sent to suppress them.[40]

Jesus preached that the "Kingdom of God" was at hand, and some called him "King of the Jews"; it was rumoured that he was descended from David. When he began to be called the "son of God," the Romans felt threatened, because they considered their own emperor to be a god. In spite of Jesus' avowed pacifism, the Romans saw him as the potential leader of a revolt, so he was arrested, tried, and crucified by order of the Roman procurator, Pontias Pilate.

Various messianic movements, including Christianity, arose out of the conviction that the "End of Days," based on the Apocalypse concept, was near. Each messianic group disappeared after the death or failure of its originator, except for Christianity, which gained power after Jesus' crucifixion. It is interesting that "Christ" comes from *Christos*, the Greek word for *Mashiach*, which is the Hebrew for "Messiah," "Saviour," or "Redeemer." Christianity is thus the religion of messianism.[41]

Current Jewish views on the Messiah are varied. In the early 1990s, some Chassidic groups in Montreal who believed that his arrival was imminent placed billboards on highways reading, "Bienvenue à Mashiach." In Jewish religious tradition, the mission of the Messiah is to bring about God's Kingdom on earth (not in heaven, as Christians hope), by establishing brotherhood, peace, and justice among all people. Many Jews, regardless of their religious views, hope that these conditions may be realized in a "messianic era," without waiting for a Messiah. A song in an Israeli film expressed hope for peace between Jews and Arabs through their own efforts, because, as the lyrics went, "The Messiah will not come, he won't even telephone!"[42]

Jews could not accept Jesus as the "son of God," for several reasons. First, only the gods of Greek mythology gave birth to children. The God of the Jewish Bible is "non-mythological" and is said to have "no body, no kindred, no human needs."[43] By calling Jesus the "son of God," the Christians were clearly adding a Greek pagan concept to the "one God" belief. Second, although religious Jews believe in the "fatherhood" of God, since he is the "Creator," they could never accept the Christian idea of the "Holy Trinity: God the Father, God the Son, and God the Holy Spirit," because this would mean that God, in addition to his supposed supernatural qualities, also has human and supra-natural qualities.

Christians also claim that the "virgin birth" was foretold in the Jewish Bible by the Prophet Isaiah, who supposedly said, "Behold, a virgin shall conceive, and bear a son, and shall call his name Immanuel." This verse, Isaiah 7:14, from the King James version of the Bible (based on earlier Christian texts), is marked as a "prophetic reference to Christ." The Jewish version of Isaiah says, however, "A *young woman* shall conceive." As well, Immanuel means "God is with us" and is the symbolic name of the son of Isaiah. The name Immanuel is not found in any part of Jewish tradition on the Messiah, and the messianic interpretation given to the name and related text in Isaiah is therefore not of Jewish origin.[44]

Christian versus Jewish Symbols

Christianity has long been known for its visual symbols, the cross and the images of Christ and the Virgin Mary, which represent an adaptation of the idol worship of ancient times. But because the early Christians were still Jews, these images were not created immediately. During the rise of Christianity, the Roman historian Tacitus observed that the Jews strongly opposed any representation of God in human form as "a profanation of heavenly nature." This stemmed from the second of the Ten Commandments, prohibiting the making of "graven images." The revered symbols came after the Christians had become accommodated to the image worship of the Romans.[45]

The commandment against graven images also extends to "any manner of likeness of any thing . . . in heaven . . . in the earth . . . or . . . in the water"; this inhibited the development of Jewish art at certain times. Nevertheless, some Jews felt a compelling need for artistic expression in the Hellenistic period and later, during the Italian Renaissance. A "clamor for visual beauty" among the Jews led some more worldly rabbis to ease the ban against art in "limited ways." Thus they reinterpreted the Second Commandment in "the spirit of the times";[46] in spite of the Commandment prohibition, Jewish art may be traced back to biblical scriptures.

The Jewish religion has no symbols comparable to those of Christianity. It is represented to this day by the tablets of the Ten Commandments, the Torah scroll of the Five Books of Moses, and the Menorah. The Menorah and the Magen David (Star of David) are the two most recognizable Jewish symbols; they are symbols not of God, but of Judaism and the Jewish people.

The Menorah was originally the symbol of the story of Creation. The first Menorah, a seven-branch gold candelabrum, is said to have been made, on the instructions of Moses, by Bezalel, an artisan, for the desert Tabernacle.[47] Biblical scholars now say, however, that Exodus was actually written in the days of the Second Temple. Thus the Menorah described there is more likely the one engraved on the Arch of Titus in Rome, which symbolizes the conquest of Jerusalem.

When the Second Temple was destroyed, it was the Menorah, not the Magen David, that became the primary art symbol of the Jewish faith. By then, the nine-branch Menorah had been created for Chanukah, the Feast of Lights. In 1948, the seven-branch Menorah was restored as the national symbol of Israel and of the Jewish people.[48]

The Magen David (a hexagram) is found in the architectural design at the Hellenisitic synagogue in Capernaum, on the Sea of Galilee, where Jesus is said to have preached, but its earliest use dates back to the seventh century B.C.E. First recognized as a Jewish symbol in the late Middle Ages, it came into frequent use in the sixteenth century. It became well known, however, only when it was adopted as the symbol of the Zionist movement. It is now featured on the flag of Israel.[49]

The Menorah and the Magen David, unlike the Christian crucifix, are clearly capable of secular adaptation. A new adaptation of the Menorah is the Humanorah, the symbol of secular humanistic Judaism. This is a "personified menorah" combining the traditional Menorah with an expression of "human-centredness." It is used particularly by the Society for Humanistic Judaism.[50]

The tablets of the Ten Commandments and the Torah scroll represent the Jews as the people of the "covenant with God," and as the "people of the Book." The Torah scroll, however, in its decorated splendour in the Oren Kodesh, the sacred Ark, and in its worshipful treatment when taken out of the ark for ritual use, may impress the casual observer as a substitute for an idol. In every synagogue, one will also find the Ner Tamid, the Eternal Light, which is kept burning as a symbol of the faith.

Traditional Judaism also has several personal religious symbols, including the yarmulke or kippah (skullcap), the tallit and tzitzit (prayer shawl and ritual fringes), the tefillin (phylacteries), and the mezuzah (doorpost symbol). Each symbol has a tradition behind it, usually emerging from ancient custom into a religious dictum.

There is no biblical law for covering the head. But Moses Maimonides, the twelfth-century rabbi, philosopher, and physician, wrote in his *Guide to the Perplexed* that the great Jewish sages "would not uncover their heads because they believed God's glory was around them and over them." Wearing a skullcap or a turban was a sign of humility or reverence adopted by Hindus, Arabs, and Persians, as well as Jews. Paul of Tarsus, when he sought to de-Judaize Christianity, determined that since Jews covered their heads in prayer, Christians should do the opposite. The most devout orthodox male Jews wear the *kippah* at all times. In Orthodox and Conservative synagogues, it is customary for the men to wear a *kippah* during services. Reform Judaism originally discarded the *kippah*, but it is now optional in Reform synagogues.[51]

The *tallit* is worn by Jewish men when they are praying. It includes the *tzitzit*, the fringes on the four corners, which are a visible reminder of the duty of the male Jew to observe all of the 613 Torah commandments! Most men usually don a *tallit* when they attend a synagogue service. The fully observant man wears a *tallit kattan*, a small *tallit*, with *tzitzit*, under his clothes at all times.[52]

Tefillin are worn by orthodox Jewish men at weekday morning prayers in fulfilment of the commandment "It shall be a sign . . . upon thy hand, and a memorial between thine eyes, that the law of the Lord may be in thy mouth."[53] The *tefillin* consist of two leather boxes with leather straps, one worn on the forehead, the other bound on the left arm. Each box contains extracts from the Hebrew prayers to God.[54]

The *mezuzah*, literally "doorpost," is a small oblong tube mounted on the right doorpost of Jewish homes. Often ornamented, it contains a parchment with Hebrew extracts from Deuteronomy and has "Shaddai," a mystical name for God, inscribed upon it. A *mezuzah* will be found on the doorpost of many Jewish homes even if the people living there are not very observant. It is a reminder of God and has also been considered an amulet for protection against evil spirits. Some Jews wear a *mezuzah* as a neck ornament.[55]

Some Jewish women, seeking equality with men in religion, are adapting male symbols for female use.[56] These personal religious symbols are considered inappropriate for secular humanistic Jews.[57]

The Right to Dissent

Since the Hellenistic age, some Jews have questioned the belief in a supernatural God. And since the era of the Talmudic sages, after the Second Temple, the intellectual right to dissent, even from cardinal theological doctrines, was tacitly recognized. But the ban of excommunication for dissenters considered heretics was introduced in the fifth century B.C.E., at the time of Ezra and the scribes, and became a full-fledged institution in the Talmudic era.[58] From the experience of Elisha ben Abuya, one might have concluded that those who recognized his right to dissent came into conflict with those who thought that he should be excommunicated. Dubnow states that ben Abuya was persecuted for his thinking and was "regarded as excommunicated,"[59] but if he had been formally excommunicated, surely a chapter of his sayings would not have been included in the Talmud's ethical book "Sayings of the Fathers" (*Avot*).[60]

There is no doubt about what happened to ben Abuya's intellectual heirs, Uriel Acosta (1585—1640) and Benedict (Baruch) Spinoza (1632—77). Acosta was excommunicated for questioning the doctrines of immortality, resurrection, and reward and punishment, among other "heretical" views. Unable to endure his total isolation from the Jewish community, Acosta publicly "recanted." He was thereupon flogged and trampled by the worshipers at the synagogue, after which he went home, wrote a reaffirmation of his views, and shot himself![61] (This is not unlike what happened to Galileo, his Italian contemporary, who was compelled by the "Holy Fathers" to recant his finding that earth was round and revolved around the sun.)

Acosta's work involved "free thought and religious rationalism," which were "embodied to a still higher degree . . . in the theory of life expounded by the immortal author of the *Theologico-Political Tractate*." This immortal author was Spinoza, who was excommunicated for his non-conformism, by the same "angry rigorists" who had scourged Acosta in the same Amsterdam synagogue.[62] Spinoza did not attend his excommunication, and did not actually disavow his belief in God. But he equated God with nature and said that nothing was supernatural, not even God. Today, he is widely recognized as an exemplary Jewish thinker.[63]

Men like Spinoza, and even Maimonides before him, with their controversial commentaries on the great books of the Jewish religion, laid the groundwork for new Jewish ideas in the Haskalah, the Jewish Enlightenment movement of the late eighteenth and nineteenth centuries. Some Jews in the ghettos, who acquired a measure of secular culture, found that they could no longer hold to traditional beliefs and observances. In Western Europe in particular, there was a religious-cultural struggle between the Haskalah adherents and the defenders of orthodoxy. This struggle eventually brought Reform Judaism into being. But some people became secularists; they were influenced by Spinoza, who had "rejected blind faith for reason and theology for science," or they came to similar conclusions on their own. Some of these people gave up their Jewish identity and left the Jewish community.[64]

By the time of the Haskalah, it was becoming clear that Judaism encompassed the cultural, spiritual, and social way of life of the Jewish people and was not limited to conventional religious expression. While the Jewish religion is based on monotheism, Jews never adhered uniformly to the same religious ideas, particularly in regard to belief in God. Some Jews have moved all the way from monotheism to atheism.

Of course, many Jews still do believe in God as a supernatural, all-powerful being, existing in an invisible state and watching to make certain that "religious laws" are followed. Many adherents of other religions also accept this type of belief.

There are also some Jews who do not believe in a supernatural God but do not reject the idea of God completely. They see God as an idea or force for good, or as the perception of the quality of goodness.

Rabbi Sherwin Wine suggests that any attempt to redefine God is immoral. He argues that "God" is not a new and "unknown sophisticated scientific term." It is an ordinary word, like "man," child," or "house," and for "the ordinary user God refers to a supernatural father figure." Wine disputes the notion that God may be reinterpreted as a "natural force of goodness or creative energy," and he argues that the word "God" does not necessarily imply "good," because "Gods can be wicked as well as benevolent."[65] I believe that Wine's view is persuasive of the idea that the spirit of goodness should not be placed on a pedestal and worshipped. One should be motivated to act out of the spirit of goodness in one's daily life regardless of the state of one's religious belief and whether or not one believes in God in the traditional way.

Through the centuries, rabbis have interpreted the idea of God in different ways. Israel Baal Shem Tov, the Master of the Good Name, taught that all people are equal before God. Baal Shem Tov was the founder of Chassidism, the movement that introduced the idea that each person possesses the spirit of God or the "divine light."[66] Other religions, particularly in the Oriental world, have also used the "divine light" idea. Some groups have turned this into such a strong belief that God is inside the person that they worship the so-called divine spirit within themselves. But this is just another version of the idea of a man as the "Son of God," an idea that Jews reject whether or not they believe in God.

There is a Chassidic story, told by Martin Buber, about a young rabbi who consulted an older rabbi concerning a personal problem. "During hours when I devote myself to my studies," the young rabbi said, "I feel life and light. But the moment I stop studying all is gone. What shall I do?"

The older rabbi replied, "This is the same as when a man walks through the woods on a dark night, accompanied by another man with a lamp. But at a certain crossroads they part and the first man must then find his way alone. If a man carries his own light within him, he need not be afraid of darkness." [67]

This story may be explained in two ways. First, the young rabbi may not be benefiting from his studies if he does not absorb some ideas to guide him in his life away from his books; perhaps he is pursuing the wrong subjects! Second, if a person must always depend on someone else's lamp, or someone else's leadership, such a person may lose his or her personal independence. If the learning imparted by a rabbi, or any teacher, is to have real value, the student should ultimately be able to use the knowledge gained without constantly returning to the teacher. Although one should be able to turn to someone for advice from time to time, ultimately one must be able to rely on one's own understanding and intellect; this is not a "divine light" but rather the spirit of humanity.

Belief in the spirit of humanity is known as "humanism," defined as concern with human beings, their achievements and interests, and their problems, rather than with abstract beings, such as God, or problems of theology. Any person who questions the existence of or does not believe in God should also have some understanding of theology, to help him or her to a clearer appreciation of his or her own belief in humanity and human creativity. Without belief in God, this approach is known as secular humanism, and it is gaining support in the Canada, the United States, Israel, and elsewhere.

Secular humanism is a choice for those who no longer believe in God. Of course, people who believe in God and continue to follow an established religion may also be humanistic in their outlook and be involved in creative secular activities. As well, secular humanists need not reject every aspect of religion because they do not believe in a God. Religion, after all, has been part of Jewish heritage and history for several millennia, although the history of the Jews goes back before the formal establishment of the Jewish religion.

The story of Abram and the idols is recalled by Abraham Sutskever, the Holocaust survivor and editor of *Di Goldene Keyt* (The Golden Chain) in a poem entitled "Outlandish Words," which offers advice for secular Jews who must deal with the seemingly outlandish and unconventional approach involved in becoming dissociated from the belief in God:

> I had no help or helper then
> (having already run away from the rabbi and his assistant),
> when light dawned and it was revealed to me
> that I, Abraham, am different from all the others:
> I don't have to overturn Terah's idols anymore.
> What next? I must construct all the rules
> for outlandish words . . . [68]

Notes

1. *Holy Scriptures*, "Encyclopedic Dictionary," p. 832.
2. Ausubel, *Treasury of Jewish Folklore*, p. 455; Trattner, *Understanding the Talmud*, pp. 65—66.
3. Ginzberg, *Legends of the Jews*, vol. 1, pp. 195—98.
4. Genesis 12:1—4.
5. Malamat, *History of the Jewish People*, pp. 32, 45.
6. Exodus 15:11.
7. Exodus 20:4.
8. Exodus 34:14, 17.
9. Exodus 23:24.
10. Joshua 24:20, 23.

11. Second Chronicles 2:4.

12. Malamat, *History of the Jewish People*, p. 107; I Kings 11:1—13.

13. Durant, *Story of Civilization*, vol. 1, *Our Oriental Heritage*, p. 312.

14. Ausubel, *Book of Jewish Knowledge*, p. 300.

15. Durant, *Story of Civilization*, vol. 1, *Our Oriental Heritage*, p. 312.

16. Ausubel, *Book of Jewish Knowledge*, p. 300.

17. *American Heritage Dictionary*.

18. Y. Kaufmann, *Great Ages*, p. 8.

19. Ibid., pp. 8—9.

20. Ibid., pp. 10—11.

21. Ibid.

22. Ibid., pp. 14—15.

23. Ausubel, *Book of Jewish Knowledge*, pp. 303—04.

24. Ibid., p. 303.

25. Ibid., pp. 142—43; Bentwich, *Hellenism*, pp. 77—78.

26. See Steinberg, *As a Driven Leaf*.

27. Roth and Wigoder, *New Standard Jewish Encyclopedia (NSJE)*. See articles on ben Abuya, 613; Apostasy, 132—33; Gnosticism, 763.

28. Graetz, *History of the Jews*, vol. 2, p. 377.

29. Bentwich, *Hellenism*, 274—75.

30. G.D. Cohen, *Great Ages*, p. 193.

31. Ausubel, *Book of Jewish Knowledge* pp. 76, 485.

32. Roth and Wigoder, *Encyclopedia Judaica*, vol. 3, p. 202.

33. Dubnow, *Nationalism and History*, pp. 8, 46.

34. Dubnow, *History of the Jews*, vol. 2, pp. 104—06.

35. Ibid., 105; Safrai, "Part 4: The Era of the Mishnah," p. 335.

36. Ausubel, *Book of Jewish Knowledge*, p. 485; Dubnow, *History of the Jews*, p. 105; Safrai, Ibid.

37. Dubnow, Ibid., 106.

38. *Jewish Encyclopedia*, vol. 5, p. 139.

39. Ausubel, *Book of Jewish Knowledge*, pp. 100—01; 224—25.

40. Ibid., p. 286.

41. Stern, "The Period of the Second Temple," pp. 286—87; Ausubel, *Book of Jewish Knowledge*, p. 286; Roth and Wigoder, *New Standard Jewish Encyclopedia*, see "Apocalypse," pp. 128—29.

42. *Shattered Dreams*, Victor Schonfeld, director, 1987.

43. Roth and Wigoder, *New Standard Jewish Encyclopedia*, p. 764.

44. *Holy Scriptures*, "Encyclopedic Dictionary," p. 846.

45. Ausubel, *Book of Jewish Knowledge*, pp. 22—23.

46. Ibid.

47. Exodus, chapters 25, 37.

48. Ausubel, *Book of Jewish Knowledge*, pp. 276—78; *Holy Scriptures*, "Encyclopedic Dictionary," p. 873.

49. Gaster, *The Holy and the Profane*, pp. 217—21; Ausubel, *Book of Jewish Knowledge*, p. 263.

50. *Guide to Humanistic Judaism*, pp. 75—76.

51. *Holy Scriptures*, "Encyclopedic Dictionary," p. 921; Ausubel, *Book of Jewish Knowledge*, pp. 191—92.

52. Ausubel, *Book of Jewish Knowledge*, pp. 439—40, 485—86.

53. Exodus 13:9.

54. *Holy Scriptures*, p. 915; Ausubel, *Book of Jewish Knowledge*, pp. 458—59.

55. *Holy Scriptures*, p. 874; Roth and Wigoder, *NSJE*, pp. 1332—33; Ausubel, *Book of Jewish Knowledge*, 290-91).

56. Schneider, *Jewish and Female*, p. 77.

57. *Guide to Humanistic Judaism*, pp. 75—76.

58. Ausubel, *Book of Jewish Knowledge*, pp. 133, 151.

59. Dubnow, *History*, vol. 2, p. 105 .

60. Roth and Wigoder, *Encyclopedia Judaica*, vol. 3, p. 668; Trattner, *Understanding the Talmud*, p. 171.

61. Ausubel, *Book of Jewish Knowledge*, p. 152.

62. Dubnow, *Nationalism and History*, p. 309.

63. Roth and Wigoder, *NSJE*, pp. 1789—90.

64. Ausubel, *Book of Jewish Knowledge*, p. 231.

65. Sherwin Wine, "Symposium: Humanistic Judaism and God," p. 28.

66. Ausubel, *Book of Jewish Knowledge*, pp. 87—88.

67. Buber, *Tales of Chassidism*, pp. 62—63.

68. Sutskever, *The Fiddle-Rose Poems*, p. 47.

CHAPTER THREE

The People of the Book

Jews have been known as the "People of the Book" throughout the ages from their association with the Old Testament. This view may be traced back to a Talmudic legend: when the Israelites were standing at the foot of Mount Sinai, the *bat kol*, a heavenly voice, called out to them to choose between the Book and the Sword, both of which were suspended over their heads. And the people chose the Book, known variously as the Torah, the five books of Moses, or the Pentateuch. The legend of the Book relates to the events following the exodus from Egypt, which, according to tradition, occurred five hundred years after the start of the biblical period, beginning with Abraham, about 1800 B.C.E. From the time of Moses, 1300 B.C.E., for about seven hundred years, to the destruction of Israel (721 B.C.E.) and the fall of Judah (586 B.C.E.), the Pentateuch was written and rewritten.

The Jewish idea of the Book is so strong that rabbinical legend asserts the Torah existed before all else and that God consulted it before He created the world![1] Or, as Nathaniel Kravitz puts it, "God looked into the Torah and created the world as an architect looks at his blueprints!"[2] Taking this idea symbolically, Kravitz reinforces what others have said about the Pentateuch not being "the creation of one man but rather a conglomerate work . . . a people's book, the authors of which lived during many centuries."

Kravitz agrees with Dubnow that the post-biblical period began when the Prophet was replaced by the priest and the scribe, with the rise of the Second Jewish Commonwealth in the second half of the sixth century B.C.E.[3] However, the books of Moses were almost certainly still being revised and edited by the scribes in Babylonia before being brought back to Jerusalem for canonization after the Persian conquest. Many of the other books, from Joshua to Second Chronicles, were also compiled, written, and accepted into the Bible during the two centuries of Persian rule (538—322 B.C.E.).[4]

The Bible was finally closed by the rabbis sometime during the Maccabean era. From then on, books of Jewish myths, legends, and history became part of the Apocrypha, most of which were accepted into the early Christian Bible. This period continued until the fall of the second Jerusalem Temple in 70 C.E. From about 200 B.C.E. to 200 C.E., another series of Jewish religious works were written; these books were spuriously ascribed to various prophets and kings. Not recognized by the Jews or the early Christians, they became known as the Pseudoepigrapha. It thus appears that from biblical through post-biblical times there were three groups of ancient writings; the authors of all of them likely vied to have them included in the Jewish Holy Scriptures. The writing of the books that became the Christian gospels of the New Testament began in the first century C.E.

The Talmudic period also began in the first century C.E. and lasted about five hundred years. During this time, the rabbis produced various works of commentary on Jewish law. Discourses known as "oral law" were eventually written down as the Mishna. Supplementary commentaries were later added to the Mishna; these became the Gemara. The Mishna and the Gemara together comprise the Talmud. Added to the Talmud later were the Halacha, legal commentaries, and the Aggada, social commentaries.[5]

In the post-Talmudic period, from 500 to 900 C.E., works of critical exegis on the Talmud were produced, and the Hebrew

Prayer Book was developed. In the medieval period that followed, Jewish literature, mainly Hebrew, branched out into heterogeneous subjects from grammar and dictionaries to poetry, philosophy, and science. In fact, there was a Golden Age of Hebrew literature, based in Spain, from the middle of the tenth century to the end of the fifteenth century. The best-known writer of this era was Rabbi Solomon ben Isaac, born in France in 1040, the year the Babylonian Jewish academies were closed. His Bible and Talmud commentaries made him famous as Rashi.

Judah Halevi (c. 1075—1141), a great Hebrew poet, wrote a cycle of poems, "Songs of Zion," one of which begins, "O Zion, wilt thou not inquire about the peace of thy captives, / They that seek thy peace and are the remnant of thy flocks?" He also wrote love and wedding songs:

> Rejoice, O young man, in thy youth,
> And gather the fruit thy joy shall bear,
> Thou and the wife of thy youth . . .

Halevi declared, "The servant of God does not withdraw himself from secular contact lest he be a burden to the world and the world to him." He followed his own counsel, since he was a physician and a student of philosophy and the natural sciences.[6]

There were two Ibn Ezras, apparently not related, Moses (c. 1070—1139) and Abraham (1088—1167). In his youth, Moses wrote love poems, even describing erotic love. Later, he wrote penitential poems, some of which are found in the Sephardic Machzor (High Holidays prayer book). A manuscript of three hundred of his secular poems are in the Bodleian Library at Oxford University.[7] Abraham Ibn Ezra is known for his biblical commentaries. He is described by Kravitz as a "keen critic" who "dared to express doubts as to the integrity of the text and the Mosaic authorship of the Pentateuch; but fearful of being pronounced a heretic, he employed his great mastery of Hebrew to hide his remarks in riddle-like phrases."[8]

A variety of works from the Middle Ages and the Renaissance achieved particular renown: Maimonides' *Guide for the Perplexed* (twelfth century C.E.), the Zohar of the mystical Kabbalah tradition (thirteenth century C.E.), Joseph Caro's *Shulchan Aruch*, a code of rabbinic law for the Orthodox (sixteenth century C.E.), and Spinoza's *Theologico-Political Treatise* (1670). Another writer who may have helped to set the stage for Spinoza's critique was Levi ben Gerson (1288—1344), known as Gersonides, who, in his best-known work, *Milhamot Adonai* (Wars of God), was critical of biblical theology if it did not accord with reason: "The law cannot prevent us from considering to be true that which our reason urges us to accept."[9]

The first books in Yiddish date from 1382 and include fables and biblical epics. Perhaps the best known of the earliest Yiddish books was the *Tsene rene*, the retelling of biblical tales known as the Woman's Bible, which is still read today. Other early Yiddish works were biblical dramas, such as the *Shmuel bukh* (Book of Samuel, 1544) and the *Melokhim bukh* (Book of Kings, 1543). Adaptations from the Talmud and the Midrash appeared in Yiddish in the *Mayse bukh;* there was also some secular literature.[10]

Jewish writers began to reflect the Renaissance Age of Reason when they began to question ancient verities. Kravitz calls the sixteenth to eighteenth centuries a period of transition in a Hebrew literature "nurtured on Renaissance humanism." One of the first writers of this period was Elija Levita (1468—1549), also known as Elye Bokher, a Hebrew grammarian who was the teacher of Christian humanists. Levita was born in Germany but spent most of his life in Italy. He wrote in Yiddish as well as Hebrew, demonstrated that Hebrew vowels were invented in post-Talmudic times and not in biblical times, and wrote the first known Yiddish-Hebrew dictonary. He was also the author of the *Bove bukh*, a Yiddish book of romances based on Italian and English sources.[11]

One of the best-known writers in this period was Leon de Modena (1571—1648), a rabbi in Venice. Two of de Modena's books were *Kol Sacal* (Voice of a Fool), an attack on traditional Judaism, and *Sha'agat Aryeh* (Roar of a Lion), a defence of Judaism.[12] He took an enlightened view in criticizing the Talmud and supported choral music in the synagogue and Jewish involvement in theatre, dance, and visual art.[13] According to Cecil Roth, de Modena "stood amazed at the obscurantists who deliberately confined their reading to Hebrew."[14]

Another humanist rabbi was Joseph Solomon Delmedigo of Candia, Italy (1591—1655), who studied the sciences and attended the astronomy classes of Galileo. In addition to his scientific works, Delmedigo wrote a book, *Mazref Lahokmah* (Crucible of Wisdom), in which he tried to harmonize faith with philosophy; however, his fear of being declared a heretic kept him from expressing his ideas clearly. He also had close contact with Leon de Modena.[15]

At the high point of humanism, in the seventeenth century, two Jewish women in Venice, Deborah Ascarelli and Sarah Copia Sullam, were writing poetry. Ascarelli also translated Hebrew books and hymns into Italian.[16] Her work was first published in 1601—02, and it was republished in 1925 by a descendant.[17] She was probably the first woman to publish a Jewish literary work.[18] Accounts of Sullam's writing are given by various scholars,[19] but it seems that her work was never published. Another woman, Gluckel of Hamelin, Germany (1646—1724),[20] wrote memoirs in Yiddish, beginning in 1691, when she was a widow with thirteen children. Gluckel's memoirs were found and copied by a grandson after her death, and they were eventually published in 1896.[21] Gluckel has been called "the Pepys of German Jewry,"[22] and the importance of her work "in Yiddish literary history [and] . . . European women's history of the late medieval period" has been emphasized.[23]

Other historic personalities who contributed to Jewish literature in this transitional period were Uriel Acosta (or Da Costa) and Benedict Spinoza, both of whom were excommunicated; the Amsterdam Rabbi Mannaseh ben Israel, who appealed to Oliver Cromwell for the return of the Jews to England (they had been expelled in 1290); and Israel Baal Shem Tov, the founder of Chassidism.

The modern period in Jewish literature dates from the early eighteenth century, shortly before the Haskalah began at mid-century. Moses Hayyim Luzzatto (1707—47) of Padua, a mystic Cabalist, is regarded as the father of modern Hebrew literature. He wrote poetry, a book of psalms in imitation of the Bible, and several plays, the most notable being *Mesillat Yesharim* (The Path of the Righteous), an ethical work that became a classic and is still popular among the pious.[24]

Moses Mendelssohn (Germany, 1729—86), the father of the Jewish Enlightenment, became well known for his secular writings before he turned to Jewish works. His first published work, *Philosphische Geshprache*, was published anonymously in 1755 by his friend, poet and dramatist Gotthold Lessing. In 1756, Mendelssohn produced a German translation of Rousseau's *Discours sur l'inégalite parmi les hommes*. At the age of thirty-four, he won first prize from the Berlin Academy of Sciences for a philosophical treatise in a contest in which Immanuel Kant was also a competitor. Mendelssohn won the title of "German Socrates" for *Phadon* (1767), a work on immortality modeled on Plato's dialogues. He completed a German translation of the Pentateuch, with Hebrew commentary, in 1763, and also translated the Psalms and the Song of Songs.

In 1779, Lessing wrote a play, *Nathan the Wise*, on religious tolerance and universal brotherhood; the leading character was modelled on Moses Mendelssohn. In 1783, Mendelssohn wrote *Jerusalem,* a book defending Judaism and introducing the idea that "all faiths are good as long as they lead man to live in accordance with morality." That same year, the Haskalah movement began to produce *Ha-Measseph,* a monthly Hebrew journal for poets, essayists, biographers, satirists, and humourists.[25]

Although books by Jews became varied in subject matter and language over the centuries, the Bible remained the centrepiece or was one of the themes in many works of Jewish literature, which increasingly included biblical analysis and criticism. Even during the Haskalah, the Bible was called the "portable homeland" of the Jews. Heinrich Heine, who was baptized as a Christian but regretted it for the rest of his life, said of the Jews, "A book is their very fatherland, their treasure, their governor, their bliss, and their bane."[26]

Language, Culture, and Ideology

Language has been very important to the Jews, but not in the same way as for other cultural groups. Visual arts, music, and sometimes theatre have been minimized, even negated, under Jewish religious strictures in the past.

While Jewish culture has changed with the times, it has always been able to rise above attempts to suppress it. But it is also far from being fixed or always precisely delineated. In certain times and places, Jewish culture has been, and is, a complete pattern of living. In Canada and the United States, for example, Jews live as an ethnic or religious component within the culture of the country of which they are citizens; in Israel, Jews live as a nation in their own land.

Through the ages, Jews have often lived under complete or near- complete Jewish patterns of culture. Different forms of a total Jewish culture existed in the ancient Jewish states–in biblical Israel and Judea, and in the Second Jewish Commonwealth (following the Babylonian exile), which ended with the Hasmonean (Maccabee) empire of the Hellenistic era. A near-complete Jewish pattern of culture also existed in the segregated European ghettos. The term "ghetto" originated in Venice in 1517, but segregation of Jews was decreed by the church as early as 1179.[27]

In Eastern Europe, the Kahal, or Kehillah, initiated by a charter of the Polish king, Sigismund Augustus, in 1551, became the most highly developed form of Jewish self-government. The Jews were granted religious freedom and communal autonomy. In 1764, the Kahal was abolished in the Polish provinces by royal decree. Between those two dates, the small town *shtetl* became the stronghold of Jewish culture, and the Kehillah pattern survived through the nineteenth century.[28]

In fact, a wide-ranging Jewish culture flourished in a macabre manner in the short-lived Nazi ghettos. In his deeply moving and highly insightful book *Against the Apocalypse,* David Roskies writes, "The mirage of autonomy . . . [made] the ghetto seem like an upside down version of Herzl's Jewish State; with the landsmanshaft, the tenement committee, the soup kitchen, the underground synagogue, school and political party as the social basis for individual survival."[29]

Jewish culture today can mean anything, from the complete pattern that is possible only under conditions of nationhood to a specific interest such as education, religion, language, history, Zionist ideology, or secular humanism. In Canada, the United States, and other countries, Jewish culture benefits from the growing acceptance of cultural pluralism or multiculturalism.

When the curtain rose on the Enlightenment in Western Europe in the eighteenth century, the Haskalah began in Prussia under Moses Mendelssohn. The aim of the Haskalah was to enable the Jews to become integrated into the community at large without losing their religion and their cultural traditions. The first secularized Jewish religious school was opened in Berlin in 1781. Subjects taught included German and French, mathematics, geography, and technical subjects, in addition to Bible and Talmud. This school was the forerunner of the Jewish parochial schools that have become widespread in the twentieth century.[30]

The advocates of Haskalah were known as Maskilim, but differences developed among them over how to educate the Jewish masses and prepare them to participate in the world at large. The German leaders sought to replace Yiddish with the German language. In Eastern Europe, where the movement began a little later, one group of Maskilim insisted on Hebrew to educate the ghetto Jews in the ideas of Haskalah; the other wanted to introduce the Jewish masses to liberal ideas in Yiddish. The more religious-minded leaders of the Haskalah felt that both language groups were developing assimilationist trends.[31] Another result of the Haskalah in Germany was the birth of Reform Judaism. This gave rise to the movement of neo-Orthodoxy, formed to renew and reinforce religious traditions.

In contemporary times there are still warnings about the danger of assimilation. When Irving Abella took office as president of the Canadian Jewish Congress, in 1992, he suggested that assimilation had become a greater threat to the Jews than anti-Semitism. In the 1950s and 1960s, Dr. Nahum Goldmann, long-time president of the World Jewish Congress, had taken a similar position. In 1966, Goldmann spoke of the "menace from within–the danger of assimilation and disintegration."

The American Jewish philosopher Horace Kallen invented the concept of cultural pluralism to counter the "melting pot" approach to Americanization, because he believed the latter to be an anti-democratic form of assimilation.[32] A similar concern may also be expressed regarding Canada where, prior to the advent of the federal policies of bilingualism and multiculturalism in the late 1960s and early 1970s, English unilingualism was virtually enforced and minority groups were pressed to become completely Anglicized. That policy was changed, but bilingualism and multiculturalism still encounter considerable opposition. In the Jewish community, there is concern that "internal disintegration"–the drop in religious affiliation–also leads to assimilation. One answer to this concern is to accept and encourage every mode of Jewish cultural expression, including secularism.

Some degree of assimilation cannot be avoided. Assimilation is really like a river flowing among the nations, and the people on its banks cannot avoid being affected by it. No cultural group, including the Jews, can put up dikes to protect its people forever from the river of assimilation. In fact, it should be seen as a natural phenomenon in the social intercourse of people of all backgrounds.

While the Jews pioneered the concept of monotheism, they have never been monolithic. Ever since the Enlightenment, however, different groups of Jews have offered answers to the question of Jewish survival like evangelists preaching salvation.

Religious partisans still claim that faith in God is the only road to Jewish survival. At a recent Holocaust memorial service, a rabbi expressed thanks that "God survived the Holocaust" and deplored the idea that some Jews believe there can be Judaism without God. Some Jews, however, have questioned the idea of a supernatural God at least since the Maccabean era.

For more than a century, Hebraists have said that Hebrew is the key to Jewish survival, and since the Enlightenment there have been special efforts to revive Hebrew. During the eighteenth-century Berlin Enlightenment, efforts to revive biblical Hebrew were seen as artificial and considered an anachronism. In spite of a Hebrew literary upsurge in Eastern Europe in the 1880s and 1890s, Hebrew failed to make any appreciable advance as a spoken language. Yiddish remained the mother tongue of the vast majority of East European Jews. For that reason, the great Jewish writers of the late nineteenth century, like Sholem Jacob Abramovich (Mendele Mocher Seform) and Sholem Rabinovitz (Sholom Aleichem), switched from Hebrew to Yiddish.[33] The revival of Hebrew did not succeed until the rise of the Zionism and the eventual establishment of the Jewish homeland in Palestine, leading to the birth of Israel.

Some secular Yiddishists, such as Chaim Zhitlowsky, saw the Yiddish language as the key to Jewish national rebirth, and socialism as the road to Jewish national emancipation.[34] However, Yiddish proved not to be the sole or primary vehicle to securing Jewish cultural survival.

When political Zionism began, in the late nineteenth century, inspired by the religious longings for Zion but organized in the secular national-liberation spirit of the times, it was strenuously argued that achievement of the Jewish homeland was the solution to the Jewish problem. In retrospect, with the rise of the State of Israel, one might say that Zionism came closer to the answer for the Jews than did any other movement. But for a world people like the Jews, not even Zionism or the Jewish state can provide the complete answer. There is no way of ensuring that the Jews as an ethno-cultural group can be impregnable.

It cannot be denied that since the destruction of the second Jewish Commonwealth, the Jewish religion has been the central element in keeping the Jews together as a distinct people. As Jews became dispersed through Muslim and Christian lands in Asia, Africa, and Europe, in the medieval and middle ages, geography contributed to the creation of Sephardic and Ashkenazic practices. On the one hand, various messianic groups arose; on the other hand, efforts were made to rationalize Jewish beliefs with the philosophy of Aristotle and with the secular world. As well, the mystical Kabbalah developed among devout Jews, and later the Chassidic movement emerged. The modern divisions of religious Judaism–Reform, neo-Orthodox, Conservative, and Reconstructionist–emerged from the Haskalah. Jewish secularism also came into being via the Zionist, socialist, and Yiddishist movements.

Thus when the emancipation era began, in the mid-nineteenth century, political ideologies began to replace religious faith. These new ideologies drew upon the philosophy inherent in the Jewish religion, as well as ideas and ideals developing in the world at large at that time. Although they were centred on political Zionism, socialism also played a leavening role in Jewish ideological development; this began with the Bund, but later a fusion of Zionist and socialist ideals and more radical left-wing groups began to take root. Religion continues to play a significant role. It is clear, however, that no one religious trend, nor all Jewish religious groups together, have the full and whole-hearted support of the Jewish people.

As for Zionism, its original ideological appeal sparked wide support for humanitarian and philanthropic endeavours for the Jewish-homeland cause and later for the state of Israel. Support for Israel among the Jews is still high, but this can no longer be equated with an ideological commitment to Zionism.

The role of language in the Jewish cultural sphere also requires careful consideration. Some Hebraists may still raise the cry that only Hebrew can assure Jewish cultural survival, and it may be said that the loss of Yiddish has seriously affected the health of Jewish culture. But for many centuries, between the end of the Jewish commonwealth and the beginning of the Haskalah, neither Hebrew nor Yiddish was commonly spoken.

Assessing the rise of Jewish literature in Yiddish, Irving Howe and Eliezer Greenberg discuss other languages spoken by the Jews:

For the Jews, Hebrew has always been loshon hakodesh, the sacred tongue. But at least since the time of the second temple, Hebrew has had to compete–or at best co-exist–with a variety of languages . . . which drove it out of the market place, if not the House of Prayer. During the period of the Second Temple, Aramaic was the daily language of the Jews. After the fall of the Temple the Jews who remained in Palestine began to adopt Greek as their mundane tongue. Many Jews in the near east and North Africa have spoken Arabic for centuries. More recently the Sephardic or Spanish Jews have spoken Ladino in daily speech, while the Ashkenazic, or Eastern Jews have spoken Yiddish.[35]

Howe and Greenberg point out, further, that "bilingualism has been almost inevitable" among the Jews. Jewish culture has carried on despite, and perhaps because of, the changes in language. So why, outside of Israel, should one particular language be crucial? This does not mean that it is no longer necessary to learn Hebrew or Yiddish. One language is not enough; a greater understanding of languages is crucial to cultural survival. Therefore, any trend away from bilingualism among the Jews is a serious problem.

The largest portion of all the Jews in the world, probably a majority, now speak English. Yet, it is only since the end of World War Two that an organized effort has been under way to develop Jewish culture in the English language. At first, some Jewish cultural workers who began to seek expression in English did so grudgingly because of what appeared to be a vested interest in Yiddish or Hebrew.

It has often been claimed that Yiddish cannot be properly translated. Howe and Greenberg comment,

Among American Jews who retain vague memories of Yiddish as the tongue of their parents, there has arisen a legend that Yiddish is untranslatable. Such people always ask, with an air of suppressed triumph, how do you translate this or the other idiom. That is no problem at all: most Yiddish idioms, like most French or American idioms, are untranslatable and the translator is under no obligation to try the impossible; he need only hunt for vivid equivalents.... The idea that Yiddish is somehow uniquely untranslatable may very well arise from a hidden sentimental desire to keep it so, to preserve it as a soft sweet haze of memory." [36]

This attitude may help to bury Jewish culture. If languages were untranslatable, they would undoubtedly stand as a permanent barrier separating nations, peoples, and ethnic groups. Instead of sighing for that lost Yiddish *tam* (taste), more action is needed to save the positive Jewish values inherent in Hebrew and Yiddish literature through imaginative translations.

What about these positive Jewish values? Religious leaders suggest that the Mosaic code contains the sum and substance of positive values. The advocates of different forms of Zionism or any other Jewish idea have promoted their particular beliefs as the core of positive value. *"Es Shteit Geshriben"* (It is written thus and so for evermore), say the pundits of different ideas of Jewishness. In an essay on the Jewish heritage, I. L. Peretz remarked, "Every interpretation lays claim to being the only true form of Jewishness." [37]

Those who are now known as the writers of the "classics" of Jewish literature achieved their status because they set down the real-life experiences of the Jewish people. They criticized and praised, teased and pitied, advised and encouraged. The positive values of Jewishness are there for the seeking, in Yiddish or in translation, in the stories of Mendele Mocher Seforim, Sholom Aleichem, Chaim Bialik, and Peretz.

Howe and Greenberg present an appropriate quotation from Mendele about Jewish life in his time:

The life of the Jews, although it seems outwardly ugly and dark in color, is inwardly beautiful; a mighty spirit animates it, the divine breath which flutters through it from time to time. . . . Israel is the Diogenes of the nations; while his head towers in the heavens and is occupied with deep meditation concerning God and His Wonders, he himself lives in a barrel.[38]

Mendele's "barrel" was, obviously, the economic and political plight of the Jews of Eastern Europe. Today the Jews do not so often have their heads in the heavens, but many may be living in a barrel–a cultural barrel.

Yiddish theatre in America has virtually disappeared, except for the Dora Wasserman Theatre in Montreal and a few struggling groups in New York. The most popular Yiddish plays since the 1880s were called *shund,* a term that can be interpreted, in a pejorative sense, as "vulgar." However, one author defines *shund* as "the sort of art that most cultures and most people like best. . . . It is art for the masses."[39] Based on this definition, the contemporary equivalent of *shund* would likely be "Fiddler on the Roof," the Americanized version of Sholom Aleichem's *Tevye the Dairyman,* which hardly represents the classic Yiddish writer at his best.

Perhaps unknowingly, since he never left Poland, I. L. Peretz explained American vulgarization in his poem "Monish," first published in 1888:

Differently my song would ring
If for gentiles I would sing
Not in Yiddish, in "Jargon,"
That has no proper sound or tone.
It has no word for sex-appeal
and for such things as lovers feel.
Yiddish has but quips and flashes,
Words that fall on us like lashes,
Words that stab like poisoned spears,
And laughter that is full of fears.
And there is a touch of gall,
Of bitterness about it all.[40]

This translation illustrates that a Yiddish poem can be expressed in English and confirms the position of Simon Dubnow, who advocated strong measures in support of Yiddish. In fact, in 1888, Dubnow was the first to call attention to the great talent of Sholom Aleichem. However, he opposed "Yiddishism as a formal dogma."[41] He wrote, in 1929, "History shows us that had the Jewish people rested only on the foundation of language no trace of it would have remained by now." He pointed out that so-called foreign languages have become "mother tongues to great numbers of our people, and . . . Jewish culture must be poured into these language vessels, just as the Jews have always done in their long journey among peoples and lands." He warned against "language chauvinism" in trying to save Jewish culture.[42]

Two vital elements in the furtherance of Jewish culture are history and education, on which Dubnow also made important statements. In 1884 he wrote a strong attack on the traditional *cheder* (Hebrew school), calling these schools "prisons," where children are "criminally tortured . . . in spirit and body" and the teachers are "ignoramuses" whose style of teaching was to forcibly inject "an enormous Babylonian storehouse of wisdom . . . into the brains of these youngsters. They are told nothing about the real world, about nature and life, but only about the next world and about death."[43] Dubnow urged greater attention to Jewish history beyond the Bible and expressed concern that few people "recognize the profound, moral content of the second half of Jewish history, the history of the Diaspora."[44]

Dubnow also de-emphasized the role of religion. He believed in cultural nationalism but rejected religion as the supreme factor in Jewish nationalism: "By aspiring to secularism, by separating the national idea from religion, we aim only to negate the supremacy of religion but not to eliminate it from the storehouse of national cultural treasures." He wanted to preserve Judaism as a "cultural-historical type of nation" and considered the Jewish religion as integral to the national culture. But he took exception to the belief of orthodox Jews in a form of Judaism set for all eternity. He called for "an evolutionary Judaism . . . which adjusts itself to . . . new cultural conditions."[45]

In every era, some of the "people of the Book" have questioned "the Book." Some have questioned the religion; others have questioned the language. Many answers have been advanced, but none have been entirely satisfactory. So long as there are more questions, and more answers are attempted, and if apathy can be held at bay, the "people of the Book" will continue.

Notes

1. Ginzberg, *Legends*, vol. 6, p. 11.

2. Kravitz, *3000 Years*, p. 11.

3. Ibid., p. xvi; Dubnow, *Nationalism and History*, p. 282.

4. Dubnow, *Nationalism and History*, p. 283.

5. Ausubel, *Book of Jewish Knowledge*, pp. 442—53; Roth and Wigoder, *New Standard Jewish Encyclopedia (NSJE)*, pp. 1826—30; *Guide to Humanistic Judaism*. Special issue of *Humanistic Judaism* (Summer/Autumn 1993): 77.

6. Kravitz, *3000 Years*, pp. 231, 259-262.

7. Ibid., pp. 255—58; Roth and Wigoder, *New Standard Jewish Encyclopedia*, p. 945.

8. Kravitz, *3000 Years*, p. 268; Roth and Wigoder, *New Standard Jewish Encyclopedia*, pp. 942, 945.

9. Kravitz, *3000 Years*, p. 301.

10. Peltz, *Mama-Lochen*, pp. 7—8.

11. Kravitz, *3000 Years*, pp. 389, 393—95; Peltz, *Mama-Lochen*, p. 8; Roth and Wigoder, *NSJE*, p. 1212.

12. Kravitz, *3000 Years*, pp 397—98.

13. Ausubel, *Book of Jewish Knowledge*, pp. 26, 85, 92, 137, 167, 220, 468.

14. Roth, *Jews in the Renaissance*, p. 34.

15. Kravitz, *3000 Years*, pp. 398—99.

16. Ibid., pp. 399—402.

17. Henry and Taitz, *Written Out*, pp. 129, 132.

18. Roth, *Jews in the Renaissance*, pp. 56—57.

19. Ibid., p.57; Kravitz, *3000 Years*, pp. 400—02; Henry and Taitz, *Written Out*, pp. 132—34.

20. Kravitz, *3000 Years*, pp. 411—12.

21. Henry and Taitz, *Written Out*, pp. 169—77, 277 fn16.

22. Roth, *Short History*, p. 324.

23. Peltz, *Mama-Lochen*, p. 9.

24. Kravitz, *3000 Years*, pp. 430—32; Roth and Wigoder, *New Standard Jewish Dictionary*, p. 1248; Roth, *History of the Jews of Italy*, p. 401.

25. Kravitz, *3000 Years*, pp. 430—32; Roth and Wigoder, *New Standard Jewish Encyclopedia*, pp. 876, 1203, 1318—20.

26. Kravitz, *3000 Years*, p. 453.

27. Roth and Wigoder, *New Standard Jewish Encyclopedia*, pp. 752—53; Worth, *The Ghetto*, pp. 11—27.

28. Ausubel, *Book of Jewish Knowledge* pp. 120—21; Zborowski and Herzog, *Life is With People*, p. 34.

29. Roskies, *Against the Apocalypse*, pp. 205—06.

30. Ausubel, *Book of Jewish Knowledge*, p. 139.

31. Ibid., pp. 140—41.

32. Kallen, "American Jews," p. 21.

33. Ausubel, *Book of Jewish Knowledge*, p. 200.

34. Roth and Wigoder, *New Standard Jewish Encyclopedia*, p. 2013.

35. Howe and Greenberg, *Treasury of Yiddish Stories*, p. 20.

36. Ibid., p. 46.

37. I.L. Peretz, "What is the Jewish Heritage?," p. 129.

38. Howe and Greenberg, *Treasury of Yiddish Stories*, p. 51.

39. Sandrow, *Vagabond Stars*, pp. 109—112.

40. Howe and Greenberg, *Treasury of Yiddish Stories*, pp. 32—33.

41. Dubnow, *Nationalism and History*, p. 52.

42. Ibid., p. 53.

43. Ibid., pp. 9—10.

44. Ibid., p. 269.

45. Ibid., pp. 45—46.

CHAPTER FOUR

Women in the Bible,
the Talmud, and Beyond

Women are not accorded equal treatment with men in the Jewish Holy Scriptures (the Old Testament of the Bible), nor in the Talmud and later Jewish works. The story begins in Genesis, on the sixth day of "Creation," after all the beasts of the field had been brought to life. Then, "God created man in His own image, in the image of God created He him; male and female created He them."[1] It would seem that man and woman were created equal at that point.

But, after the seventh day, when God rested from his "creative" labours, He found that there was no helpmate for Adam.[2] God then formed all the animals a second time and brought them to Adam to be named. Yet for the man there was still no helpmate. So God caused Adam to fall asleep, took one of his ribs, and made a woman. He brought her to Adam who described her as "bone of my bones, and flesh of my flesh; and she shall be called Woman, because she was taken out of Man."[3]

To account for this apparent anomaly, biblical scholars have explained that these two versions of "Creation" were written at different times, the first one during or after the Babylonian captivity, the second one several hundred years earlier, during the original Yahvistic period.[4] What happened to the "female" created on the sixth day? Ginzberg explains, "Lilith was first given to Adam as wife. Like him she had been created out of the dust of the ground. But she remained with him only a short time, because she insisted on enjoying equality with her husband.[5] She derived her rights from their identical origin." When Adam rejected her claim, she left him and fled from the Garden of Eden. Jewish tradition then turns her into a demon.[6] According to legend, Lilith is a demon who tries to kill newborn children.

The prophet Isaiah, in recounting the evils that would befall the people of Edom for their idolatry, said, in part,

> And the wild-cats shall meet with the jackals,
> And the satyr shall call to his fellow;
> Yea, the **night-monster** shall repose there,
> And shall find her a place of rest.[7]

"Night-monster" is a reference to Lilith. Gaster confirms this view by citing the same Isaiah passage in different words: "In the future the ruins of Edom will be haunted by demons; the night-hag [Lilith, according to Gaster] will make herself at home there."[8] The story of Lilith's demand for equality with Adam is presented in the *Alphabet of Ben Sira*,[9] an eleventh-century work of Jewish folklore credited, without authority, to Jesus Ben Sira, a scribe of the second century B.C.E.[10] It is not surprising that Lilith was transformed into a demon, a witch, or a monster because of her striving for equality with Adam, for the Lilith stories, like all Jewish legends since ancient times, were written by men.

In mystical and Kabbalistic literature, Lilith is also called the queen of demons, the consort of Satan, and the symbol of sensual lust and sexual temptation. According to the Holy scriptures, however, Satan himself was not a demon or an evil spirit but a member of the Divine household who took the role of accuser.[11] In the Book of Job, where Satan is first named, he is simply someone who throws a monkey-wrench into the works. He challenges God to inflict certain hardships on Job to test him in the steadfastness of his faith.[12] The meaning of the name Satan, in this sense, is simply "obstructor."[13] Satan's identification with the demonic actually originates with other, non-Jewish traditions, including Christianity. On the other hand, the single biblical reference said to refer to Lilith, and calling her a monster or night-hag, allows for no redeeming view.

Only with the rise of the Jewish feminist movement, in the early 1970s, has a positive interpretation of Lilith been developed. Roslyn Lacks relates the changes in the Lilith story from the *Alphabet of Ben Sira* to "The Coming of Lilith," by the feminist theologian Judith Plaskow, the founding of the Jewish feminist magazine named *Lilith,* and the Bat Kol Players, the feminist theatre group that produced a play based on Lilith.[14]

There is another explanation for the quick disposal of the woman who wanted to be equal with man. Will Durant relates that in primitive times, when the family was first organized, the role of the man was "superficial and incidental, while that of the woman was fundamental and supreme," perhaps because the male role in reproduction "appears to have escaped notice." There was a time when descent was traced through the female and inheritance was through the mother. But this was not a "matriarchate," Durant asserts; "it did not imply the rule of women over men."[15]

Lacks presents pre-biblical legends, from Africa and South America, of a time when society was matriarchal and women dominated men.[16] They include the experience of the Kikuyu people of Kenya, who are said to have begun as a matriarchy, and of the Ona Indians of Tiera del Fuego, where women once ruled. The Kikuyu story, recorded by Jomo Kenyatta, which is "happily unburdened by assertions of divine authorship," according to Lacks, tells that the women practised polyandry and kept men subservient. But after a time the men staged a revolution, overthrew the women, and assumed leadership, taking all the privileges the women had enjoyed previously.

The central element in the men's revolution was to get all the women pregnant at the same time so that a revolt could be carried out when the women were in the last stages of pregnancy and unable to fight back.[17]

The myth of Genesis began where the legend of women's superiority ended, Lacks explains, and the Bible evolved in terms of woman's domination by man. Eve, because she ate of the tree of knowledge and persuaded Adam to do the same, was punished with the pain of childbirth and was obliged to submit to her husband's rule.[18]

The questionable treatment of women arises with the story of the generations of Terah, who had three sons, Abram, Nahor, and Haran; no daughters are reported. The third son, Haran, "died in the presence of his father" and left a son, Lot, and a daughter, Milcah. Nahor married his niece, Milcah, and Abram, or Abraham, married Sarah, who is referred to only as Terah's "daughter-in-law."[19]

On two occasions, Abraham passed Sarah off as his sister because she was "fair to look upon." The first time, in Egypt, where they went to escape a famine in Canaan, Sarah was taken into Pharaoh's house. For her, Abraham was given sheep and oxen, other livestock, and servants. Then "The Lord plagued Pharaoh . . . with great plagues because of Sarah." Pharaoh asked Abraham why he said that Sarah was his sister "so that I took her to be my wife," but Abraham's answer is not known.[20] Later, Abraham told Abimelech, King of Gerar, that Sarah was his sister. Abimelech took her into his house and also got into trouble with God over it. This time, Abraham claimed she was his half-sister and that they both had the same father.[21] It appears that a matrilineal system was in vogue at that time, and children of the same father but different mothers were not considered blood relatives.[22]

The treatment of women comes into question again with Dinah, the daughter of Jacob and Leah, who was taken and "humbled" by the Hivite prince, Shechem. But he loved her, spoke "comfortingly" to her, and sought her as his wife. Shechem's father, Hamor, offered an alliance between the Hivites and the Israelites, to accomplish his son's desire. But Dinah's brothers, concerned that their sister had been "defiled," said they could grant his request only if all the Hivite men were circumcised. The Hivites agreed to this demand, but the sons of Jacob, instead of honouring their agreement, went out and killed the Hivite men when they were in pain from the circumcisions. They took their sister away from Shechem and made off with the Hivite women.[23] Lacks argues that the Dinah episode is used solely to oppose the idea of intermarriage.[24]

The biblical prohibition against homosexual acts (Leviticus 18:22 and 20:13) has often been invoked in arguments against its inclusion in codes of human rights. Non-fundamentalist biblical scholars have established that the sexual prohibitions set forth in Leviticus were written at the time of the Babylonian captivity, when many Israelites had resorted to idolatry. Whatever one's belief may be, so long as one is not a fundamentalist, these biblical proscriptions should now be seen as part of the outmoded baggage of the so-called Judaeo-Christian tradition.

Apart from the Levitican prohibitions, the Old Testament episodes involving sodomy demonstrate, above all else, the exploitation and repression of women. (Because of what allegedly happened in Sodom, where Abraham's nephew, Lot, was living, sexual intercourse between men is known as sodomy.) The story relates that two angels, disguised as men, came to visit Lot, who welcomed them in his home. During the night, the men of Sodom surrounded Lot's house and demanded that he send out the two visitors so that "we may know them." Lot urged the men to refrain from such wickedness and offered them his "two daughters that have not known man; let me . . . bring them out unto you and do ye to them as is good in your eyes; only unto these men do nothing."[25] The men refused Lot's offer and broke into the house to have their way with the visiting men. But the visitors, being angels of God, "smote the men . . . at the door of the house with blindness,"[26] preventing them from carrying out their intention. What is significant, however, is that Lot was prepared to sacrifice his daughters to protect his male guests.

There is a second incident in the Old Testament in which the rape of women was considered preferable to forced sexual intercourse between men. This episode[27] involved a Levite who was travelling with his concubine through the land of the tribe of Benjamin. He took refuge for the night in the home of the only man in the town of Gibeah who would give him shelter. While they rested, "certain base fellows beset the house . . . beating at the door; and they spoke to the master of the house . . . saying: 'Bring forth the man that came into thy house, that we may know him.'"

The master of the house, went out and said to them, "Nay, my brethren, I pray you, do not so wickedly . . . Behold, here is my daughter a virgin, and his concubine; I will bring them out now, and humble ye them, and do with them what seemeth good unto you; but unto this man do not so wanton a thing."

At first the men would not listen to him, but when the concubine was brought to them "they knew her, and abused her all night until the morning." She ended up dead on the doorstep.

The Levite took his murdered concubine, cut her up into twelve pieces, and distributed the pieces throughout the land of Israel to arouse the people against the Benjaminites. This action caused the other tribes to make war against the tribe of Benjamin, and there was much bloodshed and loss of life on both sides. The men of Israel swore not to give their daughters as wives to the men of Benjamin even though all the women of the tribe of Benjamin had been slain.

Eventually, the enmity between the Benjaminites and the other tribes was ended. But the men of Israel were fearful of breaking the oath they had sworn not to give their daughters as wives to the Benjaminites. How could they get around it?

They discovered that the people of Jabesh-gilead had not participated in the war against Benjamin. So they sent an army of twelve thousand men to smite the inhabitants of that city, instructed to "utterly destroy every male, and every woman that hath lain by man." But they saved four hundred young virgins, brought them to Shiloh in the land of Canaan, and gave them to the men of Benjamin. There were not enough virgins, however, and some Benjaminites were still without women.

Still concerned about their oath, the men of Israel devised another stratagem. They informed the men of Benjamin who were still without wives of an upcoming feast day when the young women of Shiloh would come out to dance in the fields, and they suggested to their former enemies, "Then come ye out of the vineyards, and catch you every man his wife of the daughters of Shiloh." So the gang-rape of one concubine at Gibeah ended up with the forced marriage to the men of Benjamin of the four hundred virgins of Jabesh-gilead and of an additional number of young women of Shiloh.

Whether these biblical episodes are the "word of God" or the writings of a priest or scribe, their author obviously held women to be little more than the chattels of men.

There are certain exceptional situations depicting a more positive role for female characters in Jewish legend. In the Talmudic legend described at the beginning of chapter three, the heavenly voice that called out to the Israelites was the Bat Kol, suggested as the "Daughter of the Voice of God." I wondered why the Bat Kol, described as the instrument by which God proclaimed his will,[28] was presented as the "daughter." One rabbi I consulted suggested that to call the voice "Bar," meaning "son of," rather than "Bat," might imply the recognition that God had a son, which is, of course, contrary to Jewish belief. The other said that "Bat Kol" simply means an echoing voice. My English-Yiddish dictionary defines "Baskol" as "oracular," but "bas" is still "daughter."[29] Ausubel gives a further hint about the significance of the "Bat" or "Bas Kol" by relating it to the Shechina, defined in most sources as the "divine" or "holy" spirit. In the mystical literature of Kabbalah, the Shechina is described as a term for the feminine aspect of God.[30]

Lacks revives the argument about whether God is male or female by saying that the Shechina is the "pure and divine female essence" of God, who was "compelled to leave God's side to join the exiled nation on earth" after the destruction of the Temple. According to Lacks, monotheism covered up "the human need for female eminence [that] continued to erupt throughout the ages, manifesting itself . . . [as] a heavenly family [with] . . . the emergence of the Shechina, identified with the nation of Israel in conjugal relations with its god."[31] The modern Jewish feminist movement has used the Shechina myth to advance the concept of God as both female and male. Therefore, it is argued that the first human, created in the image of God, would also have been androgynous.[32]

Until the Israelites left Egypt, in the Exodus, the role of women did not extend beyond the domestic front. Sarah's only independent act was to give her servant Hagar to Abraham to produce his first child, Ishmael. Rebecca is remembered for counselling Jacob to dress in the clothes of his twin brother Esau to obtain the blessing of the first-born from his father Isaac. Leah and Rachel are noted mainly for competing for the favours of Jacob, the husband they shared. The matriarchs are thus celebrated primarily for the sons born to them and for their role in determining the course followed by their sons within the patriarchal context.[33] The Bible calls Miriam a "prophet-ess" but does not specify her role apart from her association with Moses and Aaron and her leadership of the women in a dance.[34]

Deborah, the judge and prophetess, was the first woman who apparently played an independent role. The Bible says that "the children of Israel came up to her for judgment," as she sat under the palm trees. She also commanded Barak, in the name of "the Lord, the God of Israel," to take ten thousand men and go to fight Sisera, the captain of the army of Israel's Canaanite enemy. Barak said that he would do as Deborah commanded only if she went with him, and she did just that.

Deborah is said to have risen to power at a time when the Israelites had fallen into idolatry; she brought them back into line and there was peace in Israel for forty years.[35] Recently, it has been claimed that Deborah was "the one person who . . . managed to unite the tribes [of Israel] into a nation that has endured until today."[36] The first evidence that this claim is exaggerated is in the account of the virtual civil war between the Israelites and the tribe of Benjamin in the aftermath of the dismemberment of the Levite's concubine at Gibeah. A more reasonable comment about Deborah is that when "Israel was without a leader, or a man of tried courage, a woman, a poetess and prophetess, Deborah . . . came forward as a 'mother in Israel' . . . animated the timorous people and changed them from cowards into heroes."[37]

Another woman, Jael, wife of Heber the Kenite, aided the Israelites when they were at war with Sisera. It is said that Sisera fled to Jael's tent when his army was defeated. There, for the first time in Jewish legend, a woman feigned friendship with an enemy of Israel and then killed him. Jael drove a tent-pin into Sisera's temples while he slept.[38]

The second woman prophet was Huldah, who lived in Jerusalem in the reign of King Josiah (637—608 B.C.E.). Her role may have been more significant than that of any other woman in the Jewish Scriptures, but some contemporary writers, in bringing to light the "hidden legacy" of Jewish women, have given her only passing reference.[38] She is said to have "prophesied at the gate of the Academy" and to have been a teacher of the elders.[40] Her counsel, like Deborah's, "was much sought after."[41] While very little is known about Huldah, it is certain that she "wielded some influence upon the king and the people and her words had to be listened to."[42]

Around 621 B.C.E., during the reign of King Josiah of Judah, the high priest, Hilkiah, is said to have "found the book of the Law," believed to have been Deuteronomy. When the book was read to Josiah, he "rent his clothes" and commanded Hilkiah to seek its meaning. The high priest and his aides went to consult with Huldah who told them the message of the book was that God would "bring evil upon this place and upon the inhabitants thereof . . . because they have forsaken Me and have offered unto other gods." But God's punishment would come later, after the death of Josiah, she said.

Huldah's prophecy moved the king to proclaim the book of the Law to the people and begin his campaign against idolatry.[43] Thus the male authors of the first "discovered" book of the Torah assigned a woman to utter the words that set the people of Judea, later the Jews, on the road to genuine monotheism.

The other heroic women of the biblical era are Naomi and Ruth of the Book of Ruth; Esther, of the historic novel which the Rabbis accepted into the Bible; and Judith, who emulated Jael by killing an enemy of the Maccabees. Thus there are a few women in that era who are outstanding in their own right (although the books of Judith and the Maccabees were in fact left out of the Bible), but they are hardly more than occasional exceptions that prove the rule of the negative attitude toward women that largely prevails through the Scriptures, the Talmud and later rabbinic writings.

Explanations and Apologetics

One part of the Talmud commentaries is the Aggadah, an explanatory sequel to biblical chronicles, moral instructions, and admonitions of the prophets. The Aggadah contains an explanation of why Eve was made from Adam's rib, in God's own words:

> I must not create her from the head, that she should not carry herself haughtily; nor from the eye that she should not be too inquisitive; nor from the ear that she should not be an eavesdropper; nor from the mouth that she should not be too talkative; nor from the hand that she should not be too acquisitive; nor from the foot that she should not be a gadabout. I will fashion her from a hidden portion of man's body that she should be modest. [44]

There is more than one version of God's words on the making of Eve. Another suggests that from the head she might have "arrogant pride," from the eye she might be "wanton-eyed," and from the neck "insolent." Thus a rib, "a chaste portion of the body," was chosen. [45]

The rabbis went on to suggest that God's "painstaking precautions" in creating Eve did not help. They said that women developed all the faults God tried to prevent. They were "haughty and walked with stretched forth necks and wanton eyes." Sarah is called "an eavesdropper in her own tent when the angel spoke with Abraham. . . . Miriam, a tale-bearer accusing Moses; Rachel envious of her sister, Leah; Eve put out her hand to take the forbidden fruit; and Dinah was a gadabout." [46]

The Bible proclaims women to be ritually unclean during menstruation and following childbirth. Observant Jewish women have thus been governed by the laws of *niddah* on menstruation, as set forth by the rabbis in a Mishnah tractate of the Talmud, based on the provisions in Leviticus. [47] Lacks states that *niddah* "at its root means 'banishment'"; she seems to be paraphrasing Leonard Swidler, who, in his book *Women in Judaism*, says "'banishment' [is what] the word *niddah* means in its root."[48] Lacks cites Rachel Adler to the effect that *niddah* became distorted into "controlling the fearsome power of sexual desire."[49] "The state of *niddah* became a monthly exile from the human race, a punitive shunning of the menstruant."[50]

There are also specific provisions in the Bible setting out that men are worth more than women. A woman who gave birth to a male child was held "unclean" for seven days; if she gave birth to a female child she was "unclean" for two weeks.[51] As well, a higher monetary value is set for men than for women: when a man makes "a vow of persons unto the Lord, thy valuation shall be for the male from 20 years old unto 60 . . . 50 shekels of silver . . . And if it be a female then thy valuation shall be 30 shekels.[52] This valuation was set in relation to an ancient religious practice that was long ago abandoned.

The differentiation between men and women arising from the Bible led to a series of inequities endured by women down to modern times in divorce, the taking of vows, and the ownership of property. There is an explicit provision that if a wife no longer finds favour in the eyes of her husband he may give her a "bill of divorcement" and send her away.[53] This right is the basis of Jewish religious law by which only the husband may initiate a divorce. As well, a husband may disallow the vow of his wife and a father may disallow the vow of his daughter if he does it when the vow is heard.[54]

Jewish law recognizes only the right of a man to own property; in biblical times women did not own or inherit property, except in special circumstances. Sons were the heirs of their fathers, and the first-born son had priority. In cases where there were no sons, daughters were granted the right to inherit their father's property before other male relatives, provided they did not marry out of the tribe to which they belonged. This right was established when the five daughters–Mahlah, Noah, Hoglah, Milcah and Tirzah–of Zelophedad, who had no sons, appealed for an inheritance before Moses, Eliezer the priest, the princes, and "all the congregation, at the door of the tent of meeting."[55] A husband could inherit his wife's property, but a wife could not inherit her husband's property.[56]

Discussing "contradictory Talmudic ideas about women," Ernest Trattner cites one Babylonian sage, Mar Samuel, saying that "listening to the voice of a woman is a profanation" and another, Rabbi Sheshet, saying the same about the sight of a woman's hair. Rabbi Eliezer deemed it "inadvisable" for women to "spend time in the lecture halls, studying the law."[57] (Eliezer is quoted elsewhere as saying, "Whosoever teaches his daughter Torah teaches her lasciviousness."[58]) However, Ben Azzai, a colleague of Eliezer's, held that each father should teach his daughter Scripture and the Oral Law. Trattner holds that the negative views of women resulted from "currents of immorality . . . during Talmudic times [that came from] the spread of gnostic ideas." He also writes of "the moral breakdown and licentiousness in certain periods of Greek life as the result of women's activity and leadership."[59]

"Mosaic Law," Trattner believes, protected women from misogynist ideas, since the commandment "Honour your father and your mother" places "woman on a par with man." Acknowledging that women were not considered competent witnesses in any court case, Trattner adds that "this in no manner interfered with their position in their own household!" He recalls Bible episodes seen as favourable to women, particularly the "Qualities of a good wife," who does everything for the benefit of her husband.[60] But he does not choose to see even one anti-female idea in the Scriptures![61]

Nathan Ausubel, who discusses most subjects of Jewish knowledge in an enlightened and expository manner, devotes close to half of his discourse on the treatment of Jewish women to a defensive posture. He begins with the assertion that "most of the time, Jewish women fared better at the hands of their menfolk than did the women of other peoples. This was especially true during those fervent centuries of Hellenistic times, when the Talmud was being created."

Ausubel does cite the "indignation" he feels at the "gratuitous 'insult' to womankind" in the early-morning Hebrew liturgy, in which the man, after thanking God for not being made a "heathen" or a "bondman" (slave), goes on to "exult," "Blessed art thou, O Lord our God, King of the Universe, who hast not made me a woman!"[62] Ausubel then presents detailed excuses and apologetics by the rabbis for this expression of male superiority. Their intention was to keep woman in her place, in the home, to fulfil tasks that they claimed were equal to the religious obligations of the man. Ausubel acknowledges that the Jewish woman was assigned "an inferior role in religious life as well as in society" because she was excluded from the *minyan* (prayer quorum) and from participation in public prayers or other congregational functions.

Ausubel returns to apologetics about "less attractive features" of religious laws kept on the statute books because of the "odor of sanctity attached to them." Although he concedes that the "sacred literature" of the Jews still has "laws, regulations and opinions about women that are primitive and harsh," he asserts that "the traditional Jewish evaluation" of women is "enlightened" and accords them "full equality with man as a human being."[63] It should be noted that these comments were made before the rise of modern feminism.

Since the 1970s, many women have become activists in seeking enhanced rights and status in all areas of Jewish life, religious and secular. The *Encyclopedia Judaica*, in a broad-ranging and enlightened essay on women, states, "No amount of apologetics can get over the implications of the daily blessing [on not being a woman] which orthodox Judaism has still lacked the courage to remove from its official prayer book." This comment is credited to the Anglo-Jewish scholar, Claude Montefiore, great-nephew of Sir Moses Montefiore and founder of the Liberal (Reform) Jewish movement in England.[64]

In 1973, Rabbi Saul Berman, then chairman of Judaic Studies at Stern College for Women, Yeshiva University (Orthodox) declared that it was time to "call a moratorium on apologetics" regarding the status of women in the Jewish religion. He stated that it was "dishonest . . . to attempt, through homiletics and scholasticism, to transform problems into solutions and to reinterpret discrimination to be beneficial." Apologetics "only serve to exacerbate the problem" of women seeking equality in the Jewish religion. Berman also warned that there is an "exceedingly thin line" between "apologetics and explanation." Taking this into account, he went on to consider laws and social practices that "seem" unjust to women.

First, he suggested that the "Talmudic sages" did not make "a single attempt to formulate a general principle governing the status of women." Then, on the subject of women studying Torah, he pointed out that, in addition to the views of the rabbis opposing or obligating women in Torah study, there was a middle view that women might study without being obligated. Considering various patterns of thought among the rabbis, he concluded that "the most striking of the patterns is the absence of a specific role definition for women."[65] With this conclusion, Berman probably crossed his own "thin line."

A comprehensive study on women in Judaism since pre-biblical times is presented by Leonard Swidler in what he terms a work of historiography dealing with "the place of women in human society and their relationship to men." To begin, he stresses the need to guard against "the sort of apologetic" prevalent since the Haskalah and the rise of "subsequent feminist movements." He then criticizes the tendency of Judaism and Christianity to claim that women were highly valued and even made "equal" to men. He quotes Jospehus, the Roman-era Jewish historian, as stating, "The woman, says the Law, is in all things inferior to the man," and "the Law," in effect, is the word of the Torah. Paul of Tarsus "echoed the same idea" for the Christians.[66]

To place his comments in their historical context, Swidler reviews the attitude toward women in society prior to and at the time when Judaism was in its "formative" stage (second century B.C.E. to fifth century C.E.). Before 2400 B.C.E., in the ancient Sumerian civilization of Babylonia, "woman may well have been man's equal socially and economically, at least among the ruling class." But by 2000 B.C.E., when the biblical legend of Abraham begins, male domination was the rule and the patriarchy was established.[67]

Swidler adds that some scholars dispute the idea of a long, "beneficent period of matriarchy" before patriarchy was firmly established.[68] The Kikuyu legend about the rule of women, discussed earlier in this chapter, probably corresponds to the Sumerian era. Swidler also discloses that in ancient Egypt, from the age of the pyramids to the end of the Hellenistic period (2778 B.C.E. to 30 B.C.E.), women enjoyed a high status–for example, at certain times daughters had the same inheritance rights as sons and "the wife was the equal of husband in rights." By the eighth century B.C.E., however, male dominance was no longer in doubt. In Athens, in the "golden age" of Pericles (fifth to fourth century B.C.E.), the status of women reached a "nadir in Western history."

In Periclean Athens, however, there were already the beginnings of a movement for women's liberation, which made "enormous advances from the time of Alexander to Constantine."[69] This was the period when Judea came under the sway of Hellenism. Thus Trattner's claim that negative attitudes toward women were due to Greek influence and women's leadership may be ascribed to this early women's-liberation movement. This movement, which led to improvements in the status of women in the Hellenistic sphere, brings into question the defensive claim that women were always better treated in Jewish society than in non-Jewish society.

Swidler's revelations support Lacks's conclusion that the evolution of the Talmud led to "the unequivocal assumption of separate orders of life for male and female, buttressed by a profound ambivalence towards women." The negative aspects of that ambivalence, Lacks adds, were "invariably heightened" during the times of turmoil and stress that affected the Jews periodically throughout their history.[70] Sondra Henry and Emily Taitz conclude that the Talmudic rabbis considered women intellectually inferior–"'lightminded' and extremely sexually and physically oriented, hence a constant lure and temptation to men." In addition to finding individual exceptions to the rules, customs, and practices restricting women, Henry and Taitz also report some rabbinic viewpoints favouring the teaching of women. But they quote Swidler's conclusion "that the overwhelming feelings of the Talmudic rabbis were against equality of women" and that their exclusion from certain *mitzvot* (commandments), because of household obligations "eventually amounted to a prohibition for women" from learning.[71]

During the rabbinic era, there were, nevertheless, one or two women who achieved renown as Talmudic scholars. The best known of these was Beruriah (second century c.e.), who lived in the time of the Bar Kochba revolt against the Romans. She was married to Rabbi Meir, who is said to have encouraged his wife, and other women, to study (although Meir is mentioned as the author of the male prayer giving thanks for not being made a woman[72]). Some of Beruriah's opinions are recorded in the Talmud. There is a later legend, recounted by Rashi, an eleventh-century rabbinical scholar in France, that Beruriah's husband decided to test her faithfulness by arranging for one of pupils to attempt to seduce her. When she felt herself tempted, Beruriah, realizing her weakness, allegedly committed suicide.

Lacks states that Rashi's commentary on Beruriah "endeavors to illuminate an obscure reference in the Talmudic tractate *Avoda Zara*." She calls Beruriah's seduction an "unlikely story" recounted by Rashi a thousand years later to undercut the stature of a female authority on the Talmud.[73] Swidler concurs that the alleged seduction story "was invented simply to morally annihilate Beruriah, the one woman of superior stature in the Talmud." In support of his position, Swidler cites Henry Zirndorf, a Jewish scholar who, in 1892, wrote of the charge against Beruriah, "The improbability of this occurrence is too obvious. . . . This calumny ought no longer to be permitted to tarnish the memory of the pure and noble-minded Beruriah."[74]

Swidler exposes the unequal treatment and inferior status imposed on women in Jewish society throughout the period under review in his work. They suffered the same disadvantages as children and slaves. The degree to which Jewish women could appear in public at the outset of the Common Era was far less than in the surrounding Hellenistic milieu, and when they did go out their heads and faces were covered, with just one eye free. There was a prohibition against "superfluous talk" with women. Women could neither eat with men nor serve them when a guest was present. Rabbinical documents project women as "almost totally sex objects." In marriage, the wife was in a position clearly inferior to her husband. For a married man, extra-marital intercourse was not, *per se*, a crime; but for a married woman adultery merited death in a barbaric manner. And, of course, a man could easily divorce his wife, but a wife could not divorce her husband under other than very exceptional circumstances.

Swidler declares that in the "formative period" of Judaism the status of women was based on "severe inferiority" to men and that "intense misogynism was not infrequently present." With the "sacred and secular spheres . . . so intertwined," women's subordination was present in "both the religious and civil areas of Jewish life." During the same era, the status of women was "significantly higher" in Greek and Roman society than in Judaism, and it generally improved throughout the period. The "subordinate" position of women "was so profoundly . . . bound up with Judaism" in the formative period that "the inferiority of women and misogynism . . . tended to have an overwhelming influence in the subsequent history of Judaism."[75]

Swidler's conclusion is borne out from an examination of Moses Maimonides, who placed women in a lesser role than men. In his *Guide to the Perplexed,* he listed woman with "turbid, transient matter," while man was linked with "loftier realms of the spirit." Man is urged to "transcend the baser compost of his noble form," while woman is considered "incapable of transcendence" and remains "glued to gluttonies of the flesh."[76]

In the Middle Ages, in Egypt and in other Mediterranean communities, women participated in all aspects of Jewish life, from trade and politics to philanthropy and scholarship, though they were limited in religion and formal rabbinic studies. Israel Abrahams, an English Talmudic scholar (1858—1925), states, "The rigid separation of the sexes in prayer seems not to have [occurred] earlier than the thirteenth century." In fact, "it is not impossible that they prayed together with the men in Talmudic times."[77] This tends to support Lacks's claim that the Talmud permitted women to be called to the Torah and to read from the Torah. Lacks adds that women's Torah privileges were abolished by Maimonides "to preserve the honor of men," but she cites no supporting sources. Swidler cites sources showing that women were originally called to the Torah but were later forbidden to carry out the readings. Henry and Taitz say that Maimonides, on moving from Spain to

Egypt, urged that women not be appointed to any communal office; as well, he revived the anti-feminist attitudes scattered throughout the Talmud.[78] Maimonides' view was not followed in all Jewish communities. Abrahams cites a woman in six-teenth-century Rome, "entitled *Parnessa*" (probably a vice-president) in charge of charities. The title was rare, Abraham adds, but the office was common throughout the Middle Ages.[79] Moreover, Maimonides stated, "A wife who refuses to perform any kind of work that she is obligated to do, may be compelled to perform it, even by scourging her with a rod."[80]

Isaac Klein, the 1972 translator of Maimonides, calls this a "rather amazing statement" and rationalizes that Maimonides "found it advisable to yield to the prevalent mores of the Moslem society in which he lived." But then Klein discloses that Islamic law "forbids physical abuse of the wife," although the Koran says that "perverse" women may be "chastised." Klein goes on to cite some "less brilliant" contemporaries of Maimonides who deplored wife-beating as out of keeping with Jewish tradition.[81]

Many of the foregoing negative and ambivalent positions, often leading to outright proscriptions, from the biblical era to the Middle Ages, have adversely affected women right up to contemporary times. Of course, the myths and "laws" recorded in the Bible, and the legends, elaborations and rules set down in the Talmud, were all written by men and, whether they were done consciously or unconsciously, had the primary effect of reinforcing patriarchy.

When history, no longer "divinely inspired," was being written in the Hellenistic and Roman eras, a more realistic approach to the record of human experience began to unfold. However, since writers were almost always men, a male bias was usual in the treatment of women. The Bible, the Talmud, and subsequent Jewish works have adversely affected the status of women, in both the Western and Muslim worlds. The biblical episodes and Talmudic tractates concerning women have directly influenced the Jews up to and including modern times, and the Old Testament and some Talmudic precepts on women were taken over by Christianity as part of the "Judaeo-Christian" tradition. As well, proscriptions against women in the Muslim world are strikingly similar to those in the Bible and the Talmud.

Efforts to change the restricted status of women in Jewish life have usually been in keeping with the movement for women's liberation in Western civilization. In the Jewish community, the women's movement may be traced to the Haskalah; improvements in the status of Jewish women are generally credited to the rise of Reform Judaism. However, it took almost a century from the time they first began to discuss the ordination of women until a female rabbi first took her place in a Reform pulpit in the 1970s.

Women in America began to assert their place in the Jewish community by forming their own organizations, beginning with the Female Hebrew Benevolent Society in Philadelphia in 1819.[82] In Montreal, the Hebrew Ladies Benevolent Society was established in 1877. The National Council of Jewish Women was founded in the United States in 1893, with the first Canadian chapter formed in Toronto in 1897. The feminist movement, however, did not become a serious element in Jewish life until the 1970s. Since then, all groups in Judaism have responded, in one way or another, to the demands of women for equality.

Most of the debate on redefining the role of Jewish women is linked to religion. At a major conference of Jewish women in New York in 1973, Judith Plaskow stated that the women's-liberation movement "is a secular movement whose principles we are attempting to apply to an ancient religious tradition."[83] The movement for the dignity and equality of women began over a century ago and included issues such as suffrage for women. It began as a secular movement, but it has moved into the sphere of organized religion in a big way. Feminism is now shaking the foundations of all denominations of Judaism and Christianity, and the debate about the place of women in religion is still raging.

Susan Weidman Schneider discusses efforts "to reconcile Judaism and feminism" and quotes a range of answers from "complete rejection to loving rebuke."[84] She cites Naomi R. Goldenberg, a feminist theologian, who, while expressing pride in her Jewish origin, stated, "[I] want to be identified with my people, but I wish to separate myself from the religion. Actually, I do not have to separate myself from the religion—Jewish sages and rabbis have done that for me."[85] It is Schneider's view, however, that there are "undisputed links" between Judaism and the ongoing movement for gender equality. She points out that social justice and ethical human relations are stressed by Judaism and brings to her support the view of Batya Bauman, a New York Jewish lecture bureau manager, who said, "Many Jewish feminists are feminists because we are Jews. . . . Stripped of male dominance, the Jewish world view may not be so different from the feminist world view."[86] Schneider also quotes Blu Greenberg, the Orthodox Jewish feminist, on the effect of feminism on her "sense of harmony." Greenberg longs to be "the deeply devout person" she once was, when "everything God said was sacred." She "can never go back," but she hopes that "when the dust settles" and when women's equality becomes natural in traditional Judaism, "I'll be touched by the spirit again."[87]

What will really happen in the religion of Judaism "when the dust settles"? Goldenberg is not optimistic: "If women win, Judaism (and Christianity) cannot survive." Goldenberg's basic position is, "If men are no longer considered better than women, and if equal numbers of both sexes are involved in all the work of society then Judaism cannot survive."[88] In seeking a non-sexist religion, feminists are asking for a religion that is "radically new," even if it contains elements of tradition. It cannot be a "mere cosmetic alteration" of the old religion. Therefore, these "reformed religions should, perhaps, not be called by the old names." Goldenberg believes that the Jewish feminist has nowhere to go but "out of traditional and conventional Judaism." This option is fine for those who are prepared to "radically [reconceive] the whole enterprise."[89] Recognizing the right to free choice, however, it should be realized that many feminists, who are not prepared to follow Goldenberg, are still working to improve the status of women within the traditional and conventional streams of Judaism.

Some women have adopted male symbols, such as the *tallit* (prayer shawl), *tfillin* (phylacteries), and the *kippah* (skull cap), although some feminists would agree with Rabbi Sherwin Wine, the founder of Humanistic Judaism, who says, "Certain Jewish symbols are so tied into male chauvinist behavior and clothing style that their use by women becomes a desperate travesty . . . honoring those traditions . . . built on the exclusion of women. Self-respecting Jewish women do not seek to rescue the signs of humiliation."[90] Nevertheless, women, "to be complete Jews with their brothers . . . are entitled to rewrite the definition . . . of these admittedly powerful symbols. Rabbi Wine may see casting off these symbols as part of his own agenda for change, but others have been trying to transform the symbols."[91] The efforts of some women to redefine and redesign the established streams of Judaism should be respected and appreciated as should their efforts to reinterpret and rewrite Jewish history.

Wine makes some other important points, however. One is that before the Haskalah began there was "no context" in which a women's liberation movement could have existed. It was the "dramatic effects" of scientific, industrial, and urban revolutions that undermined the male-dominated family unit.

He is also correct in saying that Jewish feminism, like Jewish humanism, "must be future oriented."

Notes

1. Genesis 1:27.
2. Genesis 2:20.
3. Genesis 2:19—23.
4. Gaster, *Myth, Legend and Custom*, p. 8.
5. Ginzberg, *Legends of the Jews*, vol. 1, p. 65.
6. Zuckoff, "The Lilith Question," p. 5; Lacks, *Women and Judaism*, pp. 38—39; Roth and Wigoder, *New Standard Jewish Encyclopedia*, p. 1226.
7. Isaiah 34:14; emphasis added.
8. Gaster, *Myth, Legend and Custom*, p. 578.
9. The Lilith story told in *Alphabet of Ben Sira* is excerpted in Zuckoff, "The Lilith Question."
10. Roth and Wigoder, *New Standard Jewish Encyclopedia*, p. 266.
11. Ibid., pp. 1691—92.
12. *Holy Scriptures*, p. 899; Job 1:6—12.
13. Gaster, *Myth, Legend and Custom*, pp. 785—86.
14. Lacks, *Women and Judaism*, pp. 38-61.
15. Durant, *Story of Civilization*, vol. 1, *Our Oriental Heritage*, pp. 30—32.
16. Lacks, *Women and Judaism*, p. 23.
17. Ibid., pp. 16—22.
18. Genesis 3:16.
19. Genesis 11:27—31.
20. Genesis 12:10—20.
21. Genesis 20:1—18.
22. Plaskow, *Standing Again at Sinai*, p. 42; Teubal, *Sarah the Priestess*, p. 14.
23. Genesis 34:1—31.
24. Lacks, *Women and Judaism*, p. 32.
25. Genesis 19:5—8.
26. Genesis 19:8—11.
27. Judges 19—20.
28. Ausubel, *Book of Jewish Knowledge*, p. 32.
29. Weinreich, *Modern English-Yiddish Dictionary*, p. 355.
30. Roth and Wigoder, *New Standard Jewish Encyclopedia*, pp. 1096, 1737.
31. Lacks, *Women and Judaism*, pp. 40, 49—50, 87.
32. Schneider, *Jewish and Female*, p. 80; Plaskow, *Standing Again at Sinai*, pp. 124, 138—40.

33. Lacks, *Women and Judaism*, chapter 6 and p. 99.

34. Exodus 15: 20—21; Micah 6:4.

35. Judges 5:7—8, 31.

36. Henry and Taitz, *Written Out*, p. 26.

37. Graetz, *History of the Jews*, vol. 1, p. 61.

38. Judges 4:1—24.

39. Henry and Taitz, *Written Out*, p. 23; Lacks, *Women and Judaism*, p. 92.

40. Rashi comment elaborating on Hulda's role in II Kings 22:14 in his commentary on the Pentateuch, *Microt Gedollot*.

41. Graetz, *History of the Jews*, vol. 1, p. 286.

42. Kravitz, *3000 Years*, pp. 41—42. See also Plaskow, *Standing Again at Sinai*, pp. 39—40.

43. II Kings 22:8—20, 23:1—14.

44. Trattner, *Understanding the Talmud*, p. 83.

45. Roth and Wigoder, *Encyclopedia Judaica*, vol. 16, p. 626; Lacks, *Women and Judaism*, p. 31.

46. Ginzberg, *Legends*, vol. 1, pp. 66; see also Lacks, *Women and Judaism*, p. 31

47. Lev. 15:19—24, 12:1—5.

48. Lacks, *Women and Judaism*, p. 157; Swidler, *Women in Judaism*, p. 134.

49. Quoted in Lacks, *Women and Judaism*, p. 157.

50. Adler, "Tumah and Tahara," p. 26.

51. Leviticus 12:2—5.

52. Leviticus 27:2—4.

53. Deuteronomy 24:1—4.

54. Numbers 30:4—16.

55. Numbers 27:1—8, 36:2—12.

56. Deuteronomy 21:15—17.

57. Trattner, *Understanding the Talmud*, p. 81.

58. Roth and Wigoder, *Encyclopedia Judaica*, vol. 16, p. 626. See also Trattner, *Understanding the Talmud*, p. 81; Lacks, *Women and Judaism*, p. 122.

59. Trattner, *Understanding the Talmud*, p. 81.

60. Proverbs 31:10—31.

61. Trattner, *Understanding the Talmud*, p. 82.

62. Hertz, *Authorized Daily Prayer Book*, p. 21.

63. Ausubel, *Book of Jewish Knowledge*, pp. 494—95.

64. Quoted in Roth and Wigoder, *Encyclopedia Judaica*, vol. 16, pp. 623—28.

65. Berman, "The Status of Women," pp. 116—20.

66. Swidler, *Women in Judaism*, pp. 1—2.

67. Ibid., pp. 4—5.

68. Ibid., p. 7.

69. Ibid., pp. 7, 12.

70. Lacks, *Women and Judaism*, p. 120.

71. Henry and Taitz, *Written Out*, pp. 3, 7—9.

72.Ausubel, *Book of Jewish Knowledge*, p. 494.

73. Lacks, *Women and Judaism*, pp. 122—23, 129—34; Henry and Taitz, *Written out of History*, pp. 54—58.

74. Quoted in Swidler, *Women in Judaism*, p. 173. See also Zirndorf, *Some Jewish Women*.

75. Ibid., pp. 167—69.

76. Quoted in Lacks, *Women and Judaism*, pp. 1-3.

77. Abrahams, *Jewish Life*, pp. 25—26.

78. Lacks, *Women and Judaism*, pp. 139—40; Swidler, *Women in Judaism*, p. 92; Henry and Taitz, *Written Out*, pp. 8—9.

79. Abrahams, *Jewish Life*, p. 54.

80. Klein, *The Code of Maimonides*, p. 133.

81. Klein, "Introduction," *The Code of Maimonides*, pp. xxxv—xxxvi.

82. Marcus, *American Jewish Woman*, p. 46ff.

83. Plaskow, "The Jewish Feminist," p. 3.

84. Schneider, *Jewish and Female*, p. 23.

85. Quoted in ibid., p. 23. See also Goldenberg, "Judaism: Where Does the Feminist Go?," p. 15.

86. Bauman, *On Being a Jewish Feminist*, pp. 132—33.

87. Quoted in Schneider, *Jewish and Female*, p. 24.

88. Goldenberg, "Judaism: Where Does the Feminist Go?," pp. 14—15.

89. Ibid., pp. 17—18.

90. Sherwin Wine, "Perspective," p. 25, quoted in *Schneider, Jewish and Female*, p. 77.

91. Schneider, *Jewish and Female*. p. 77.

92. Sherwin Wine, "Perspective," pp. *24—25*.

CHAPTER FIVE

Secular Judaism
and Jewish Humanism

During the 1970s, I heard a rabbi, a socialist author, a Yiddishist educator, all from New York, and an Israeli educator each address aspects of Jewish secularism from his personal perspective. They might have been part of a panel discussion, except that they each spoke at a different time. The rabbi was Dr. Judah Shapiro, who headed the American Labor Zionist movement. The author was Irving Howe, best known in the Jewish community for his book *World of Our Fathers*. The Yiddish educator was Itche Goldberg, director of the Zhitlowsky Foundation for Jewish Education, and the Israeli educator was Dr. Berl Frymer, education director of the Histadrut, the national labour organization in Israel.

Shapiro drew a distinction between secularism and "secularity." Secularism, he said is "a movement which I don't feel part of, they go around secularizing people. But secularity is the reality of accepting the fact that one can rationally engage in such activities as bear out the [Jewish] values."[1] He drew a distinction between being a secularist–a person who does not observe religious practices–and one who is active in the secular program of the Labor Zionist movement. The avowed Jewish secularist, he said, used to know "what the tradition was and what the Bible says . . . and what was traditionally expected to be done." It is therefore "not a rejection of tradition which makes the secularist; the secular person is the individual who has accepted the value system but has altered the way in which [the values] are to be acted upon."

As an example, he cited his own belief that "Zionism, in its essence, is a heresy," since it was the first great Jewish "do-it-yourself movement." The heresy consisted in "rejecting the belief that all you had to do was pray to God and ultimately some kind of salvation would come. . . . And the Zionists came to say . . . we will not rely on God . . . we will take this matter into our own hands."

Shapiro explained that the secular person, "having been freed from . . . the fear of the Godly, the Divine retribution that could be visited upon a person" could re-examine what had produced some of the religious traditions. He described, for example, the experience of the Jews who returned from Babylonian exile, when Ezra the Scribe wanted to "whip his people back into shape." The Samaritans, who never went into exile, had married women outside the faith and were suspected of indulging in idolatry. Therefore, when Jerusalem was restored Ezra was determined to exclude the Samaritans from the Jewish people. When the daughter of SanBalad, the Samaritan leader, married the grandson of the high priest, there was concern that in the dynastic succession, the grandson of the Samaritan might eventually become the high priest.[2] The priests therefore ruled that a person would be regarded as a Jew only if he or she had a Jewish mother. Thus, as Shapiro explained, when a Jewish immigrant arrives in Israel today with a non-Jewish wife, he has trouble registering his children as Jews because of a political decision made in Jerusalem in the fifth century B.C.E.

Some aspects of Kashrut, the Jewish dietary laws, were introduced for economic reasons, Shapiro believed. Dishes of metal or earthenware were subject to ritual impurity and had to be kept separate for meat and milk. The provision for dishes did not mention glass pots, however. The Jews of ancient

Palestine therefore began to make pots, wherever practical, out of imported glass. The manufacturers of metal dishes and earthenware began to go broke. So the rabbis, to protect the makers of pots and pans, introduced a law saying glass was also subject to ritual impurity. Thus economic controls were imposed on the people through religion.

Turning to modern times, Shapiro explained that the Labor Zionist movement was built by people who recognized that observing Kashrut, attending synagogue, and praying three times a day were not enough. These people had to become "sufficiently heretical to go out and act" on essential issues in society. "This became the great new tradition and it came . . . from every person who had been a *Yeshiva bocher* [seminary student], who had studied and . . . knew Bible . . . and Talmud." Shapiro cited David Ben Gurion as an example of this type of person: at age sixteen or seventeen, he began to see that the traditional Jewish commitment of his parents was not enough. "The issue was not remaining Jewish, or breaking with Jewishness. The issue was extending the tradition in a practical way [to] go out and act on it." Shapiro also stated that secular Jews were familiar and comfortable with synagogue rituals, while many of those who defined themselves as religious were really ignorant of the rituals. "The importance of the secular tradition is not that it was a break with [the old] tradition [but that it moved] into the realm of the practical, of the active, of the programmatic, of the attempt to change the society and bring about the necessary salvation of the Jewish people in a realistic sense. This was Zionism, and Socialist Zionism."

Shapiro's interpretation of how Jews should act in a secular way was not intended for relations with Jews alone; he also expressed the belief that Jews should aim to make the world a better place for all people.

Irving Howe was a secular Jew who made an outstanding contribution to the transformation of Yiddish culture into English. He co-edited *A Treasury of Yiddish Stories, A Treasury of Yiddish Poetry,* and *Ashes out of Hope* (Soviet-Yiddish fiction), with Eliezer Greenberg, and *The Best of Sholom Aleichem,* with Ruth Wisse, an alumna of a Montreal Yiddish secular school and later head of the Yiddish-studies program at McGill University. Through his labour and socialist writings, Howe also demonstrated how a Jew could contribute to the better understanding of social and political issues by editing an anthology called *Essential Works of Socialism.*

In 1978, Howe gave a speech in Winnipeg titled "East European Jewry and American Culture." He pointed out that the Jewish immigrants of the late 1880s and 1890s were "barely literate." Neverthless, "Jews carried more cultural baggage with them [than did other groups] because they were less able to store it back home." An Italian professor of art would have no reason to come to America. But there were no Jewish professors in Eastern Europe. The Yiddish-speaking intelligentsia consisted of journalists and writers, representatives of the political parties, and *luftmenschen* (people living on air, that is, without visible means of support), who all worked side by side with ordinary people.

At the turn of the century, the Jewish immigrants became more diversified; intellectuals came to help create a "cultured immigrant milieu." The Jews brought with them a rich fund of culture, a world outlook, and a closeness to their folk origins, as well as a language. They also brought "an unstable mixture of religious views and radical thought." At the same time as Yiddish culture began to be "exported" to America, the immigrants were already "losing touch with its sources." The first generation of American Jewish children were "stamped with the immigrant experience [but] it was already thinned down from its sources. Thus, after a few generations, most American Jewish writers today [1978] are painfully ignorant of Jewish culture."

On the other hand, Jews made a big contribution to American culture: "The Jews contributed the European old world back to the people who [had] fled from it. Jews brought a new sense of the past to a nation which made a virtue of denying the past. [They brought] not only Jewish culture but elements of nineteenth-century Russian humanist culture as represented by Tolstoy, Turgenev, and Chekhov."

Of course, Jews began to move "eagerly" into Western culture, and the question arose, Would they remain Jews? Howe was questioned closely by his audience on the decline of the Yiddish language and culture. This decline, he explained, "was the fault of a historical development over which none of us had any control, [yet it was one] to which Jews contributed. [But] the decline of Yiddish culture does not mean the end of Jewish life."

Howe called it "something of a mystery" that the Jews have been able to live in many languages and to transmit their culture from one language to another. In the past, however, this was done not at the expense of abandoning their own language, but by creating something new. He cited the two great linguistic achievements of the Jews in recent times: Yiddish as a new *lingua franca*, drawn largely from the languages of the people among whom they lived, and developed into a comprehensive means of Jewish expression; and the revival of Hebrew, the holy tongue, into a modern language as part of the experience of building a new Jewish state. In fact, Yiddish was not the first language developed by the Jews, drawing from the linguistic resources of other people. Jews in Spanish-speaking countries developed Ladino, and, much earlier, Jews in Muslim lands spoke Judaeo-Arabic, as extensively as Yiddish and for a longer period of time.

One reason that Jews in North America began to shed important parts of their own past, Howe suggested, is that "Jewish culture was plebeian because most Jews were former workers." The immigrant Jew also "intruded a new voice, the voice of ironic questioning and skepticism." To retain this faculty, to be a "nay-sayer and an eyebrow-raiser," it was necessary to feel "not quite at home." But Jews wanted to become "normal," and many groups, including Zionists and socialists, tried to make Jewish life normal. They wanted to change the status of the Jews as "a pariah people," a condition that had persisted through many changes of time and place.

This "pariah" condition had decreased considerably by the 1970s, Howe added. But there was enough of a residual "outsider" feeling to make Jews continue to feel insecure. It may be suggested, however, that Jewish feelings of insecurity arise not only from the real or imagined attitudes of non-Jewish neighbours, but because many Jews have largely turned their backs on their plebeian roots and folk origins. Thus the current "not-quite-at-home" feeling rarely produces the skeptics and nay-sayers of an earlier generation.

Howe pointed out (citing U.S. sociologist W.R. Thomas) that the process of Americanization led to the destruction of immigrant memories. Many Jews, in Canada as well the U.S., have moved away from their past, especially in regard to language. In Europe, the long tradition of multilingualism helped the Jews to develop their own new language. In the United States and Canada, however, English has been fostered for centuries as the only language worth speaking. Thus Jewish parents who worked so hard to enable their children to get a college education actually helped to speed the decline of Yiddish. For the same reason, other major elements of Jewish culture in Yiddish, such as the theatre and the press, have virtually disappeared.

Howe was asked about relations between Yiddish speakers and religious Jews. Speaking as a secularist Jew, Howe declared that, even if other secularists might be "uncomfortable" with his answer, "organic Jewish culture" had been held together by religion as a "total way of life." The secularists sought to break away from religion, he added, but they wanted to keep Yiddish. "This was only possible in a world that was neither totally free, nor totally unfree," Howe asserted. He cited inter-war Poland as one example of this kind of society, and suggested that the United States, in the early decades of the twentieth century, was similar. The secularists "depended on religious tradition as something to rebel against." The defiant secularists of a departed era, the "Yom Kippur mockers, knew what real prayers were all about, otherwise they could not write parodies," Howe added.

On the question of Yiddish in Israel, Howe pointed out that the "socialist Jews" who were dominant in the development of the Jewish state realized that a Yiddish background was "not enough for the building of a national consciousness." Unfortunately, this belief led to a situation in which "the attitude to Yiddish in Israel ranged from hostile to scandalous," but this started to change when the Israelis began to feel more secure about Hebrew. As well, events such as the "trauma of the Yom Kippur war" led Israelis to realize they could not live in isolation from Jews elsewhere, and they began to develop an interest in Jewish life in other parts of the world.[3]

Howe's view on Yiddish in Israel was substantiated by Dr. Berl Frymer, who had been, for twenty-five years, educational director of the Histadrut, the Israel labour organization. In a 1979 interview, Frymer remarked that for many years Yiddish had been ignored, "in a certain measure," by the Israelis, and "especially by the younger generation." But at the time of the interview, "a certain revival" of Yiddish in Israel was under way. Previously, all efforts had been directed toward reviving Hebrew as "the unifying historical language to assure the cohesion of the Jewish people, composed of elements from so many countries and speaking many different languages." The revival was "miraculously" accomplished, and Hebrew is now "the everyday language as well as the literary language" of the country.

Despite many problems, Yiddish never ceased to exist in Israel, Frymer affirmed. "There has always been a Yiddish literature with Israeli motifs and some writers in Israel, of great name and fame, fought for Yiddish because that language is their natural form of expression. But in the past these were rather isolated cases." He gave four reasons for the changed circumstances of Yiddish in Israel: a re-evaluation of the search for roots and tradition; the growth of Holocaust consciousness; the arrival of Yiddish writers among new immigrants; and the change in attitude to Yiddish of the champions of Hebrew.

> We came to the conclusion that political independence, Jewish statehood, and the emblems of sovereignty are not sufficient to give content and meaningful significance to Jewish life. Israel is not a revolution but a continuation of the thousand years of Yiddish culture created in the Diaspora, which was not a wasteland. The chief beneficiary of the new national mood in Israel [1979] is Yiddish as a most significant and meaningful expression of Jewish life. . . . Holocaust consciousness also found expression in the development of respect for the language of the victims, which was Yiddish. Among the Holocaust survivors and the olim [immigrants] from Soviet Russia there are Yiddish poets, writers, and journalists who sought cultural expression in Yiddish. And the champions of Hebrew now saw that both languages help to strengthen the cultural forces of the Jewish people against the common enemy of rampant assimilation.

Frymer reported that Israel had three hundred Yiddish writers and a Yiddish daily, *Di Letzte Naies*. There had been a revival of Yiddish theatre, and over thirty active Jewish clubs. Some high schools were offering Yiddish classes, there was a Yiddish faculty in every university, and there were publishing houses and literary awards for Yiddish. The progress of Yiddish in Israel was still "rather marginal" in comparison to the "great cultural upsurge of Hebrew," Frymer felt, but he believed

Yiddish had "found its place in Israel for continuation and development." [4]

Rakhmiel Peltz confirms that Israel has become the major centre for Yiddish literature, especially since the emigration of many writers from the Soviet Union in the 1970s. Since World War Two, the major publication for Yiddish literature has been *Di goldene keyt* (The Golden Chain), a quarterly published in Tel Aviv and edited by Holocaust survivor Abraham Sutskever. [5]

The three basic expressions of modern Jewish life with which most Jews identify are Israel, Jewish religion in all its varieties of expression, and Jewish secularism. These were the key concepts in the speech "Secularism and Jewish Tradition," given by Itche Goldberg, director of the Zhitlowsky Foundation for Jewish Education in New York, in Winnipeg in 1979, [6] and later in a lecture at a conference to establish the *New Jewish Agenda,* which became an alternative Jewish advocacy organization in the United States.

Recognizing that secularism is an intangible concept to many people, particularly in comparison with their understanding of Israel and of religion, Goldberg explained Jewish secularism as "a combination of historic and cultural elements outside of the Jewish religion but not against it." He related his interpretation of secularism to the concept of Jewish peoplehood and said, "You don't have to be a Zionist to see the Jews as a *velt folk* [world people] and to recognize the special importance of Israel for the Jewish people. Our common roots are in our national memories, that is, our history of nearly 4,000 years." He traced the cultural origins of secularism back to some of the "historical collisions and schisms of Jewish life" that were not only inevitable, but sometimes desirable. As examples, he cited the trials of the biblical Prophets; the struggles of the Maccabees against Greek Hellenism and of the Jews, under Bar Kochba, against Roman oppression; the efforts of Maimonides to reconcile faith and reason for his age; and Benedict Spinoza's advocacy of God as a nature phenomenon instead of as a supreme being.

Goldberg called Spinoza "the father of secularism among the Jews." He recalled Dubnow's view that the excommunicated Amsterdam philosopher "would not have removed himself from Jewish life if he could have reached the conclusion that you can be a national Jew without being a believer in the traditional sense. But the seventeenth century was not ready for secularizing the Jewish national idea."

Dr. Chaim Zhitlowsky and Horace Kallen were "two modern fathers of Jewish secularism," according to Goldberg. Zhitlowsky espoused Yiddish secularism in the socialist movement, while Kallen spoke of life as "an orchestration of future with past" and originated the concept of "cultural pluralism" in opposition to the "melting pot."

In a Winnipeg lecture in 1943, the last he gave before his death, Zhitlowsky declared, "The Jewish religion is a branch of the tree of Jewish culture and not the root or the stem. Religion and secularism are equally valuable branches of the tree." Zhitlowsky was critical of those who demanded "religious passports" as proof of Jewish identity. Traditional Jewish religion was weakened in the nineteenth-century era of emancipation, and new branches had to be grown. One of these new branches was the secularism movement, Goldberg asserted. Secularism should not be equated with atheism, which, like religion, is the private choice of the individual, he stressed. "Secularism is not against religion; it is only against foisting religious dogma upon everyone." Goldberg recalled Dubnow's words, "The lack of faith does not remove the Jew from his people as long as he does not accept conversion to another religion."[7]

Traditional elements of Jewish values should be reconsidered in building a meaningful structure for today, Goldberg said. He recalled his experience in compiling, in 1943, what was probably the first secular Haggada for Passover. A modern Haggada, he suggested, may begin with the Passover Exodus story, but may also include the story of the Sephardic Jews in the Muslim world and in Catholic Spain. It could take into account David Einhorn (1809—79), an early Reform rabbi in the U.S., who spoke against slavery, and August Bondi (1833—1907), an Austrian Jew who came to America after the failed 1848 revolution and joined John Brown's Abolitionists. As well, Emanuel Ringelblum, the Warsaw Ghetto archivist, and Simon Dubnow, both of whom perished at Nazi hands, may be recalled at the Passover seder.

The Yiddish language remains a major part of Jewish tradition, Goldberg said. Yiddish is important not only for those in the older generation who still speak the language, but for members of the younger generation now studying it and seeking out its significance at universities. Recalling that of the six million Jews killed in the Holocaust, four million had spoken Yiddish, Goldberg said, "While Hebrew is still *loshen kodesh* [the sacred language], Yiddish is now *loshen hakedoshim* [the language of the martyrs]."

Goldberg spoke of the influence of I.L. Peretz on the growth of modern Jewish secularism. Peretz drew widely on all aspects of Jewish tradition, using Yiddish as a medium for creative expression. In his essay *Vegen Geshikte* (About History), on the death of the historian Heinrich Graetz, Peretz wrote, "A people's memory is history; and as a man without a memory, so a people without a history cannot grow wiser, better." [8]

Jewish tradition also involves "a process of selectivity," Goldberg said. "Different people select different sets of values. I reserve the right to select my set of values. But if we secularists do not maintain our link with tradition, we shall not have a future. . . . The secular philosophy is a break with religion but not with the Jewish people. Still, not everyone who . . . is unsynagogued is a secular Jew."

Secularism also needs symbols, holidays, heroes and a way of life, though it should be without ritualism, Goldberg said. "We want involvement and commitment to an inner sense of Jewishness. We want a sense of contemporary relevance for us and for our children . . . [and] a historic peg with all the overtones of our history." To counteract the alienation, fragmentation, and divided loyalties that affect people in current times, especially the younger generation, Goldberg concluded, it is necessary to think in terms of the concept of Jewish humanism.

Jewish Secular Humanism–a Well-kept Secret!

The story of secular humanistic Judaism, was, for many years a well-kept secret in Jewish life. Many people don't like to talk about the secular idea, and some still tend to deny that it exists. One rabbi told me "a secular Jew is an oxymoron"! In 1991, a report on a 1990 study on Jewish identity in Canada revealed that there are secular tendencies among Jews in this country. The executive summary mentioned only "Yiddishism," as a notable tendency in Winnipeg in particular.[9] In 1993, Stephen M. Cohen, the author of the report, presented a more detailed account of his report in *The Jews in Canada*, a book of essays on the history, demography, and sociology of the Canadian Jewish community, in which he admitted, "Canada has been home to a visible and institutionalized Jewish secular population."

Saul L. Goodman has made a major contribution to revealing the secret regarding secular Judaism in his book *The Faith of Secular Jews*. Yeshiva educated in Poland, Goodman later earned degrees from Harvard and Columbia universities. He was the director of the Sholem Aleichem Folk Institute, and later became a professor of Jewish philosophy and Yiddish literature in the graduate faculty of the Herzliah Jewish Teachers Seminary, New York.

In his introductory essay, Goodman states that the roots of Jewish secularism go back to the time of the ancient kings, the socio-ethical ideals of the Prophets, and the "philosophical disputations of the creators of the Talmud." [10]He explains that secularism, "a central motif" in earlier Jewish history, was reborn with modern Hebrew and Yiddish literature, Jewish nationalism, and socialism "in their various shadings." He then presents an impressive array of twentieth-century Jewish authors, teachers, philosophers, and historians, many of whom are well known, but not usually as secularists.

The pronouncements of Simon Dubnow, Ahad Ha'Am, and Chaim Zhitlowsky provided the launching pad for twentieth-century Jewish secularism. In Europe, Dubnow, an exponent of spiritual nationalism, and Ha'am, an advocate of spiritual Zionism, were the recognized theoreticians of the Jewish secular idea. In America, Dubnow and Zhitlowsky, an advocate of Yiddishist socialism, were the most influential among *veltliche* (secular) Jews, even though the former never left Europe. The influence of these men, and of the Zionist movement and the socialist Bund, led to efforts to secularize Jewish education.

A conference of Jewish writers and scholars held in Czernowitz (then in Austria) in 1908 proclaimed Yiddish the national language of the Jewish people. It also helped to crystallize the concept of secularity, which enlightened non-Orthodox immigrants began to bring with them to America.[11] The establishment of non-religious schools based on Yiddishism, nationalism, and socialist ideals broadened the scope of Jewish education in United States and Canada between 1910 and 1920.

From 1904 on, Zhitlowsky lived mainly in America and influenced the Jewish secular groups that established the radical and national folk schools. He favoured secularization of

Jewish life not out of hostility to religion, but to make it possible for every Jew, believer or non-believer, to belong to the Jewish community, and held that the Jewish holidays, including the Sabbath day of rest, "contain national, lofty moments which render them worthy of celebration by secular Jews."[12] His ideas on the holidays were considered heretical by American Jewish radicals in 1909.

Dubnow's conception of Jewish secularism differed from Zhitlowsky's. The latter based his theory of progressive Jewish nationalism on socialism, while the former developed his belief in cultural nationalism on his studies as a historian. A people held together by culture–like the Jews of the Diaspora–was, Dubnow said, "the very archetype of a nation, a nation in the purest and loftiest sense."[13] He stressed "spiritual-cultural ingredients," arguing that spiritual strength, rather than political power, was "the essence" of the culture of the Jewish people. His conception of "spiritual" did not mean religion alone, but included attitudes, values, and folkways: "Religion and race do not account for our survival because the agnostics are in the front ranks of all our national movements. The 'something' that holds us together is the common historical destiny of all the scattered parts of the Jewish people."[14] Furthermore, "The Jewish spiritual nation survived without a land of its own for almost 2,000 years." He saw the victory of the Pharisees over the Saducees in the second Jewish Commonwealth as the triumph of "spiritual and cultural nationalism over political and military nationalism" and concluded that the Jewish nation was "defined by spirit rather than territory" before it was driven into exile.[15]

Dubnow evaluated the role of the Pharisees and the Saducees in the context of their times. The latter, called a sect, came from the priestly elite; the former, described as a religious and political party, were closer to the people. Each developed different approaches to the teachings and laws of the Torah.

The Saducees aspired to well-being in this world and did not believe in a world to come, but they adhered slavishly to the Written Law and the eye-for-an-eye concept. The Pharisees were lenient in their legal interpretations and developed the tradition of Oral Law that the Saducees rejected.[16]

The Pharisees emerged from the Soferim (scribes), "the scholarly class that proclaimed the revolutionary gospel of the twofold Law" (oral and written), when the high priests became "radical Hellenists."[17] As a result, rabbinic Judaism eventually displaced the priestly tradition. Dubnow's view of the Pharisees is sustained in the Jewish Encyclopedia: "Pharisaism was responsible for strengthening morality and introducing the elasticity which enabled Judaism to withstand its subsequent tribulations; the movement was continued in the stream of historic Judaism."[18]

Dubnow's conception of Jewish secularism is summed up as follows: The Jews are the most *historical people*, which has created cultural values that have put their stamp upon all of humanity. The religious and ethnic components of Judaism seem identical, but are not indissoluble. One may be considered a rooted Jew without accepting the religious component of the Jewish heritage, for "every type of Jew may select from our culture whatever element or current is more pertinent to him."[19]

In considering whether religion is essential for Jewish survival, Goodman cites a secularist, Shmuel Niger, and a religionist, Mordecai Kaplan, to the effect that it is not. Niger declared that secular Jews need not profess religion, because "we are Jews even though we are not religious and do not profess any faith. . . . A Jew is a historic ethico-cultural, and socio-politico-economico-psychological phenomenon. A Jew is a Jew, a Jew, a Jew . . . Jewish identification is not a screen for Jewish theology, but the truth of Jewish history."[20] Kaplan pointed out that "the survival of Judaism . . . depends on the survival of the Jewish people," and proof of this fact is found in those countries where the "only distinctive bond of unity [of the Jews] has been the Jewish religion"–for example, France, England, Germany, Holland, and Scandinavia, where Jews have been "gradually disappearing."[21]

Originally Orthodox, Kaplan founded the Jewish Reconstructionist movement in 1934, which drew adherents from Reform and Conservative Jews as well as among "some so-called secularists."[22] One of the principles of Reconstructionism calls for belief in God to be interpreted "in terms of universally human, and specifically Jewish, experience." Kaplan sees God as a cosmic process and advocated "Judaism without supernaturalism." His book on this topic is subtitled *The Only Alternative to Orthodoxy and Secularism.*

Many Jews in the United States, who are nonconformists in religion, seek to identify with the Jewish people through secular organizations such as the American Jewish Congress, the Labor Zionist Alliance, the Workmen's Circle (Arbeiter Ring), and the American Jewish Committee.[24] Since the 1960s, there has been the Society for Humanistic Judaism, with twenty local groups or congregations and one temple. There is also the Congress of Secular Jewish Organizations, with local branches in the U.S. and Canada.[25] By the 1980s, American Jews also had options such as the New Jewish Agenda.[26]

To be a conscious secularist, however, it is not enough to be areligious or atheistic; one should understand the place of religion, language, and culture as part of the history and living experience of the Jewish people. As Goodman puts it, the modern Jewish secularist should be "linked with the Jewish tradition but not shackled by it." Jewish secularists may participate in traditional observances, on a voluntary basis, to help their children develop an association with Jewishness, or to honour ancestral values. It is possible to discern relevant secular values in Jewish history apart from references to established religion. Moreover, Jewish secularism should be able to perceive "all that is good and valuable in non-Jewish cultures, as seen through the prism of Jewish history." [27]

Goodman suggests that Jewish secularity may be termed "religious secularism." This apparent contradiction may be resolved by considering the difference between religion, the noun, and religious, the adjective. "Religion" primarily denotes dogmas, institutions, rituals, and practices related to belief in the supernatural. However, a person may be religious in the conscientious pursuit of any cause in which one believes strongly.[28]

Dubnow and Zhitlowsky are probably the two best-known "prophets" of the modern Jewish secular movement. Dubnow's views appear to be more consistently applicable to the revival of Jewish secular humanism in the late twentieth century than do Zhitlowsky's; nevertheless, the latter was correct in stressing the important role of Yiddish in the development of modern secularism. Yiddish was never considered sacred; it was always mundane and secular and used "for all the needs of a human life [in the] linguistic sphere."[29] Primary among these needs was education; even in religious schools, *chedorim* and *yeshivot,* teaching had to be done in Yiddish, and special prayers for women were in Yiddish. But the *mame-loshen* never lost its secular character, as is evident in the works of the Jewish writers of the late nineteenth and early twentieth centuries, who achieved popularity and greatness only when they turned to Yiddish. Of course, the Yiddish writers have now achieved popularity in English translation; this is but one sign of the hopeful prospects for Jewish secularism in the language now commonly spoken by Jews in United States, Canada, and other countries.

Zhitlowsky stated that in ancient times, "Israelite cultural life, including literary creativity, was almost entirely secular." Only with the rise of the so-called "sacred books" did a differentiation develop "between the sacred and [the] 'external' (apocryphal) books," which may now be called "secular."[30] The authors were scribes, mortal beings, and the books were therefore secular before they were canonized as "the word of God" and made sacred. As Zhitlowsky also pointed out, the so-called sacred books are "filled to the brim with purely secular episodes." Furthermore, secular elements in Jewish literary and cultural creativity, unrelated to religious belief, are found in Jewish works from the Spanish-Arabic period through the period of the Haskalah and into current times. For example, Immanuel ben Solomon of Rome (1270—1330),[31] known as Romi, wrote love songs and satirical poetry in Italian and Hebrew. He introduced the form of the sonnet into Hebrew poetry and wrote one long poem, *Ha-Tofet weha-Eden* (Hell and Paradise), patterned on Dante's Divine Comedy.[32]

Regarding the relationship of secularism to religion, Zhitlowsky also stressed, "Secularity is never and nowhere connected with anti-religiosity. . . . Secularism has two meanings: one for the general life of the state, the other for the educational system and conscious cultural activity . . . that bears a general national character. [In a democratic state] religion is a private affair, and anti-religion is a private affair."[33] In relation to the educational system and cultural activity, he adds, "Secularism denotes the exclusion of everything that comes in the name of any superhuman, supernatural *authority*."[34]

Dubnow agreed with Zhitlowsky that secularists did not want to eliminate religion from Jewish culture. Where they differed, in addition to the emphasis on Yiddish, was in Dubnow's view of "spiritual nationalism." He took issue with those who confused the terms "nation" and "state," arguing that a people with its own culture had the right to call itself a nation even if it lacked its own territory: "Usually the shell of political or territorial independence is placed around this precious kernel–the freedom of the nation–to protect it. From time to time, however, a nation is forced to forgo this protective shell of political autonomy and to remain content with social and cultural autonomy." [35]

Dubnow also pointed out that "two opposing camps" among the Jews, "the orthodox and the freethinkers," had rejected Jewish nationalism. Because religion dominated Jewish life for two thousand years, the mass of Orthodox Jews concurred in the view that Judaism "is not a nationality in the accepted sense but a religious community." What the people failed to see was that "all the ancient national values of the Jewish nation—the historical festivals, customs and usages, laws, social institutions, the whole system of self-administration retained in the Diaspora—all had been incorporated gradually and artificially into the sphere of religion. The national body became wrapped in the garb of religion so that . . . its true form was unrecognizable." [36]

A Jew has many options regarding how to be Jewish, according to Dubnow. One could select from the teachings of the Prophets or of the Talmud; from the views of Moses Mendelssohn, founder of the Haskalah; from those of Abraham Geiger, founder of Reform Judaism; or from those of Samson Raphael Hirsch, enunciator of neo-Orthodoxy. But one must not "reject entirely the national idea, which is not a matter of theory but of historical fact," Dubnow emphasized.

Dubnow believed that enlightened Jews tend toward rationalism; thus, if Jewish religious principles do not suit these people, Christian symbols and mysticism also would not do for them. He cited the French philosopher, Diderot, to the effect that "the way of science leads from Christianity to Judaism and thence to philosophical Deism." [37]

In recent times, many people have been leaving the synagogue and the established churches and some have sought out so-called spiritual sects; others say that religion no longer has meaning for them. [38] It is surely appropriate, therefore, to bring

Jewish secular humanism into the open. Even enlightened Jewish historians and scholars, however, tend to ignore or play down Jewish secularism. The essay on Dubnow in the *Encyclopedia Judaica,* for example, has only the scantiest reference to his views about secular culture.[39]

One outstanding American secularist Jew was Morris Raphael Cohen (1880—1947), a Russian-born, U.S.-educated philosopher. In *The Piety of an Agnostic,* Cohen quoted Santayana, the Spanish-born American philosopher, who defined piety as "reverence for the sources of one's being." From this definition, Cohen pointed out that people are born not only as individuals but as members of historic groups. They are taught to take pride in the achievements of "anyone who in any way belongs to our race, nation or family." Taking pride alone is insufficient; for self-respect, Cohen said, the Jew, living in a predominantly non-Jewish world, should understand the "actual history of his own people"–not only the Bible, "which is generally just as well or even better known by his non-Jewish neighbour," but also the Talmudic and more recent historic eras.

When he "most consciously" rejected the supernaturalism of Orthodoxy, Cohen devoted a great deal of attention to Biblical history and criticism and comparative religion. He taught the Book of Job, the Hebrew Prophets, and other religious subjects, and he continued his own studies in religion at Harvard, where he obtained his Ph.D., in 1906. Cohen's interest in Jewish affairs was more than intellectual; he worked to help his fellow Jews and for the rights of other oppressed minorities, following the precept "The world is my country, to do good my religion."[40] He also worked to promote studies in the Talmud in 1928—29, a time when the "cult of unreason had made . . . 'Talmudic disputation' a popular term of contempt–even among Jews."

Cohen is recognized in the Jewish encyclopedias, but, like others of his kind, his secularism is overlooked. Nevertheless, he is a role model for Jewish secular humanists.[41]

Like other Jewish thinkers who became secularist, Horace M. Kallen (1882—1947) came from a traditional religious family and was the son of an Orthodox rabbi. He was German born, with a broad Jewish and general education and a Ph.D. in philosophy from Harvard, under William James. He also studied at Oxford and at the Sorbonne.

For over seventy years, Kallen stressed the right to be different. He took a creative approach to Jewish and American culture and developed a secularist rationale, emphasizing the need to harmonize the Jewish heritage with the world view of Jewish humanists, and he was convinced that Jewish assimilation is crippling to the individual personality, mentally and spiritually:[42]

> The Jewish way of life is no longer a religious way of life. Judaism is no longer identical with Jewishness [which now] is a focus of modernity. It is the Jewish way of life become necessarily secular, humanist, scientific, conditioned on the industrial economy, without having ceased to be livingly Jewish. Judaism will have to be reintegrated with this secular, cultural form of community which is Jewishness if Judaism is to survive. [43]

Kallen was among those who believe that the history of the Jews goes back to before the Jewish religion was established. This implies that the secular tradition came before religion in Jewish history. Moreover, Kallen accepts the view of George Foote Moore, his teacher of religious history at Harvard, that "the Judaistic tradition owns no theology in the Christian or Greek sense of the term. . . . Its dynamic essence was the rule of life or the system of observances . . . finally codified in the *Shulhan Arukh.*"[44] This view can be better understood in the realization that theology refers especially to religious questions posed by Christianity.

Liebman Hersch (1882—1955) was born in Lithuania to a Maskil (enlightened) father, became a noted scholar and professor at Geneva University, and represented the Jewish Socialist Bund in the Socialist International. Calling himself a "positivist" agnostic, Hersch explained how modern secular morality differs from religious morality. Religion believes that the earthly world is at best the "anteroom" to the eternal life hereafter and cultivates humility. Secularism holds that life in this world is "the entire life and the goal of everything" and cultivates human dignity.

When Hersch was very young, he declared himself "without religion." In later years, however, he began to ask more questions about Jewish tradition. Among his questions were: If Jewish Scriptures are merely legends and superstitions, why did these books serve as "a foundation for the three great religions of the white race and of a considerable part of other races?" If the differences between the three main religions are insignificant, why did "generations of Jews [prefer] to be slaughtered or burned alive rather than to accept Christianity?" Did every religion result from the confusion of the "natural" empirical world and the "supernatural" extra-empirical world? If so, how is it that one of the great religions, Buddhism, "is basically a religion without a god?" Hersch also wondered if his "non-religiousness" was really as remote from Judaism as from other religions. "My deviation from religious Jewishness," he concluded, "cannot be compared to my enormously greater distance from Catholicism, for instance."[45]

After setting out the differences between Judaism and Christianity as he saw them, he concluded, "For me, the Jewish religion, like every other religion, is a social product. [It was] not God [who] created man according to His image but man creates his God according to his own image. It is not God who chose the people of Israel, but Israel selected its God, fashioned its conception about the world and life and its rules of practical conduct."[46] It is safe to conclude that Hersch remained a secularist, but with a deeper appreciation of the Jewish religion.

Shmuel Niger (1883—1955), born to a learned Chassidic family in Russia, was about to be ordained as a rabbi when he became interested in Russian literature, the revolutionary movement, and Jewish secularism. In 1908, he became the representative figure of the Yiddish renaissance. He studied the humanities in Europe and served as editor of *Die Yiddishe Velt,* in Vilna, before settling in New York in 1919. He agreed with other secularists that even "a non-religious Jew [had to believe], at the very least, in the spiritual values that are latent in Jewish history."[47]

Niger shared Dubnow's view of Jewish history in the two millennia since the destruction of the Temple by the Romans: "The Jewish people [are] more the product of the last two thousand years of history than of the first thousand years. . . . The Diaspora epoch is more . . . Jewish history and Jewish heritage than the history of the Jewish tribes in *Eretz Yisroel.*"[48]

Calling ancient Israel "our cradle," Niger said, "as a people we matured . . . in the Diaspora . . . [where] Jewish culture [became] what it is." Prophecy was "the mightiest protest against the Jewish reality" of that ancient time. "It was in the Diaspora that the dream of the Prophets was translated into the language of reality."[49] Niger stressed the need to select from each epoch, each stream and current in Jewish history the "religious and ethical values or . . . intellectual and artistic achievements that can help bind us to our historical tradition without our being bound by it."[50]

Considering the nineteenth-century flare-ups in Europe between Orthodoxy and Reform in the West and between Chassidism and Haskalah in the East, and the later conflict between social and national ideas, Niger stressed the positive contributions of each of these elements to Jewish development. [51] "It is not only necessary but possible to be nourished by all the currents that have watered and fructified our folk-soil." As an example, he cited I.L. Peretz's story "If Not Higher" as a "true synthesis of Hassidism and Haskalah." This is demonstrated in the story's social-ethical moral–"the Rebbe's helping a poor woman is a superior achievement to flying to heaven." But, he warned, there is still "a tendency to become extremist, one-sided, and to destroy the synthesis" of forces that once quarrelled but later reconciled. [52] Niger's conclusions about Jewish culture, and his warnings about the continuing danger, are still valid as new ways are sought to ensure Jewish survival in the closing years of the twentieth century.

Lithuanian-born Yudel Mark (1897—1975) was educated in Vilna and at the Petersburg University. He served as secretary-general of the Jewish National Council of Lithuania and was a founder of the Yiddish Scientific Institute (YIVO) in Vilna, before settling in New York in 1936. A pillar of Yiddish secularism, Mark worked for the perpetuation of Yiddish. He published grammars and texts for Yiddish schools, and after moving to Israel in 1970 he edited the *Great Yiddish Dictionary*. But, like Dubnow, he did not believe that the language was a cure-all for Jewish survival.

In *Jewishness and Secularism*, Mark said that measured by the criterion of other religions, *Yiddishkeit* (Jewishness) is much broader than a religious creation: "Jewishness is the way of living among the nations of the world . . . among the Gentiles [but] not as Gentiles." [53] Jewishness, to him, was a combination of "religiousness of a high grade plus ethnicity on a very high level" to which should be added "the fact of being a minority." [54] Mark believed that "deeply rooted Jewishness is a fusion of religious, ethnic and folk-ways." [55] He wrote, "Secularism then is anti-dogmatism, it is the need and the possibility of thinking more or less freely. It is the theory that there can be a Jewishness that is viable without the walls of a spiritual ghetto."[56] Secularism also implies accepting and facing the whole world, accepting the valuable and essential things created by non-Jews, from scientific achievements to the "profoundest and finest" of cultural creativity. However, it should not be uncritical in its pursuit of non-Jewish things. It should, rather, be "exceedingly fastidious" and weigh everything on "the scale of our perennial ethics," reaching only "for the best flour from alien mills."

Finally, secularism does not negate "what is Jewishly traditional, but rather complements it. Secularism [does not] . . . repudiate all that is old but rather . . . create[s] new additions. Secularism . . . does not wish to sever itself from roots, but rather [seeks] . . . more sun-rays for the leaves of our tree, and wants our roots to get nourishment . . . from all kinds of soil. . . . One need not be ashamed of the term *secularism* any more than of the expression *Yiddishkeit*."[57]

Albert Einstein (1879—1955) was recently classified by Ivan Kalmar as an "EJI," one of a so-called class of embarrassed Jewish individuals who achieved greatness in a variety of endeavours at least partly due to the fact that they were allegedly uncomfortable with their Jewishness. Kalmar is an anthropologist at the University of Toronto who is the son of Holocaust survivors. He also calls "EJIs" non-Jewish Jews for their non-adherence to Jewish tradition.[58]

I prefer Saul Goodman's description of Einstein as a humanitarian who was "not only an intellectual giant but a conscious Jew and an active supporter of Zionism."[59] Einstein expressed the view that it was "superficial" to say that a Jew is someone who believes in the Jewish religion. Just as a snail that casts off its shell remains a snail, he declared, a Jew who formally gives up his faith remains a Jew. He believed that the bond uniting the Jews for thousands of years is, "first of all, the democratic ideal of social justice, with the addition of the ideal of mutual help and tolerance among all human beings."[60]

"The second characteristic feature of Jewish tradition," Einstein continued, "is its high esteem for every form of intellectual striving and spiritual effort. I am convinced that this respect for intellectual work is completely responsible for the contribution that Jews have made to the progress of every type of knowledge in the broadest sense of the word."[61]

Einstein stated his belief in Jewish ideals as "pursuit of knowledge for its own sake, an almost fanatical love of justice and the desire for personal independence–these . . . features of the Jewish tradition . . . make me thank my stars that I belong to it."[62] He felt that "there is no Jewish world outlook in the philosophic sense," and believed Judaism to be concerned "almost exclusively with the moral attitude in life and to life," which he explained as "the essence of an attitude to life which is incarnate in the Jewish people rather than the essence of the laws laid down in the Torah and interpreted in the Talmud."[63] He considered the great Jewish books the "most important evidence" of the Jewish concept of life in earlier times, and "the essence of the Jewish view of life . . . to be affirmation of the life of all creation." It was also evident to Einstein that "serving God" was equated with "serving the living," and he said, "The best of the Jewish people, especially the Prophets and Jesus, contended tirelessly for this. . . . Judaism is thus not a transcendental religion; it is concerned with life as we live it." He therefore doubted whether Judaism could be called a religion in the accepted sense of the word, "particularly since no 'faith' but the sanctification of life in a suprapersonal sense is demanded of the Jews."[64] Einstein's views may be regarded as the epitome of a secular humanist credo for Judaism.

Many proponents of secular Jewishness grew up in Eastern Europe, where the physical survival of Jews was in constant jeopardy. Thus modern Jewish secular thought has focused, until recently, primarily on the collective survival of the Jews, rather than on the content and meaning of life for the Jew as an individual. Nowadays, however, in the United States and Canada, Jewish survival depends on the content and quality of Jewish life. Jewish creative continuity demands ceaseless and all-encompassing efforts, including the development of secular philosophy and practices for Jews who are nonobservant in the practice of religion.

Before 1989, no Jewish encyclopedia, including the *Jerusalem Encyclopedia Judaica* of 1972, had ever published an entry on secularism. The *Encyclopedia of Social Sciences*[65] and the *New Catholic Encyclopedia* published essays on secularism decades ago; the latter gives secularism a succinct definition: "A form of humanism that limits true value to those temporal qualities that contribute to man's natural perfection, both individual and social, to the actual exclusion of the supernatural. More than an abstract theory, secularism, a generic term for the forms it assumes, is a philosophy of life, a movement of thought, and in the broad sense of the word, a religion." An essay on secular humanistic Judaism was published for the first time in 1989 in the Encyclopedia of Judaism. Thus, the secret is out, but it has not yet been disclosed in the update volumes of the Encyclopedia Judaica or the New Standard Jewish Encyclopedia(1992) – and Geoffrey Wigoder is the chief editor of these latter three works.[66]

Notes

1. Shapiro, "Zionist Heresy," pp. 7—8. I always thought of Judah Shapiro as a rabbi. He had a teacher's diploma from Yeshiva University (Orthodox); he attended CCNY, Columbia U. and Harvard, where he obtained his Ed. D.; he lectured in history and sociology at Hebrew Union College (Reform) and taught Hebrew at the Sholem Aleichem Mittleshul (secular). He served as executive director at several B'nai Brith Hillel Foundations, a post usually held by a rabbi, and rose to the post of national Hillel Director. He also

served as civilian chaplain at Harvard before going on to varied other endeavours. But he was apparently not a rabbi in the formal sense.

2. Roth and Wigoder, *New Standard Jewish Encyclopedia*, pp. 1677—78, 1685.

3. Arnold, "Irving Howe on Jews and American Culture," *Western Jewish News*, 26 Jan. 1978; 9 Feb. 1978; 16 Feb. 1978.

4. Berl Frymer, "Yiddish Revival in Israel, *Western Jewish News*, 9 Feb. 1979.

5. Peltz, *Mama-Loshen*.

6. Goldberg, "Secularism"; see also Abraham Arnold, various articles in *Western Jewish News*, 1979.

7. Quoted in Goldberg, "Secularism," p. 30.

8. Quoted in Baron, *Treasury of Jewish Quotations*, p. 180.

9. Stephen M. Cohen, *An Overview*, p. 39.

10. Goodman, *Faith*, p. 3. See also Finkelstein, *The Pharisees*, vol. 1, pp. 93—94.

11. Goodman, *Faith*, p. 8, p. 40, fn16.

12. Goodman, *Faith*, p. 11.

13. Goodman, *Faith*, p. 13.

14. Goodman, *Faith*, pp. 13—14.

15. Quoted in Goodman, *Faith*, p. 14. See also Dubnow, *World History*, vol. 1, pp. 15—17.

16. Roth and Wigoder, *New Standard Jewish Encyclopedia*, pp. 1521—22, 1667—68.

17. Rivkin, *Shaping*, p. 88.

18. Roth and Wigoder, *New Standard Jewish Encyclopedia*, p. 1522.

19. Quoted in Goodman, *Faith*, p. 18.

20. Quoted in Goodman, Faith, p. 27.

21. Quoted in ibid.

22. Roth and Wigoder, *New Standard Jewish Encyclopedia*, p. 1606.

23. Kaplan, *Judaism without Supernaturalism*. For the Reconstructionist view of God, see Kaplan, *Questions Jews Ask*, pp. xii, 80—82.

24. Goodman, *Faith*, p. 36.

25. Schenker, "North American Jewry."

26. The national office of the New Jewish Agenda is now closed, but several local groups are still functioning.

27. Goodman, p. 37.

28. Ibid., p. 38. Goodman bases this approach on Dewey's definition in *A Common Faith*, pp. 9—10, 27.

29. Quoted in Goodman, *Faith*, p. 49.

30. Goodman, *Faith*, p. 49.

31. Ibid., p. 49.

32. Kravitz, *3000 Years*, p. 299.

33. Quoted in Goodman, *Faith*, p. 54.

34. Ibid.

35. Ibid., p. 178. See also Dubnow, *Nationalism and History*, p. 88.

36. Ibid., p. 179. See also Dubnow, *Nationalism and History*, p. 89.

37. Ibid., p. 182. See also Dubnow, *Nationalism and History*, pp. 92—93.

38. Jack Kapica, "Canadians rejecting traditional forms of religious workship," *Globe & Mail*, 7 Dec. 1993, p. A6.

39. Roth and Wigoder, *Encyclopedia Judaica*, vol. 6, pp. 252—57.

40. Goodman, *Faith*, p. 61.

41. Ibid., pp. 57—65; Roth and Wigoder, *New Standard Jewish Encyclopedia*, pp. 453, 1482—83.

42. Kallen, "American Jews," p. 21.

43. Kallen, *Judaism at Bay*, pp. 4—5.

44. Quoted in Goodman, *Faith*, pp. 69-71.

45. Quoted in ibid., p. 78.

46. Quoted in ibid., p. 83.

47. Quoted in ibid., p. 87.

48. Quoted in ibid., p.89.

49. Quoted in ibid.

50. Quoted in ibid.

51. Quoted in ibid., p. 90.

52. Quoted in ibid., p. 91.

53. Quoted in ibid., pp. 97—98.

54. Quoted in ibid., p. 98.

55. Quoted in ibid., p. 99.

56. Quoted in ibid., pp. 99—100.

57. Quoted in ibid., pp. 100—01.

58. Kalmar, *The Trotskys*.

59. Goodman, *Faith*, p. 111.

60. Quoted in Goodman, *Faith*, p. 113. See Einstein, *Out of My Later Years*, p. 249.

61. Quoted in Goodman, *Faith*, p. 114. See Einstein, *Out of My Later Years*, pp. 249—50.

62. Einstein, *Ideas and Opinions*, p. 185.

63. Ibid., pp. 185—86. See also Goodman, *Faith*, p. 197.

64. Einstein, *Ideas and Opinions*, p. 86. See also Goodman, *Faith*, p. 198.

65. Vol. 13/14, pp. 631—35.

66. See Bibliography at Encyclopedia, also at Roth and Wigoder.

Part Two

HOLIDAYS, CEREMONIES, AND CELEBRATIONS

CHAPTER SIX

The High Holidays

Rosh Hashonah: Remembrance, Judgment, and Call to Social Action

Rosh Hashonah, the Jewish New Year, and Yom Kippur, the Day of Atonement, comprise the High Holidays, the most important observances on the Jewish calendar from a religious perspective. They also lend themselves to interpreting the Jewish heritage from a secular point of view.

Rosh Hashonah, literally "the head of the year," is celebrated as the anniversary of "Creation," as told in the Book of Genesis. Perhaps more important, it is seen as the "renewal" of creation, as though the world is reborn from year to year. The primary message of the festival is that the process of creation is continuous and that God is involved on an ongoing basis.[1] In secular terms, Rosh Hashonah, the beginning of the year, is a time for assessment of one's personal achievements.

The dates of Rosh Hashonah are Tishri 1 and 2, in the seventh month of the Jewish calendar, although Nissan, the first month of the Jewish calendar, comes in spring, when nature re-creates itself. In the early history of Judaism, celebration of the New Year varied between the spring and the fall until the rabbis settled on the autumn date for Rosh Hashonah.

While some of the Rosh Hashonah themes come from the era of the Babylonian exile, the autumn date goes back to the time when Solomon employed Phoenician workers to help build the Temple in Jerusalem. The building was constructed to allowthe first rays of the rising sun to shine directly through the eastern gate on the semi-annual equinox days; the day of the autumn equinox was celebrated as New Year's Day.[2] But this was not yet known as Rosh Hashonah; at that time of year, there was competition with the harvest festivals: the Feast of Matzo (Passover), the Feast of Weeks (Shavuot), and the Feast of Tabernacles (Sukkot), based on the lunar calendar.

The Bible makes no direct reference to Rosh Hashonah. It calls only for a day of "solemn rest" on the first day of the seventh month, "as a memorial proclaimed with the blast of horns."[3] The day was thus known, from the beginning, as the Day of Memorial and Remembrance (Yom ha-Zikaron) and the Day of Blowing the Horn (Yom Teruah).

The designation "Rosh Hashonah" is first found in the Mishnah,[4] the code of oral tradition in the Talmud. The addition of the Day of Judgment (Yom ha-Din) theme gave Rosh Hashonah its solemn character. The synagogue rites, however, are not divorced from secular themes, particularly those involving ethical concepts.

A commemoration of the departed, involving communal visits to the cemetery, takes place in the week preceding Rosh Hashonah. The memorial is intensely personal, but it is also a shared remembrance of Jewish lives lost through the centuries. Contemplating the tragedies of Jewish history, and given the view in some quarters that all things are divinely ordained, it is no surprise that Jews tend to take a pessimistic, even fatalistic, view of themselves and their position in the world. But fatalism is almost completely foreign to Jewish tradition; in fact, the rabbis rejected it. Moses Maimonides stated that man's acts are entirely under his own control; a fatalistic approach would make the commandments meaningless. Moreover, the Jewish view of the struggle between good and evil implies that humans are free to think, to choose and to act–a repudiation of fatalism.[5]

The fatalistic view has, however, contributed to the Day of Judgment theme, which still looms large in synagogue ritual. This theme derives from an ancient Babylonian myth that the gods gathered in convocation in the autumn to determine the fate of individual human beings for the coming year. Judaism appropriated this idea, but added to it the belief in a relationship between man and God by which redemption might be achieved. Central to the idea of Rosh Hashonah as the Day of Remembrance is "the power of Memory itself [as it] defies oblivion, breaks the coils of the present, establishes the continuity of the generations and rescues human life and effort from futility. . . . New Year's Day is at once a day of judgment and a new beginning. If it looks backward, it does so only on the way forward; and its symbol is the trumpet of an eternal reveille."[6]

The third Rosh Hashonah theme, Yom Teruah, the Day of the Blowing of the Horn, involves the sounding of the *shofar,* the Ram's Horn. Here there is a clearer intermingling of religious and secular ideas. In biblical times, the *shofar* was used for public affairs as well as for religious purposes: it was sounded as the call to battle and also to bring tidings of peace. It proclaimed the new moon, signifying the beginning of each new month in the Jewish calendar, and announced the coronation of a new king or the convocation of a solemn assembly.

Maimonides declared that the only reason for blowing the *shofar* in the synagogue was to stress the urgency of individual repentance, sounding a personal clarion call:

Sleepers awake! Reflect upon your actions! Remember your Creator and turn back to him in repentance! Do not be among those who, while they grasp at shadows, miss that which is real, and waste their lives in pursuit of empty things that neither bring them profit, nor deliver them. . . . Sleepers awake! Look after your souls! Reflect upon your actions![7]

Maimonides believed in the concept of the soul, possessed only by humans, but he held that life after death involved the survival only of that part of the mind that had become actualized,[8] a view reflected in the modern-day secularist belief that the only immortality is in one's progeny and in other creative works that last beyond one's death. His comments on the call of the *shofar* may be seen in the same way. His emphasis is clearly on the importance of reviewing one's individual actions. In this sense, he is in line with other rabbinic thinkers, who said that participation in the ritual observances of the High Holidays was insufficient to bring anyone to true personal repentance.

The rabbis also warned against seeking formal repentance through lip service, and the Talmud recalls the distinction drawn by the Prophets between righteous conduct and mechanical piety. It teaches that redemption will not come by fasting or donning sackcloth. True repentance can come only through the performance of good deeds for their own sake and not as atonement. The rabbis called for *gemilut chasadim*, acts of loving kindness toward others.[9] On this basis, the faithful are asked to support Jewish charity appeals brought into the synagogue during the High Holidays. Deeds of helpful response to family members and friends and meaningful support of worthy groups and causes helps to keep faith with past generations and saves Jews from futility.

There is one ritual that takes place outside the synagogue, usually on the afternoon of the first day of Rosh Hashonah. During *tashlich* (casting off), Jews empty their pockets into the water of a river or lake. This gesture seeks to fulfil the promise of the Prophet Micah (7:19): "And thou wilt cast all their sins into the depths of the sea." This custom is not of Jewish origin; it was borrowed from gentile neighbours and reinterpreted to suit Jewish needs. Scholars believe that *tashlich* originated in Germany in the fourteenth century, but it was first mentioned in the writings of Rabbi Jacob Moln of Mainz (1355?—1427). The custom was denounced three hundred years later by Rabbi Abraham Horovitz of Cracow as "sheer mummery." Some Christians laughed at the Jews shaking their sins into the water, while other Christians performed similar ceremonies. Eventually, Jews performing *tashlich* were accused of casting poison into rivers and lakes to wipe out Christians. Such an accusation led to the massacres of Jews following the Black Death of 1348—49.[10]

The sombre mood of Rosh Hashonah is counteracted in the works of some historians, who emphasize the positive role of the Jews, beyond the martyrdom and suffering that have been stressed so often in the past. Barbara Ward, the English philosopher and historian, said that the Jews were "the first to believe that history itself has meaning and that progress, not repetition, is the law of life,"[11] and that the "Jewish vision is profoundly concerned with man's social existence here and now." She pointed to "the Jewish prophetic tradition that stubbornly rejects any accommodation with the stratification of society, the wealth of the few, the misery of the many, the pride of the rich, the long-suffering of the poor." She interpreted this tradition as the rejection of "the alienation and exploitation of man that comes into society with the division of labor, the property relations and the privileges of post-tribal society." She ascribed to the "unruly visionaries of Israel . . . [a] hunger for justice" shown by no other culture, and she linked this with one of the central religious themes of Rosh Hashonah by describing the Jewish search for justice as "an egalitarian passion backed by a terrifying vision of divine judgment." Finally, she asserted that the passion for justice of the Jewish prophetic tradition "has provided a lasting and irresistible dynamite of social change ever since!"[12]

Ward's views are in keeping with those of Simon Dubnow, who said Judaism was "not merely a religion, like Christianity or Islam . . . [but] a body of culture." Dubnow believed in "historical Judaism":

> Unique historical conditions which brought . . [the Jews] under the dominance of religion converted Judaism into an all-embracing world view which encompasses religious, ethical, social, messianic, political and philosophical elements. . . . . Judaism is broad enough and variegated enough so that any . . . [Jew] can draw from its source according to his spirit and outlook.[13]

Dubnow, who was born on the second day of Rosh Hashonah in 1860 to a family of Talmudic scholars, broke with formal religion and called himself a "'free thinker' after the model of Elisha ben Abuyah in the Talmud."[14] In 1884, Dubnow returned to his native Mstislav, in Mohilev province, White Russia, for a visit on the eve of the High Holidays. Everyone wondered whether he would attend services in the synagogue, and he did not. Later, he wrote in his autobiography, "The town of traditional piety witnessed an unheard of experience: the grandson of Rabbi Bentsion, the spiritual leader of the community, appeared in the synagogue, neither on Rosh Hashonah nor on Yom Kippur, days on which even the most 'wicked Jews' attend services." When he walked in the streets on Sabbath with a cane in his hand, people cast evil glances at him and youngsters called out, "Carrying a cane on Sabbath, heretic *[apikoros]!*"[15]

Dubnow's broad view of the Jewish experience is shared by contemporary interpreters like Gaster, who says, "Judaism is the culture of the Jewish people–the quintessence of its collective experience throughout the ages. It is a term like *Hellenism* or *Americanism,* and does not imply any kind of rigid, authoritative creed."[16]

Yom Kippur: Fasting, Scapegoats, and Humanistic Philosophy

The cycle of remembrance, repentance, and judgment that begins on Rosh Hashonah comes to a climax on Yom Kippur, the Day of Atonement, the last of the Ten Days of Penitence. Observance of Yom Kippur originated at the dawn of Jewish history, and it is therefore replete with ancient rites. Gaster asserts that the concept of "the heavenly tribunal, with God as the presiding magistrate and man as the defendant craving His pardon, is nothing but a survival of outmoded mythology."[17] Despite its primitive origins, Yom Kippur became "a sounding-board for all the inchoate yearnings of a people driven by an idealistic compulsion for self-improvement and social justice to examine their individual consciences. . . . The real significance of Yom Kippur [is] as an instrument for a higher individual morality directed toward the good of social progress."[18]

Yom Kippur is actually mentioned in the Bible as the day of atonement. It is a "holy convocation" on the tenth day of the seventh month calling for "a sabbath of solemn rest, and ye shall afflict your souls; in the ninth day of the month at even, from even unto even, shall ye keep your sabbath."[19] This injunction is the directive for twenty-four hours of fasting and prayer.

Earlier, the Book of Leviticus specified that "on the tenth day . . . shall atonement be made for you." On this day, a bull and two goats were to be sacrificed in the Jerusalem Temple. The bull was sacrificed on behalf of the high priest, and one goat was picked by lot to be killed as a sacrifice to God. The sins of the people were then magically transferred onto the head of the second goat–the scapegoat–which, as an appeasement to Azazel, the demon of the wilderness, was led out and cast over a cliff.[20]

After the destruction of the Temple (70 C.E.), when sacrifices came to an end, the rite of *kapporah* was introduced. The
word *kapporah*, derived from *kippur*, is said to come from a
Babylonian term meaning "to wipe out"; the rite was transformed into a ceremony of sin-cleansing. It is now observed
only by the most devout orthodox Jews, with a rooster for a man
a hen for a woman. The fowl is circled around the person's
head, while he or she recites the appropriate prayer; the fowl
is then taken to the *shochet* for ritual slaughter. But even the
"scapegoat chicken" has fallen into disuse; it has been replaced
by money, in multiples of eighteen (the numerical term for
chai, meaning life), which is then donated to charity. Although
the *kapporah* rite has been largely eliminated, at the synagogue,
the day before Yom Kippur has become a day for giving and
collecting donations for charitable organizations. A religious
rite has thus been almost completely replaced by a secular
practice.

On the eve of all holidays except Yom Kippur, the festive
meal takes place after sundown, when family members return
from the synagogue. On the Day of Atonement, the meal takes
place before sundown, when the twenty-four-hour total fast
begins. Everyone then hurries to the synagogue for the haunting chant of *Kol Nidre*.

If there were an inter-faith hit-parade of hymns, *Kol Nidre*
would probably be near the top, with Ave Maria. Indeed,
perceptive Gentiles, hearing it in its synagogue setting, have
been deeply moved by *Kol Nidre*. Beethoven used part of its
melody for the opening bars of one of his quartets. And when
Leo Tolstoy first heard *Kol Nidre* in a Russian synagogue he
described it as the saddest, yet the most uplifting of all melo-
dies, one "that echoes the story of the great martyrdom of a
grief-stricken nation."[21]

While *Kol Nidre*, at first, stood only for the annulment of
religious vows made voluntarily to God, "it suddenly under-

went a dramatic transformation . . . similar to that which turned the primitive rites of spring among the Hebrews . . . into the Passover Feast of Liberation."[22] In the Middle Ages, a formula was introduced as a prologue to *Kol Nidre,* which allowed "transgressors" to worship in the synagogue on Yom Kippur. In the Byzantine Empire in the eighth century, thousands of Jews had been massacred for resisting conversion, but many more thousands had survived by converting. The prologue to *Kol Nidre* allowed these people, who had secretly remained Jews, to show that they had involuntarily broken their vows to their Jewish God. Thus, from the thirteenth century, *Kol Nidre* became "the supreme penitential prayer and rite of reconciliation."[23]

During the Middle Ages, enemies of the Jews propagated the view that because of *Kol Nidre,* the oath of a Jew should be disallowed in legal proceedings. In many places, Jews were obliged to take a special and degrading oath, *more judaico,* to counteract the provisions of the *Kol Nidre.* In June, 1240, several rabbis were compelled to appear before King Louis IX of France and a group of Christian theologians to answer the accusation of an apostate that the *Kol Nidre* absolved Jews from moral guilt in breaking oaths made in dealings with Christians. The rabbis succeeded in proving that the dispensation of *Kol Nidre* had no bearing on obligations, vows, or promises a Jew made to any other person, including Christians. The main authority cited was the Mishnah, the Hebrew code of oral law.

Nevertheless, the stereotype of a Jew as one who breaks his promises persisted through the centuries. Another example occurred in 1655, when Rabbi Manasseh ben Israel of Amsterdam appeared before a commission appointed by Oliver Cromwell, the Lord Protector, on the desirability of readmitting Jews to England, from which they had been expelled in 1290. The commission asked the rabbi how a Christian can trust a Jew whose religion gives him dispensation to break his word. [24]

Because of the attitude of non-Jews, the Reform wing of Judaism abolished the recitation of Kol Nidre more than a century ago, though it never gave up the melody. In more recent times, as Reform has resumed traditional practices, the *Kol Nidre* has been reinstated.[25]

The Yom Kippur synagogue ritual includes the confessional prayer, *al chet*, begging forgiveness, with breast-beating, for sins against God. The Hebrew *al chet* is comparable to the mea culpa confessional recited by Roman Catholics. The nature of forgiveness in Judaism is defined in the Mishnah; it was declared at the end of the first century that only a man's sins against God can be atoned on Yom Kippur. Offenses against other people can be atoned only when the wrong done has been redressed.[26]

Some people are drawn to the synagogue on Yom Kippur only for the Yizkor memorial prayer for dead relatives, which is also recited on the last days of Passover, Shavuot, and Sukkot. This ritual is said to have originated during the Crusades of the Middle Ages, when many Jews living in the Rhineland communities were massacred by Knights of the Cross, and the names of those massacred were read aloud in the synagogue. In current practice, the names of the dead relatives of congregation members are recited. Folk superstition, however, forbids those whose parents are still living from attending the service for fear of the "Evil Eye."[27]

As the sun sets on Yom Kippur, the last prayer, Neilah, the final appeal to God, is chanted before an open Holy Ark. This prayer is traced back to the days of the first Jerusalem Temple. It has been asserted that the entire ceremony of Neilah relates to the "closing of the gate" at the end of Yom Kippur.[28] The last long blast on the *shofar* seems to declare, "You have fasted and prayed enough; you have wept enough. Now gather your strength and go forth to fulfill your high resolves."[29]

After the Yom Kippur sundown, most families break the fast with a festive meal. In the early decades of the twentieth century, some secular Jews in United States and Canada turned against their orthodox past when they joined nationalist, labour, or left-wing organizations. Taking the view that religion was the "opiate of the people," they rejected the supernatural concept that is prevalent in the High Holidays practices. Some went to the point of eating purposely in front of the synagogue on Yom Kippur, and radical groups organized *af tsa-loches* (for spite) dances on Kol Nidre night. Such extreme manifestations are now a thing of the past, but the number of secular and humanistic Jews who reject the religious practices of the High Holidays is probably growing. Some opt out of Rosh Hashonah and Yom Kippur because these holidays do not have the same kind of historical background as do Passover and Chanukah.

Rabbi Sherwin Wine, a leader of the Humanistic Judaism movement, has suggested that the High Holidays, "precisely because they are personal rather than national, have a special significance for Humanistic Jews. . . . If human judgment replaces divine judgment, and if human power becomes the alternative to divine power, then Rosh Hashonah and Yom Kippur become perfect vehicles for celebrating a humanistic philosophy of life." [30]

At the time of the Jewish New Year and the Day of Atonement, secular humanistic Jews may therefore find it appropriate to reflect on the moral quality of their lives and on how to improve themselves, through contemplation and discussion. And while ritual need not be entirely rejected, it is not required to seek the desired results.

Thanksgiving: Sukkot to Simchat Torah and Beyond

Sukkot is one of three seasonal harvest events when all Jewish males are enjoined to "keep a feast unto the Lord thy God." [31] The other two are the Feast of Matzo, which later became Passover, and the Feast of Weeks, Shavuot. Originally the main autumn festival on the Jewish calendar, Sukkot was long ago displaced by Rosh Hashonah and Yom Kippur. It begins four days after the latter. Of the three seasonal festivals, it has suffered the most from modern conditions and possesses the least contemporary relevance.[32] All synagogues are filled on Rosh Hashonah and Yom Kippur; on Sukkot, however, the congregation dwindles to the devout and the curious.

Sukkot is a seven-day festival that commemorates the wandering of the Israelites in the desert. Some time after receiving the "word of God," seven weeks following the flight from Egypt, the Israelites built a tabernacle as a portable Holy Sanctuary. They also lived in temporary tabernacle dwellings. These are exemplified by the Sukkah, a booth of palm and . willow branches erected by observant Jewish families, in which they eat at least once a day. The Sukkah is also symbolic of the huts in which the Jews resided in the fields during the harvest in ancient Israel, and thus Sukkot is known as the Festival of Booths.

The seventh day of Sukkot is Hoshana Rabba, the Great Hosanna, when worshipers make seven circuits around the synagogue, some carrying the *lulav*, a festive bouquet of palm, myrtle, and willow, and the *etrog*, a citron, others the Torah scrolls. Willow branches are beaten against the *bimah*, the raised prayer dais. According to ancient tradition, the Yom Kippur decision on the fate of Jews for the year to come is confirmed on Hoshana Rabba.

Sukkot observances are especially popular in Israel, and in Jerusalem many hundreds of *lulavs* and *etrogs* are sold on the festival eve; at least 30 percent are bought by non-religious Jews who do not go to the synagogue. It has been suggested that these people acquire them out of some superstitious belief![33] But the *lulav* and the *etrog* are quite appropriate for decorative purposes at a secular harvest celebration.

The Sukkot rituals include a ceremony in which devout Jews ask God to remember Jewish historical events involving the numbers one to seven: on the first day, Abraham, "the one true believer in his generation"; on the second day, the "two tablets of stone" brought down by Moses from Mount Sinai; and so on, to "the seven worthies, Abraham, Isaac and Jacob, Moses and Aaron, Phineas [grandson of Aaron and forebear of the Zadokite priests], and David."[34] The ceremony of numbers lends itself to secular adaptation to commemorate Jewish "worthies" and historical events beyond the confines of religion.

The seventh day of Sukkot does not bring the end of this festive period; two more days build to a grand climax. On the eighth day, Shemini Atzeret, there is a ceremony of water libation. Since the days of the Second Temple, Shemini Atzeret is also the day on which a prayer for rain is offered for the first time each year. This is not done earlier for fear of dampening the open-air Sukkahs.[35]

As with other festivals, the Sukkot rituals may be traced back to primitive times, and other religions observe similar harvest rituals. But one ritual of this festive period, truly exclusive to Judaism, highlights the ninth day, Simchat Torah (Rejoice in the Law). On Simchat Torah, completion of the annual reading of the books of Moses, the Torah, constituting the first five books of the Bible, is triumphantly celebrated. In the *hakofes* ceremony, the worshipers parade seven times around the synagogue carrying the Torah scrolls and every adult male gets an opportunity to carry a scroll. Even in synagogues in which women are usually segregated, they are allowed into the main sanctuary to touch and kiss the Torah. Children may also take part, each carrying a flag, with an apple impaled on it and a candle burning on top of the apple.

In Chassidic synagogues, *hakofes* are followed by frenzied dancing by the men only. One observer describes the ceremony as follows: "To witness the haunting rhythms and fancy footwork of the Vishnitzer rebbe's special *hakofe . . .* is enough to make even the most rationalistic of Jews suspect that there might be something to mysticism after all."[36] The reading of the Torah then starts again from the opening verses of Genesis.

What is this Sefer Torah, written in Hebrew script on fine parchment, dressed in a rich embroidered garment and enthroned in the Oren Kodesh–the Holy Ark? Why is this scroll, containing the books of the Genesis, Exodus, Leviticus, Numbers, and Deuteronomy, carried about the synagogue on Simchat Torah like a sacred object? Why is it kissed and adored by its adherents? Any person may be moved by the outpouring of emotion and impressed by the Chassidic dancing; this adoration of the Torah may also impress a dispassionate observer almost as a form of idolatry.

The five books in the Torah are known as the Pentateuch, a term derived from Greek origins. Authorship of the Pentateuch has been ascribed to Moses, "except for the last eight verses,"[37] which deal with Moses' death. But how could Moses himself have written the story of the Exodus, of which he was the prime instigator–unless, of course, God dictated the whole story to him on Mount Sinai?

Several theories have been advanced as to the authorship of the Pentateuch. Biblical criticism may be traced back to the seventeenth-century descendants of the Marranos. One was Benedict Spinoza, who claimed that Ezra, scribe of the Babylonian exile of the Jews, had written or rewritten the Pentateuch and then attributed it to Moses.[38] Spinoza was excommunicated for his views, but he is now recognized as a major Jewish philosopher. Even before Spinoza, Uriel Acosta, a son of Marranos, expressed views considered heretical by Christians as well as by the rabbis. Acosta wrote in his autobiography, "I doubted whether Moses' law was really God's law, and decided that it was of human origin."[39]

Early in this century, Julian Morgenstern, a leading scholar of Reform Judaism, was castigated by some of his own colleagues when he declared that, "contrary to the traditional Jewish view, the Torah . . . is not the work of one man, Moses, but of many persons." Thus, according to Morgenstern, the Torah cannot be, "in an absolute literal sense, the divinely revealed word of God. This conclusion is based upon an almost overwhelming mass of evidence, and is now generally accepted, except by extremely conservative and orthodox scholars."[40]

Yehezkel Kaufmann, one of Israel's leading biblical scholars in the first half of the twentieth century, has written about the "Josianic reform" in 622 B.C.E., when King Josiah "purged the Jerusalem Temple and the entire land of . . . pagan cults and of the pagan vestiges . . . from earlier days. The immediate cause of the reform was the discovery of 'the book of the Torah' in the Temple. This book was, according to current scholarly consensus, the Book of Deuteronomy." Deuteronomy called for the prohibition of worship outside Jerusalem; Josiah fulfilled this demand by bringing all the priests to Jerusalem. He then called all the people to the Temple, read them the "newly found" book, and made a covenant "obligating them to obey all that is written therein." Josiah thus gave "'the book of the Torah' . . . the force of state law." In the time of Ezra and Nehemiah, some two hundred years later, after the return from Babylonian exile, the other books of the Torah were brought to light and "an event of enormous significance took place: the Torah was fixed and canonized."[41] Some sources deny "formal canonization of the Hebrew Scriptures," claiming that the sanctity of the books was accepted "in the course of time."[42] However, on New Year's Day in 444 B.C.E., the completed Torah was "publicly read before the assembled throng in Jerusalem." The reading, which took six hours, was conducted by the priest-scribe Ezra, with benedictions, "Amens," and interpreters to explain the difficult passages. "The people

[were] moved to tears." [43]Of course, the Torah was presented as God's words, written by Moses. All this certainly seems like a formal canonization, and in fact the Hebrew Bible is described as "the sacred canonical books."[44]

Who really wrote the Torah? Morgenstern has likely come as close as anyone to answering this question. He states that the five books of Moses and the book of Joshua, together known as the Hexateuch, were written (except for a few ancient fragments) between 932 B.C.E., the date of the division of the Kingdom of Judah and the Kingdom of Israel, and the third century B.C.E., at about the time when Ezra brought the Torah book back from Babylonia with him. Morgenstern asserts, "It is absolutely certain that not one word of the Hexateuch goes back to the traditional period of desert wanderings." These first six books of the Bible were "the work of various writers and epochs"; different portions were written under various conditions and for various purposes, and they thus have "unequal historical value."[45]

Bringing to light the mundane origins of the Torah does not negate the place of Simchat Torah among the Jewish festivals. Not everyone who participates in the synagogue *hakofes* ceremony is necessarily a believer in the Mosaic books as the word of God. Some may see them as part of historic tradition and as a means of expressing solidarity with Jews who, over the centuries, and particularly during the Nazi Gehenna (hell on earth), witnessed the burning of Torah scrolls and the destruction of synagogues before their own lives were destroyed.

A recent example of Jews dancing on Simchat Torah, not necessarily for the sake of the Torah, but for their rights as Jews, occurred in the Soviet Union in the 1960s. Young Jews began to celebrate the *hakofes* ceremony outside the Moscow and Leningrad synagogues as a means of affirming their Jewishness in public, "even if they defined it in secular rather than Torah-centered ways."[46] Some Western Jews began attending the celebrations of the Soviet Jews, and Jewish communities in Canada and United States began to organize outdoor Simchat Torah rallies in sympathy with Jews in the Soviet Union.

What, then, is the status of the Torah in Jewish life? For Orthodox and traditional Jews, it retains its sacred status. For nontraditional and secular Jews, the Torah, as part of the Jewish Bible, should be recognized as the best-known literary work in the library of Jewish culture. "Torah" may also be considered a generic term for education. Israel Chipkin, founder of the American Association for Jewish Education, once wrote, "Torah represents the accumulated literary and spiritual heritage of the Jewish people throughout the centuries." As well, the Talmudic scholar Louis Ginzberg has written, "Torah is not law. It is an expression for the aggregate of Jewish teachings."[47]

Moreover, Simon Dubnow, a descendant of rabbis who gave up religious observance and became a "free thinker," was devoted to *Torah lishmah*, study for its own sake."[48] Torah, divested of divine status, may be taken as denoting the broadest range of Jewish education and study–from the religious to the secular. And the Jews, as the "People of the Book," have a heritage that extends far beyond the Torah in its religious guise.

Notes

1. Gaster, *Festivals*, p. 109.
2. Morgenstern, *As a Mighty Stream*, pp. 233—35.
3. Leviticus 23:24.
4. The Mishnah was compiled by Judah Ha-Nasi, rabbinic head of the Palestine Jewish community under the Roman emperor, Marcus Aurelius Antonius, in the second century C.E. See Ausubel, *Book of Jewish Knowledge*, pp. 372-373; Roth and Wigoder, *New Standard Jewish Encyclopedia* pp. 1082—83.
5. Roth and Wigoder, *New Standard Jewish Encyclopedia*, pp. 669—70. See also Ausubel, *Book of Jewish Knowledge*, pp. 505—06.
6. Gaster, *Festivals*, pp. 108—09.

7. Quoted in Ausubel, *Book of Jewish Knowledge*, p. 373.

8. Maimonides' view of the active intellect is derived from Aristotle's theory about the universe. See Halkin, *Great Ages*, p. 250.

9. Ausubel, *Book of Jewish Knowledge*, p. 373. For a story describing *gemilut chasadim*, see Peretz, "If Not Higher!," in *In This World*, pp. 76—79.

10. Ausubel, *Book of Jewish Knowledge*, pp. 457—58; Gaster, *Festivals*, pp. 121—22; Roth and Wigoder, *New Standard Jewish Encyclopedia*, p. 1836.

11. Ward, *Faith and Freedom*, p. 47.

12. Ward, *Spaceship Earth*, p. 114.

13. Dubnow, *Nationalism*, p. 91.

14. Ibid., p. 8. See also Roth and Wigoder, *New Standard Jewish Encyclopedia*, p. 613.

15. Ibid., p. 9. Religious law forbade the carrying of anything in one's hands on the Sabbath.

16. Gaster, *Festivals*, p. 3.

17. Ibid., p. 136.

18. Ausubel, *Book of Jewish Knowledge*, pp. 519—23.

19. Leviticus 23:27—32.

20. Leviticus 16:1—32; Ausubel, *Book of Jewish Knowledge*, p. 521.

21. Ausubel, *Book of Jewish Knowledge*, p. 252.

22. Ibid., p. 253.

23. Ibid.

24. Ibid. Manasseh ben Israel went to great lengths to answer all charges, from usury to the blood libel, brought against the Jews by the commission. He published "a brief but comprehsneive work, in defense of the Jews," and he won over Cromwell. But there was still too much opposition to permit the Jews to return "through the great portal, [so] they were let in by Cromwell through a back door." Graetz, *History of the Jews*, vol. 5, pp. 38—49.

25. Ibid., pp. 252—53; Greenstone, *Jewish Feasts*, pp. 29—32.

26. Ausubel, *Book of Jewish Knowledge*, p. 522.

27. Ibid., p. 519.

28. Morgenstern, *As a Mighty Stream*, pp. 233—35.

29. *Holy Scriptures*, p. 931.

30. Wine, "A Short Humanistic History." See also suggestions for the secular observance of the High Holidays in *Humanistic Judaism* (Summer 1986): 25—44.

31 Deuteronomy 16:13—17.

32. Gaster, *Festivals*, p. 96.

33. Lowin, "Sukkot," p. 9.

34. Gaster, *Festivals*, pp. 88—89.

35. Waskow, *Seasons of Our Joy*, pp. 68—69.

36. Lowin, "Sukkot," p. 6.

37. *Holy Scriptures* (Menorah Press), p. 1.

38. Ausubel, *Book of Jewish Knowledge*, p. 39.

39. Baron, *Treasury of Jewish Quotations*, p. 509.

40. Morgenstern, "The Foundations of Israel's History," in *As a Mighty Stream*, pp. 3, 19. This essay was first published in 1915.

41. Y. Kaufmann, *Great Ages*, p. 71.

42. *Holy Scriptures*, p. 1.

43. Ibid., pp. 82—83.

44. Roth and Wigoder, *New Standard Jewish Encyclopedia*, p. 305.

45. Morgenstern, *As a Mighty Stream* p. 37. See also Kaufmann, *Great Ages*, p. 82.

46. Waskow, *Seasons of Our Joy*, p. 84.

47. Baron, *Treasury of Jewish Quotations*, p. 504.

48. Dubnow, *Nationalism*, pp. 5, 8. *Dubnow was murdered by the Nazis in a roundup of Jews in Riga in 1941.*

CHAPTER SEVEN

Festival of Lights
to Feast of Lots

Reinterpreting Chanukah–From Zadok to Apikoros

The traditional story of Chanukah comes from Maccabees I and II, two of the fourteen books in the Apocrypha, which deal with the period of ancient Jewish history following the return from Babylonian exile. The Apocrypha books, largely written between 300 and 30 B.C.E, are not part of the Bible because of a decision made by the rabbis some twenty-five years after the Roman destruction of the Temple. The word "apocrypha" comes from a Greek word that means something secret or hidden away,[1] and is now used to denote works of questionable authorship or authenticity.[2]

Probably because the books of the Apocrypha were excluded from the Bible, their authenticity has been questioned. The charge has been made that several books were left out of the Bible without justification. Maccabees I and II were written during or shortly after the period they describe. They were omitted from the Bible for the same reasons that the ancient rabbis tried to downplay Chanukah and the Maccabees.

The unnamed author of Maccabees I followed the biblical pattern in writing of the establishment of the "Hasmonean state." A contemporary scholar describes this author's work as an "invaluable" historical source for the Hasmonean (Maccabean) Revolt. He is praised for his descriptive talent and fluent style, and for his ample documentation and wealth of chronological data, which place him "among the leading Jewish historians."[3]

The Apocrypha book of Judith, called a historical novella, relates the heroism of the woman who beheaded the Greek general Holofornes, throwing an entire army into disarray. It has been described as "one of the most perfect works of ancient Jewish literature."[4] Another woman in the Chanukah story is Hannah, who allowed her seven sons to sacrifice their lives rather than succumb to idolatry. This story is one of the best known of Jewish martyrology.[5] In the Christian tradition, Hannah's sons are called the Maccabees, and there are shrines to their memory in many parts of the Christian world.[6]

For several centuries, Judea was part of the Persian Empire, until that regime was destroyed by Alexander the Great, who created the Greek Empire. The Greeks were the ancient Hellenes, and Greek rule brought the struggle between Hellenism and Judaism to Judea. At first, the Hellenes did not try to impose their ways on the conquered people. It was the policy, before the untimely death of Alexander the Great (323 B.C.E.), to allow "vassal peoples" to enjoy cultural and religious independence. Indeed, Hellenization succeeded in western Asia through the popular appeal of Greek culture and not by military imposition.[7] The freedom, wealth, and beauty of Hellenism attracted many Jews as a compelling alternative to the "dull, repetitive routines of a Semitic theocracy."[8]

After Alexander died, his successors fought for control of the empire. Judea ended up in the domain of General Ptolemy, based in Egypt, while General Seleucus won control of Syria and the lands to the north and east. Under Ptolemy, the Jews still enjoyed a large measure of self-government, but Hellenization continued to spread. In current interpretation, early Ptolemaic experience is used to support the belief that Jews are more susceptible to assimilation in times of peace and freedom than in times of war and repression.

Under the Ptolemies, the Jews underwent a "partial secularization," which ran counter to the Torah-based control of the

Zadokite priests. The Jews had been primarily agricultural, but under Greek rule they developed an urban class, which produced intellectuals who sought a new approach to religious traditions. They wanted rational meanings for old rituals and a scientific explanation for old myths; the Zadokite priests were considered illiterate and incapable of adapting the Torah to the times. For the first time in Jewish history, secular schools were started for the children of the new urban class, as an alternative to the Temple religious schools. Here, pupils could acquire skills for business and leisure pursuits.[9]

In 198 B.C.E., Antiochus III, known as "the Great," defeated Ptolemy V, took control of Judea, and was actually welcomed by the Jews as a liberator. In 175 B.C.E., however, Antiochus IV, or Epiphanes, succeeded to the Syrian throne. He imposed more taxes on Judea and banned Jewish religious practices. (One commentator claims that the Maccabean cause transcended specifically Jewish interests and extended to all national groups within the empire; he says that the measures directed against the Jews were also used against other groups.[10] This view is questioned by others; one states that "Antiochus did not resort to religious compulsion in respect to other nations in his kingdom."[11]) The events now began that are the basis for the traditional story of Chanukah.

In the current era of multiculturalism, it has been suggested that Chanukah celebrates the first major attempt in history to champion the principle of religious-cultural diversity. The Maccabees are seen, in some quarters, as having fought for the principle that the state has an obligation, in a diverse society, to permit the creative development of its varied cultural groups, rather than to impose a single pattern on all elements. By contemporary standards, this would seem to be a favourable interpretation. But before accepting its retroactive application, it is necessary to re-examine the clash of cultures between Greek Hellenism and Maccabean Judaism.

The Jewish ruling class cared little about the religious and national traditions of their fellow Jews.[12] Some priests and lay aristocrats encouraged the invasion of Judea by the Syrian army; they hoped to turn Jerusalem into a Hellenistic *polis*, a Greek city-state. In fact, Jason, the Syrian-appointed high priest, was in the process of doing just that, with the approval of Antiochus. He was going to call Jerusalem "Antiochia." This situation has been termed the "desperate illness of the Jewish nation [which] found its desperate cure in the armed revolt led by the Hasmonean, Mattathias and his sons."[13]

When Mattathias started the rebellion in Modin, only a small number of Jews followed him. Except for the pietists, the Zadokite priests all collaborated with the Syrian Greeks. The Hasmoneans (later the Maccabees, under Judah), were described as "destitute, non-Zadokite Levites who aspired to priestly power." The pietists, who wanted to resist Antiochus, believed that the Maccabees were more nationalistic than religious, but they joined the Maccabees because many Jews had become so assimilated that they cared nothing about religion or a distinctive Jewish identity. In fact, the Jewish leaders of that day could be described as "Hellenes of the Mosaic persuasion," and the Maccabees had to conduct "a fanatical vigilantist campaign" to bring Jews back into the fold before gaining the strength to mount open opposition to the Syrian-Greek power. As Elias Bickerman, a German-Jewish scholar of the 1930s, has written, "The Maccabean movement was primarily a civil war."[14]

The Zadokites had opted for the Greek style even while seeking to maintain priestly control over the people. Thus it was possible for the Maccabees to develop a lower-class rebellion that was pietistic and based on a fanatical attachment to Torah lifestyle. This was an ironic development because "The Torah was originally a document of the Zadokites, by the

Zadokites, and for the Zadokites, which they created to impose their control upon the Jewish masses."[15]

The Maccabean uprising was thus directed against Antiochus and his Zadokite collaborators. It succeeded partly because of the aggressiveness of the Syrian Greeks in promoting Hellenization. In trying to turn Jerusalem into a Greek city, Antiochus plundered and desecrated the Temple and sought to equate the Jewish god, Yahveh, with the Greek god, Zeus. The Jews could never accept a god who liked pork and preferred uncircumcised males.[16]

While the Maccabees and their followers did demonstrate heroic efforts in the campaign against the armies of Antiochus, their victory was not due solely to their own strength. Antiochus had other enemies to contend with at the same time. The Maccabees also turned for help to Rome, the new rising power.

The Maccabees recaptured Jerusalem in 164 or 165 B.C.E and sought to rededicate the Temple. The one-day flask of oil said to have been found at this point supposedly burned for eight days. But the Chanukah "miracle" story was created long after the fact. There is another legend, a *midrash* in rabbinic literature, relating that on entering the Temple the Maccabees found eight iron spears. They lit eight candles, placed one on each spear, and erected them in front of the Temple as a signal to the people of Jerusalem that the Temple was liberated. Of course this *midrashic* explanation is not as dramatic as the "miracle" of the oil.[17]

The choice of date for the celebration of Chanukah also relates to the belief of primitive people that the sun was dying as the days grew shorter in December. They tried to encourage the sun to stay by lighting fires on the hilltops. Of course, immediately after the winter solstice the sun seemed to renew itself as the days grew longer. It is said that the Maccabees recaptured Jerusalem two months earlier, but Judah knew the winter solstice story, so he delayed proclaiming the victory until the magical date.[18] Kislev 25, 164 B.C.E., the time of the winter solstice, chosen for the start of Chanukah, was the New Year's Day of the Syrian-Hellenistic religion and the third anniversary of the day the Syrians captured the Temple. In rededicating the Temple on Kislev 25, instead of on Tishri 1, the Jewish New Year, Judah Maccabee was following Syrian-Hellenistic practice rather than Jewish tradition.[19]

With the usually close coincidence of Chanukah and Christmas, comparisons of the two festivals are natural. Chanukah is considered a lesser Jewish festival played up only to offer an alternative to the attractions of Santa Claus and the Christmas tree. However, Chanukah celebrates the highly significant role of the Maccabees, who stepped onto the stage of Jewish history at a most important period in world history, the flourishing of Greek Hellenism. The rise of the Maccabees also coincided with the beginning of rabbinic Judaism. The early rabbis sought to minimize Chanukah because they saw the Maccabees reviving priestly Judaism, which the rabbis sought to replace. Actually, Chanukah ranks second to Passover in its historical importance to the Jews.[20]

The struggle of the Maccabees did not end with the rededication of the Temple. Judah and his followers were driven out of Jerusalem a year later, and three more years of military action followed. They won their last great victory on Adar 13, 161 B.C.E., when they defeated General Nicanor in battle and captured Jerusalem for the second time. The Jews began to celebrate this victory as Nicanor Day,[21] a festival that was superseded by Purim. But the Maccabean struggle was still not over.

Judah died in battle a year later. He was succeeded by his brothers, Jonathan and Simon, and between them they campaigned for an independent Judea for another twenty years. In 152 B.C.E., Jonathan made peace with the Syrian Greeks and became high priest, a post held by the Hasmoneans for the next

115 years. Judea achieved full independence only in 141 B.C.E., when Simon succeeded Jonathan and was able to expel the Greek garrison from Jerusalem.[22]

Simon's successor, his son, John Hyrcanus, had himself proclaimed king around 135 B.C.E.; the Hasmoneans then ruled as monarchs for almost seventy years. Among them was a woman, Salome Alexandra, who succeeded her husband, Alexander Jannai. She ruled from 76 to 67 B.C.E. and is said to have reversed the policy of opposition to the Pharisees. She also brought peace to the land.[23]

During the Hellenisic period in Judea, some Greek philosophers, influenced by advanced thought and scientific knowledge, began to question the existence of the gods and to challenge the authority of religion.[24] One of these dissidents was Epicurus (341—270 B.C.E.), who disputed the view that the universe was governed by divine power; he also denied the legitimacy of the Greek gods. Epicurus was considered an atheist and a hedonist among traditional Hellenists. The charge of hedonism is said to have been unjustly used against him by his critics, and his philosophy has been called "epicurean in name only." In fact, he is said to have lived "in Stoic simplicity and prudent privacy."[25]

A small circle of Jewish intellectuals took to epicurianism in Hellenistic Alexandria in the third century B.C.E., and the philosophy spread to similarly disposed Jews in Judea. A Jew who followed Epicurus was considered a heretic and came to be called an *apikoros*. The first *apikorsim* were denounced by the rabbis as moral libertines who denied the fundamental principle of religion. As heretics, the rabbis said, they would be deprived of the blessings of the world to come. From references in Jewish religious writings, however, it appears that the apikorsim were not true atheists but free-thinkers and vocal skeptics who challenged cherished Jewish beliefs.[26] One had to be knowledgeable to do this. Thus anyone who was ignorant of Jewish traditions and customs could not qualify as an *apikoros* but was simply an *amorets*, an ignoramus.

During the Hellenistic era in Judea, the urban intellectuals questioned the theology of the Zadokites on secular grounds, while the Maccabees and their peasant followers questioned the Zadokites' devotion to traditional Torah. The latter won the struggle not only over Antiochus, but over more liberal elements among the Jews. The Maccabees may have been willing to tolerate differences between Pharisees and Sadducees in the matter of adherence to the Mosaic code, but they were unwilling "to extend any living space to Jewish pagans, skeptics or Hellenists."[27] A bona fide *apikoros* would therefore have been in trouble under the Maccabees. In today's world, however, an *apikoros* should be able to make common cause with Jews in the secular humanist movement, and Chanukah may therefore also be celebrated for the origin of Jewish secular tradition.

The clash of Judaism and Hellenism marks the beginning of post-biblical Jewish history. The Maccabees established a new independent Judea–a Jewish state–without the help of "miracles," as in biblical times. While they achieved independence, they could not maintain the Jewish religion in its monolithic form. There was, in fact, a complex of religious trends and sub-trends that began in the period of the Second Temple and flourished as the Maccabees established their Hasmonean Kingdom and carved out their Judean mini-empire. The main trends were represented by the Pharisees, the Saducees, and the Essenes.

The Pharisees maintained unswerving faithfulness to the Torah but they also introduced the living tradition of Halakhah, the "oral Torah," which evolved over generations. In addition, they tried to humanize penal law. The Saducees were conservative when it came to the Torah and did not recognize the Halakhah, but they believed in free will and rejected some of the popular beliefs of their time, such as resurrection of the dead and the functions of angels. The Essenes were determinist in their outlook, subscribed to holiness in daily life, and believed in prophetic inspiration.[28] Jesus of Nazareth is said to have been attracted by them.[29] As well, amidst the complex of trends that gave expression to the fervent spiritual life of the times, there was undoubtedly the occasional no-name secularist who didn't know he was an *apikoros* unless he had that epithet hurled at him for asking a heretical question.

One last point about the Hasmoneans: they came to power with the support of Rome, and they fell from power when they lost favour with the Romans after the assassination of Julius Caesar. The celebration of Chanukah may thus be accompanied by the telling of tales covering over one hundred years of Jewish history during the Second Commonwealth. There are a host of exciting characters in the Maccabean era, who can be brought to light on each of the eight days of the Feast of Lights.

Tu b'Shevat: New Year for Trees and Earth Day

In Jewish tradition, there are four New Years on the lunar calendar according to which Jewish festivals are observed. The New Year for Trees, known as Tu b'Shevat, shortened from Chamisha Oser b'Shevat (15th day of Shevat) is the first Jewish New Year on the C.E. calendar (usually in February). It is the day on which the sap begins to rise in the fruit trees of Israel, and it is celebrated by eating fruits and nuts that come from Israel. Fruits eaten include apples, figs, dates, carob, pomegranates, and almonds and other nuts. The carob is known as "boxer" in Hebrew and also as St. John's bread, after John the Baptist, who supposedly ate carob when he was in the wilderness. The fruits have symbolic meanings: the carob, considered the lowliest fare, is the symbol of humility. The fig, on the other hand, is the symbol of peace and prosperity, according to the biblical injunction "Make your peace with me . . . and eat ye every one of his vine and everyone of his fig-tree."[30] In recent times, a seder for Tu b'Shevat has been developed,[31] during which passages from the Bible dealing with trees, fruits, and fertility are recited.

Tu b'Shevat itself is not mentioned in the Bible. It is regarded as the survival of a prehistoric festival when Israelites were not yet monotheists, but, probably, nature-worshipers. The forebears of the Israelites celebrated the festival of Asherah, the goddess of fertility; this festival became the New Year for Trees.[32]

From ancient to modern times, the planting of trees on Tu b'Shevat has had special significance. According to the Talmud, there was a custom in Jerusalem that when a male baby was born, a cedar tree was planted; when a female baby was born, a cypress tree was planted. When a man and a woman were to be married, the trees, or branches from the trees, planted when they were born were cut down to be used as posts for the *chuppah*, the wedding canopy, under which they were wed.

There is a rabbinic legend that says, "If the Messiah arrives while you are in the midst of planting a tree, finish your planting before you go out to greet the Messiah." The Bible prohibits the cutting down of fruit trees even in time of war (Deuteronomy 20:19). The rabbis permitted the cutting down of such trees only when space was needed to build a house. The recognition that trees hold back the desert clearly goes back a long way.

Tu b'Shevat is now a national tree-planting festival in Israel, and Jews throughout the world participate by contributing to the Jewish National Fund, which raises monies for land reclamation and reforestation in the Jewish State. It is also becoming the Jewish Earth Day, and Jews are being urged to join the fight against pollution and to work to protect the environment.

Rabbi Wine cautions that Earth Day may lead to nature worship; he warns against accepting the idea that everything produced by nature is good: "Understanding nature makes a lot more sense than worshiping it."[34] A reasonable atttitude is that a Tu b'Shevat seder may be appropriate and enjoyable, but it might become ritual without substance if the problems of the environment are not discussed.

Other Jewish New Years

The best-known Jewish New Year is Rosh Hashonah, the religious new year on Tishri 1 (September—October). Since Rosh Hashonah coincides with the major fall harvest, it is also considered the economic new year.

However, the first month on the lunar calendar by which Jewish festivals are calculated is Nissan. (Passover begins on Nissan 15.) Nissan 1 (March—April) is therefore the New Year for counting the months. In ancient Israel, it was the date from which the reign of the king was counted. Nissan 1 has no special ceremonies, but it remains important, even in modern times, as the day from which the dates of all other Jewish festivals are set. The lunar year consists of 353 or 354 days, divided into twelve months of twenty-nine or thirty days each. The lunar calendar has a leap year every fourth year, but instead of an extra day, a whole month is added. This thirteenth month comes before Nissan, adjusting the lunar to the solar reckoning. Each festival is delayed about three weeks following a lunar leap year.

The fourth new year, Elul 1 (August—September) is the date for tithing cattle, an ancient custom that has fallen into disuse. Tithing was the practice of contributing one-tenth of one's annual income, in money or produce, for charitable purposes. In ancient times, any cow born before Elul 1 could be offered as a tithe for cattle born after that date. This custom, while discarded in its original form, has its modern equivalent in the recognition of charitable contributions for income-tax deductions.

Purim: The Book of Esther, Fact or Fiction?

The story of Purim, in the Book of Esther,[35] begins with what would be considered today the sexist and unequal treatment of women. The King of Persia, Ahasuerus, commands his wife, Vashti, to parade her beauty before him and his carousing cronies, wearing only her royal crown. She refuses to humiliate herself in this way.

Becoming "very wroth . . . his anger burn[ing] in him," Ahasuerus calls on "his wise men, who knew the times" asking, "What shall we do unto the Queen Vashti, according to law," for not doing the bidding of the King? The wise men warn him that the queen's deed will be reported to all women and will "make their husbands contemptible in their eyes." They recommend that "Vashti come no more before King Ahasuerus and that the king give her royal estate unto another that is better than she." They also advise him to circulate his decision throughout his empire in a decree that all wives shall give honour to their husbands. It is surprising to find this episode described, by a usually credible source, as a "spoof of . . . marital relations."[36]

Vashti's treatment at the hands of Ahasuerus and his wise men is given little attention in most works on the Book of Esther. Those that do mention her call her cruel and arrogant, and suggest she was as lascivious as the king. They also ascribe to her certain anti-Jewish acts to leave her without sympathy.[37] But these are unsubstantiated add-ons to the story. One feminist writer, Esther Gendler, has charged that the rabbis wanted to make certain that Vashti's refusal to debase herself would not be seen as noble or courageous. The rabbis were in a bind,

Gendler suggests: "On the one hand they could not possibly approve of the demand Ahasuerus makes on Vashti. On the other hand, to support her would be to invite female disobedience in other situations." The rabbis therefore tried to show that Vashti got what she deserved.[38]

With Vashti gone, the stage is set for Ahasuerus to call for a bevy of beautiful virgins from across his empire to parade before him so that he might pick a new wife. Esther, a Jewish maiden living with her cousin Mordecai in Shushan, the ancient capital of Persia, wins the marital beauty contest. Mordecai had urged Esther to enter the royal matrimonial sweepstake, but had advised her not to reveal that she was Jewish; he was concerned that she might eventually experience the same fate as Vashti. Mordecai also felt that if Esther fell out of favour with the King, and he knew she was Jewish, he might turn against all the Jews.

Soon after Esther becomes queen, Mordecai, sitting at the King's gate, overhears two of the king's chamberlains, Bigthan and Theresh, plotting to "lay hands" on Ahasuerus. Mordecai reports the plot to Esther, who passes the word on to the king "in Mordecai's name." The two conspirators are hanged and the matter is recorded in the King's chronicles.

A little later, the King raises Haman, his chief advisor, above all the princes in the realm and orders all his subjects to bow before him. Mordecai refuses to do this. Haman becomes enraged at him and, on the advice of his wife, Zeresh, decides to seek revenge on all the Jews. He tells Ahasuerus that "a certain people . . . dispersed among all the provinces of thy kingdom" have their own laws and do not "keep . . . the king's laws" and urges "that they be destroyed," and he offers to "pay ten thousand talents of silver . . . into the king's treasuries." The king gives Haman the ring from his hand and says to him, "The silver is given to thee, the people also, to do with them as it seemeth good to thee." It is recorded that even before

Haman won the agreement of the king he had already "cast *pur*"–chosen a date by lot on which to slaughter all the Jews in Persia–Adar 13. (*Pur* is Hebrew for lot and *Purim* is the plural; thus, the holiday is also known as the Feast of Lots.)

Before the fatal date set for the Jews, the King cannot sleep one night, so he calls a courtier to read to him from his chronicles. The courtier reads about how Mordecai, the Jew, had saved his life by exposing the two men who had plotted against him. Ahasuerus decides that he should convey some honour on Mordecai. He asks Haman "what should be done unto the man whom the King delighteth to honor." Haman, thinking that he himself is to be the recipient of the honour, suggests that the man be dressed in royal garments, placed on the royal horse with a crown on his head, and led about the city by one of the King's "most noble princes," who would proclaim, "This is the man whom the King delights to honour." The king tells Haman to "make haste" and do what he had suggested "to Mordecai the Jew." Haman is greatly chagrined at hearing the King's order, but he does as he has been bidden and his hatred of the Jews grows stronger.

Meanwhile, Mordecai hears of the plot against the Jews and goes to see Esther. He asks her to risk her life by going to see Ahasuerus and telling him that the Jews are her people, and that if they were to be slaughtered she would also have to die. She agrees to do so. The story is prolonged through several banquets that Esther gives for the king and Haman. But in the end, she denounces Haman to the king, who gives in to the wishes of his beautiful queen, agreeing to cancel the attacks on the Jews, and allowing Jews to resist where the attack cannot be called off. He also agrees to arrest Haman and to condemn him to be hanged for his plot against the Jews. The rest is history, as they say–or is it really fiction?

Before exploring Purim as fiction, it is necessary to consider that the Book of Esther is one of the last books of the Jewish

Holy Scriptures–the Bible. Popularly known as the Megillah, it is required reading in the synagogue every Purim. My Jewish Bible describes the Book of Esther as a "historical novel."[39] The story of Esther and Mordecai may be fiction, but Purim has been celebrated by Jews for many centuries as an example of how a tyrant who sought their destruction was foiled in his villainous intentions.

Of all the festivals and holidays on the Jewish calendar Purim is the only one based completely on a secular story with no mention of God. As well, the Book of Esther is the only Bible story recognized by most scholars as pure fiction. There appears to be no solid evidence that the characters in the Purim story ever lived or that they are based on real people who may have had similar experiences. But Purim, like every other Jewish holiday, has taken on a history of its own through centuries of practice.

According to some sources, Purim was originally a primitive new-year festival celebrating the arrival of spring with fertility rites. The leading participants were Babylonian deities: Marduk, god of the heavens, Ishtar, goddess of fertility on earth, and Humann, an underworld devil. Ishtar, representing life, triumphs over Humann, who represents death. The festival was celebrated with a dramatic re-enactment of the story; it also apparently included sexual liaisons to promote fertility.[40]

For the Jews to celebrate a festival in this way was seen by the priests and rabbis as a form of idolatry, so they changed the gods into people: Marduk became Mordecai, Ishtar became Esther, and Humann became Haman.[41] The basis for the traditional Purim story was thus established. But the rabbis, who first came into prominence in period of the Second Temple, didn't really like Purim, probably because the Jewish God, Yahveh, is not in the story. Because they were hostile to the Maccabees, however, they encouraged the celebration of Purim in preference to Nicanor Day, another Maccabean victory.[42] The rabbis' attitude is confirmed by the inclusion of the Book of Esther in the Bible, while the Book of the Maccabees was relegated to the Apocrypha.

In fact, the story of the Maccabees reflects Jewish history, while the Book of Esther is fiction. Heinrich Graetz, the noted nineteenth-century historian, devotes several chapters in his *History of the Jews* to the story of the Maccabees. The closest he comes to events in the Book of Esther is his suggestion that the Persian King Xerxes was Ahasuerus, who ruled from 485 to 464 B.C.E.[43] A more recent work devotes two chapters to the Hasmonean state. On Purim it reports, "No documents have been discovered that validate the story preserved in the Book of Esther, though it describes vividly and accurately the manners in the court of the Persian Emperor."[44] This statement tends to confirm the view of the Book of Esther as a historical novel written by someone who lived in the Maccabean era, was well acquainted with the history of the Jews under Persian rule, and belonged to the new school of rabbinic Judaism.

Although the Book of Esther is fiction, it represents Jews fighting persecution and "pogromchiks"–those who would carry out pogroms against them. There have been real-life Hamans, Esthers, and Mordecais, and Vashti can be seen as a prototype for women resisting sexual discrimination.

In a psychological assessment of the main Purim characters, male and female, Gendler observes that males have a "well-rounded range of psychological qualities with which to identify," but women have fewer options. She therefore calls on women to look to Vashti to "discover our own sources of dignity, pride, and independence" while remembering the "positive non-aggressive qualities embodied in Esther." She further proposes "that Vashti be reinstated on the throne along with her sister Esther, together to . . . guide the psyches and actions of women."[45]

Jewish festivals have changed through the centuries, and they continue to change. In the celebration of Purim it is well to recall that the Purim Shpiel laid the groundwork for Jewish theatre. Purim observances need be limited only by the imagination and creativity of those taking part, and it may be the occasion to celebrate real events and real heroes of Jewish history, both women and men.

Notes

1. *Holy Scriptures*, p. 783; Ausubel, *Book of Jewish Knowledge*, pp. 8—9.
2. *American Heritage Dictionary*.
3. Stern, "The Period of the Second Temple," p. 291.
4. Ibid.
5. Greenstone, *Jewish Feasts*, pp. 103-106.
6. Roth and Wigoder, *New Standard Jewish Encyclopedia*, pp. 1256—57.
7. Gaster, *Festivals*, p. 235.
8. Wine, "Hanukka," p. 3.
9. Ibid., pp. 4 & 5.
10. Gaster, *Festivals*, pp. 238, 243.
11. Stern, "The Period of the Second Temple," p. 205.
12. Kaufmann, "The Hellenistic Age," p. 105. See also Stern, "The Period of the Second Temple."
13. Ibid., pp. 105—06. See Stern, "The Period of the Second Temple," p. 203.
14. Bickerman, "Maccabean Uprising," p. 80. See also Gaster, *Festivals*, p. 239.
15. Wine, "Hannuka," pp. 7—8.
16. Ibid., pp. 8—9.
17. Barr, "Hannuka."
18. "Introduction," *Humanistic Judaism* (Autumn 1983): 2.
19. Morgenstern, *As a Mighty Stream*, p. 291. Other sources give 163 or 165 B.C.E. as the year in which the Maccabees rededicated the Temple.
20. Gaster, *Festivals*, p. 78.
21. Stern, "The Period of the Second Temple," p. 211; Greenstone, *Jewish Feasts*, p. 97.
22. Stern, "The Period of the Second Temple," pp. 212—16; see also "Maccabees on the March," *Humanistic Judaism* (Autumn 1983): 6.

23. Stern, "The Period of the Second Temple," pp. 216, 222—38; Graetz, *History of the Jews*, vol. 2, pp. 47—56; Roth and Wigoder, *New Standard Jewish Encyclopedia*, p. 1672.

24. Morgenstern, *As a Mighty Stream*, p. 287.

25. Durant, *The Story of Civilization*, vol. 2, *The Life of Greece*, p. 645.

26. Ausubel, *Book of Jewish Knowledge*, pp. 142—43.

27. Wine, "National Liberation," pp. 20—21.

28. Stern, "The Period of the Second Temple," pp. 235—36.

29. Graetz, *History of the Jews*, p. 150.

30. Isaiah 36:16.

31. "A Seder for Tu Bi-Shevat," *Humanistic Judaism* (Winter, 1993); 39—43.

32. Ausubel, *Book of Jewish Knowledge*, p. 78; Wine, "Tu Bi-Shevat," p. 5.

33. Greenstone, *Jewish Feasts*, p. 132.

34. Wine, "Tu Bi-Shevat," p. 7.

35. *Holy Scriptures*, pp. 672—78. This version of the Purim story, including quotations, is from this source unless otherwise indicated.

36. Landman, "The Book of Esther," pp. 17—18.

37. Ginzberg, *Legends of the Jews*, vol. 4, pp. 375—79.

38. Gendler, "Restoration of Vashti," pp. 241—47.

39. *Holy Scriptures*, p. 672.

40. Wine, *Judaism Beyond God*, p. 167.

41. Gaster, *Festivals*, pp. 216—17.

42. Wine, *Judaism Beyond God*, pp. 167—68.

43. Graetz, *History of the Jews*, vol. I, pp. 361, 442—531.

44. Tadmor, "The Period of the First Temple," *p. 160; see also Stern, "The Period of the Second Temple," pp. 201—38.*

45. Gendler, "Restoration of Vashti," pp. 246—47.

CHAPTER EIGHT

From the Exodus
to Mount Sinai

Passover: Ancient Festival Overlaid with History

Passover celebrates the biblical exodus of the Israelites from slavery in Egypt under the leadership of Moses, who spoke and acted in the name of God. The origins of Passover may be traced back many centuries before the departure from Egypt, and the festival has become overlaid with many other historic events in the more than three millennia since the Exodus.

Known as the Festival of Liberation and the Festival of Freedom, Passover developed out of two earlier holidays that preceded the exodus from Egypt. One was Pesach, a shepherd holiday that featured the sacrifice of lambs; the other was Matzot, the festival of unleavened bread celebrated by farmers. The rituals by which Passover is celebrated are set out in the Haggada, the book recording the Exodus in parable, poetry, and prayer. The Haggada declares, "All who enlarge upon the story of the going forth from Egypt shall be deemed praiseworthy."

This brief homily has been taken seriously in every age, from the interpretation of the history and events of the original exodus to the linking of Passover with various historic experiences that are significant not only to the Jews but to other peoples as well. For Jews, it is easy to do this because of the Haggada's urging that in every generation they must look upon themselves as though they personally have come out of slavery.

The Haggada also warns that in every generation new would-be destroyers of the Jews will appear. In fact, ever since the charge of deicide was brought against the Jews, based on the New Testament story of the crucifixion, anti-Jewish attacks have often occurred at Passover. Perhaps one reason for this is that the "Last Supper," before Jesus was condemned, was actually a Passover seder.

In past centuries Jews were often accused of ritual murder to obtain human blood for the making of Passover matzos (unleavened bread). These allegations, which usually led to pogroms, ignored the fact that the Jewish dietary law of *kashrut* forbade the use of blood in the preparation and eating of food.

The charge that Jews would slaughter a non-Jew for sacrificial purposes dates back to pre-Christian times, but the first recorded charge of ritual murder was brought against the Jews of Norwich, England, in 1144. When the body of the alleged victim was found, there was no evidence of murder, so no one was punished. Another early ritual-murder charge, in Blois, France, in 1171, resulted in the Jews of that town being burned alive. In Lincoln, England, in 1255, a ritual murder case had "fantastic consequences," leading to the expulsion of the Jews from all of England in 1290. The blood *bilbul* (myth) later reached epic proportions in Germany and spread to other European countries; it has lasted into the twentieth century. In 1911, Mendel Beilis, a Ukrainian Jew, was charged with ritual murder in Kiev. After a thirty-four-day trial in 1913, he was acquitted by the Russian court when the witnesses against him retracted their testimony under defence cross-examination.[1]

Passover has acquired even greater significance since World War Two: on the night of the first Passover seder on April 19, 1943, the German Nazi army launched an all-out attack to destroy the remnant of Jews in the Warsaw Ghetto. The Passover seder now also commemorates the heroic Warsaw

Ghetto fighters, and the memorial to all the victims of the Holocaust takes place a few days after Passover. A week later, the anniversary of the independence of the state of Israel is celebrated.

Linked with the liberation tradition of Passover is the renewal of family ties, a custom traced back to the rites of spring practised by primitive people before the rise of modern religion. The liberation of the Exodus story is different from the concept of freedom we have today. The Jews were released from bondage, say the religious traditionalists, so that they might be free to accept God and the Torah.[2] However, the Passover tradition of freedom has served to inspire other peoples in other contexts.

Some leaders of the American Revolution, for example, saw their situation as similar to that of the Israelites in ancient Egypt. Thus they chose, for the seal of the Declaration of Independence, a scene depicting Moses leading the Jews out of Egypt, and they added the motto "To rise against tyranny is to walk in the way of God." The American leaders, Benjamin Franklin, Thomas Paine, and John Adams, saw freedom as an escape from their pharaoh, King George III, and the opportunity for their people to be free to follow their own religions—as well as to have economic freedom. But they did not see freedom as something to be shared with their slaves. Ironically, after American independence, the Negro slaves saw their plight reflected in the Biblical Exodus story which included an injunction against slavery and so they sang,

> When Israel was in Egypt land—let my people go!
> Oppressed so hard they could not stand—let my people go!
> Go down Moses, way down in Egypt land, tell old Pharaoh,
> Let my people go.

And, of course, the black people's pharaoh was in Washington.

The dictum to enlarge on the Passover story has led to new seders embodying the idea that freedom should be enjoyed by all peoples. For instance, in the 1960s, during the civil-rights and anti-war movements in the U.S., a new Haggada was written for a "freedom seder," which first took place in Washington; in the late 1960s and early 1970s, new Haggadas expressed "more or less radical political feelings [and] the determination of Jewish women to enter Jewish life as full equals with men." As well, new versions were published by many non-religious socialist kibbutzim before and after the establishment of Israel.[3] Jewish feminists have introduced new elements to make up for the exclusion of women from the traditional Haggada. They have also produced a "Jewish Women's Haggada." One modification in the passage about matzo (unleavened bread) reads, "This is the matzo, the bread of rebellion, that our foremothers baked and ate at the time when they had to be organizing more and cooking less. We eat it to remind ourselves that, like our foremothers, we can and will overcome our bondage–that we and our sisters and our daughters will be free women."[4]

The Passover Seder

Passover is known as the Festival of Freedom because it celebrates the time, more than three thousand years ago, when the Jews, then known as Israelites, were freed from slavery in Egypt. The first result of becoming a free people was that every Jewish family was able to gather together in its own home. That is why the most important part of the Passover festival is the family gathering called the Seder, when relatives and friends gather to celebrate Passover with stories and food and songs and more food. The word *seder* is Hebrew for the order in which the Passover ceremony is carried out. The main feature of the Passover table is the special Seder plate, from which everyone gets to taste the different foods symbolizing and recalling the story of how the Israelites escaped from slavery in Egypt.

The ceremonies begin with Kiddush, the traditional blessing over the wine; the Haggada calls for four glasses of wine to be served during the Seder. Innovations on the wine and other rituals are introduced in nontraditional Haggadas.

The historical account of Passover begins with a special invocation, *Hoh achmo Anyo,* which is also an invitation:

> Behold the bread of poverty which our ancestors ate in the land of Egypt. Let all who are hungry come and eat; let anyone who is needy come in and make Passover. Now we are here; next year may we observe Passover in the Land of Israel. Now many are still enslaved; next year may everyone be free.

Now the youngest child usually asks the "four questions":

> Why do we eat only Matzo on Passover?
> Why do we eat bitter herbs?
>
> Why do we dip twice at the Seder?
> Why do we sit reclining on this night of Passover?

In response to the four questions, the story of Passover may be related through the items on the Seder plate.

The matzo is the most important item at the Passover table. We eat matzo at Passover instead of bread. When the Jews of ancient times learned suddenly that Pharaoh was going to let them go free, the story goes, they were told to prepare to leave quickly, before the king changed his mind. They didn't have time to let the dough rise or to bake it properly in their ovens, so it came out flat.

There are three cakes of matzo on the Passover plate, representing the three categories of Jews in ancient times. The top matzo represents the Kohen or priest; the middle matzo, the Levi, who assisted the priest; and the third matzo, the ordinary people of Israel. The father, or Seder leader, breaks the middle matzo in half. The first half is divided among the guests at the table to be eaten after a blessing. The second half is hidden away as the *afikomen*, to be eaten with dessert at the end of the meal; the children are invited to search for it, and whoever finds it receives a reward.

Another item on the Seder plate is *karpas* (greens: parsley or celery). Passover also marks the beginning of spring and the green vegetable symbolizes the spring rebirth of plants that grow in the earth. Everyone eats a piece of *karpas* dipped in salt water. The salt water symbolizes the tears of the Israelites who suffered as slaves; it may also be suggested that it represents the tears of the Egyptians who were made to suffer punishments because of the hard-heartedness of Pharaoh during the period when he would not let the Jews go free. Before eating the karpas with salt water, a traditional or other form of blessing may be recited for the fruits of the earth.

Also on the Passover plate is *z'roa*, a roasted shankbone. This represents the lamb each Jewish family was called upon to sacrifice on the night before they left Egypt. According to the legend, blood of the lamb was smeared on the front door of each home to protect Jewish families from the punishment the Egyptian families suffered because of the stubbornness of Pharaoh.

A popular seder item is a confection called *charoses,* made of apples, nuts, and wine; this symbolizes the mortar that the Jews used when they were slaves in Egypt, to make the bricks to build the ancient cities of Pithom and Ramses. Then there are the bitter herbs, known as *moror,* represented by white horse-radish, which symbolizes the bitter life that the Jews experienced as slaves in Egypt. The bitter herbs are tasted after being dipped in the sweet *charoses,* now the symbol of hope for a better life. The last item on the Seder plate is a *baytsa,* a baked egg, which symbolizes the sacrifices brought to the Temple to remember the hardships of the Jews while they were slaves in

Egypt. The Christian Easter celebration also includes an egg, providing an example of traditions and customs that date back to the time before the respective religions were established.

Every Jewish holiday and festival has its generally accepted historical version based on the Holy Scriptures, but this has not stopped rabbis and other scholars from studying, analyzing, and reinterpreting the traditional record. The exodus from Egypt on which Passover is based is no exception to such reinterpretation. One of the leading Jewish scholars of this century has written that the Exodus story, "with its markedly religious coloration and its emphasis on the supernatural 'signs and wonders,' is more of a romantic saga or popular legend than an accurate record. Written down centuries later than the period which it describes, it is clearly more indebted to folklore than to sober fact."[5]

This view is confirmed by Nathan Ausubel, the Jewish folklorist, who calls the Passover saga "part history and part folk legend."[6] Moreover, from twentieth-century research it is considered to be "virtually certain" that the Exodus story is a shortened and "anachronistic account of what really took place."[7] Historical and archaeological findings show it to be highly unlikely that *all* the tribes of Israel, "as they later existed," actually went to Egypt or came out of it. The "confederation" of Israelites developed gradually, after the Conquest of the Holy Land, and so "the story of a common ancestor who went down to Egypt with all his sons is as anachronistic as it would be to speak of 'Uncle Sam' and his 48 children at the time of the [U.S.] Revolutionary War."[8]

Other historical accounts relate that there were several invasions of Egypt by Semitic tribes four thousand years ago over a three-hundred-year period. Among them were the forefathers of the tribes that became the nations of Israel and Judah. The Semites ruled Egypt for about two centuries, until they were overthrown in an Egyptian rebellion. Most of them were driven out of the country, while the rest became slaves. Those who left Egypt eventually joined with other Semitic tribes, known as Hebrews ("people living across the river"), in a federation called Israel and invaded the West Bank of the Jordan River under the leadership of Joshua. This means that Joshua came to Canaan some 350 years before Moses.

Meanwhile, the Semites who remained in Egypt as slaves began a rebellion under the leadership of Moses, of the tribe of Levi. Several thousand of these slaves, most of them of the tribe of Judah, eventually escaped from Egypt without divine intervention. Led by the Levites, headed by Moses, they invaded southern Canaan. These people became known as Jews and called their land Judea. Almost three hundred years later, a movement to unite Judea and Israel led the priests to write a common epic, which became the story of the Exodus.[9]

Another important source confirmed, much earlier than others, that Moses really led only one tribe, most likely Judah, out of Egypt. This source recalls that the five books of Moses were all written to emphasize "Israel's peculiar obligation to God." It was unavoidable, therefore, that the writers of these books would take "many and considerable liberties with historical accuracy." [10]

Nevertheless, the Passover story is a reminder that Jews–Israelites, or Hebrews–were, at one time, slaves in Egypt. And in being enjoined to act as though "we" had come out of slavery, the more recent bondage endured by Jews should also be remembered: the persecution and destruction of Ashkenazic forebears in eastern Europe, and the repression endured by the Sephardic forebears of a growing number of Canadian Jews from North Africa and the Middle East.

Some 150 years ago, Heinrich Heine wrote, "Jews who long have drifted from the faith of their fathers . . . are stirred in their inmost parts when the old familiar Passover sounds chance to fall upon their ears."[11] The Passover festival is the outstanding example of how Jewish customs and practices are linked from historic to contemporary times. There is a wide selection of Haggadot that may be used for the Passover seder, from the traditional to the secular and humanist. Old rituals may be followed or new ones may be introduced. There is also a vast literature on Passover and the historic events linked with it, from which appropriate readings may be selected.

Shavuot: From the Sheaf to the Word

The Festival of Shavuot, seven weeks after Passover, is traditionally related to the escape from slavery, which was not to freedom, in the abstract, but to accept the covenant with God and the "yoke" of the Torah. Shavuot is also Chag ha-Bikkurium–the Festival of the First Fruits–another example of an agricultural observance changed into a religious festival after the rise of Judaism. On the Jewish calendar, the dates of Shavuot are Sivan 6 and 7, in late May or early June.

In the days of the Temple, Shavuot was the second of the three festivals when male Jews were commanded to come to Jerusalem with offerings to God. To commemorate the ancient harvest rites, synagogues are now decorated with greenery and flowers. Since the spring harvest includes an abundance of dairy products, the Shavuot festival is celebrated with foods such as cheese blintzes.

From the third century B.C.E., Hellenistic Jews called Shavuot "Pentecost," the Greek term for fiftieth. The Christian Pentecost is on the seventh Sunday after Easter, but the similarity with the Jewish festival ends there. Christian tradition claims Pentecost as the birthday of the church, when "the Holy Spirit was miraculously poured forth upon the original disciples of Jesus."[12] Judaism asserts, "Not the Church, but the community of Israel had been founded on that day. Not to a select few but to a whole people had come the revelation of God."[13]

The Book of Ruth is read in the synagogue on Shavuot, to show how a Moabite "pagan" woman, who married an Israelite, embraced her husband's faith and, after her husband died, accompanied Naomi, her mother-in-law, back to the land of Judah. This story is one of the great Biblical romances. Ruth and Naomi were gleaners[14] in the fields of Boaz. Ruth eventually married Boaz, a kinsman of her dead husband. Out of this marriage was born Obed, who fathered Jesse, who was the father of David. Thus, Ruth was David's great-grandmother. Shavuot is also said to be the anniversary of the death of David.

In Jewish tradition, Shavuot is associated with Zeman Matan Toratenu, the "Season of the Giving (to us) of our Torah." This was not an easy giving. When Moses was delayed on Mount Sinai, the Israelites became impatient, and they called on Aaron to make them a god they could see. In response, Aaron asked the people for their gold earrings, which they willingly gave him; with these he fashioned a golden calf for them to worship. When God saw what the Israelites had done, he told Moses, "I will consume them: and I will make of thee a great nation." Moses pleaded in behalf of the people, and God "repented of the evil which he said he would do."

When Moses came down from the mountain with "the two tablets . . . with the writing of God" and saw the people worshiping the Golden Calf, he became very angry and "cast the tablets out of his hands and broke them." He asked Aaron, What did the people do "that thou hast brought a great sin upon them?" Aaron told Moses how the people had asked him for a god they could see and how he had asked them for their gold. He said that he had cast the gold "into the fire and there came out this calf." He did not disclose that he himself had made the Golden Calf and built an altar before it.

Moses saw that "the people were broken loose–for Aaron had let them loose," but he uttered no further rebuke to Aaron. Instead he said, "Whoso is on the Lord's side . . . come unto me." The sons of Levi gathered around him and he told them that the "God of Israel" had said, "Put ye every man his sword upon his thigh . . . and slay every man his brother, and every man his companion, and every man his neighbour. And the sons of Levi did according to the word of Moses; and there fell of the people that day about three thousand men."

The account of the Golden Calf speaks of how the people sinned until the last verse: "And the Lord smote the people, because they made the calf, which Aaron made."[15] Yet, no punishment for Aaron is mentioned.

Another source states that while Moses was on Mount Sinai, "Aaron was enticed by the multitude to lead them while they made a Golden Calf, for which he received divine censure." For evidence of this "censure" it cites chapter 32 of Exodus plus Numbers 12:1-11. However, the Exodus section cited contains no such evidence. The section of Numbers, titled "God punishes the sedition of Miriam and Aaron," relates how Aaron and Miriam spoke out against Moses for marrying a Cushite woman. God chastised them verbally for this and He made Miriam leprous, but no similar punishment was given to Aaron. Miriam apparently recovered in ten days.[16]

For one not given to seeking divine answers, the two foregoing episodes indicate that the Levites, whether they sinned or not, were held superior to other Israelites, and that a woman was considered more culpable than her brother. It also seems that the exemption of Aaron from any punishment set a precedent for the exalted status of the high priest in the hierarchy of ancient Israel.

After the inequitable and iniquitous punishments the Israelites endured on account of the Golden Calf, the broken tablets with the Ten Commandments were replaced. The

Israelites entered into the covenant with God and received the Torah, which is celebrated at Shavuot. At this point, Moses became known as Moshe Rabbenu, our teacher Moses. The designation "rabbi" derives from *rabbenu*.

In the early years of their ascendance, the rabbis embellished the account of the events at Sinai. According to rabbinic legend, the Israelites were afraid to accept the laws Moses brought down from the mountain. They had to be persuaded, even coerced, to accept the "revelation." (The coercion is apparent from what the Levites did to those three thousand idolators.) It is also related that "Moses first approached the women and acquainted them with the ... principles of the Law, not only because women are more careful in their observance of religious laws, but also because they would instruct their children to follow the laws of the Torah."[17]

In the Middle Ages, dedication to the Torah was translated into education for children. Parents began to enrol their young boys in *cheder*, the religious, or Talmud Torah, school, at the time of the Shavuot festival. The *cheder* was dominant until the end of the nineteenth century. Early in the twentieth century, *veltliche* (worldly) or secular schools were inaugurated by Jewish socialist and Labour Zionist groups. These schools, known as the Yiddish Radicale Shule (Jewish Radical School) or the Yiddish Folk Shule (Jewish People's School), began teaching Jewish history and literature in Yiddish, as distinct from religious studies conducted in Hebrew. Different types of religious schools also developed with the growth of Reform, Conservative, and other Jewish denominations.

The Reform movement originally gave up the practice of Bar Mitzvah for thirteen-year-old boys and introduced a group confirmation ceremony for religious-school graduates–girls as well as boys–at the time of the Shavuot Festival. Conservative synagogues have also introduced this practice. Since Shavuot falls close to the end of the school term, it is natural for Jewish schools, religious or secular, and synagogues to recognize educational achievements during this festival.

From its beginnings as a harvest festival, Shavuot became a religious festival with the rise of God-based Judaism; it continues in that role for the devout of every Jewish denomination. For the secular and the humanist, the agnostic or the *apikoros*, Shavuot may serve as an occasion to celebrate Jewish educational and cultural achievements without religious ritual.

There is a *midrash*, an interpretive commentary, in the book of Jubilees, from the first century B.C.E., which is based partly on a pun on the Hebrew words: *shavuot*, meaning weeks, and *shevuot*, meaning oaths, including covenant oaths. A number of special *shevuot* are said to have been made on Shavuot, two of which merit consideration.

One of these is the covenant God is said to have made with Noah after the Flood: "I will not again curse the ground for man's sake," nor "shall there any more be a flood to destroy the earth."[18] Since World War Two, the death and destruction known as the Holocaust have, not unreasonably, been compared with the destruction caused by the Flood. The question may therefore be asked, If God really had the power to prevent such destruction, why did He fail to uphold his covenant with Noah?

It was also on Shavuot, this *midrash* relates, that Abraham's two estranged sons, Isaac, forebear of the Jews, and Ishmael, forebear of the Arabs, met at Abraham's deathbed, to mourn together and make an oath of peace between them.[19] It is therefore reasonable to hope that Israelis, Arabs, and Palestinians will learn to live in peace in the Middle East in the spirit of Isaac and Ishmael's Shavuot pledge for peace.

Lag b'Omer: Spring Interlude

In ancient Israel, the barley harvest began on the second day of Passover, marked by the presentation to the priests of the first *omer* (sheaf of grain). This day also marked the beginning of the curious ceremony of the counting of the *omer* for forty-nine days, until the eve of Shavuot, when the barley harvest ended and the wheat harvest began with another offering. The seven weeks of *omer* counting are also described as a "lenten period" comparable to the Christian Lent that precedes Easter. No one seems to know the origin of this penitential Jewish Lent, except that it is traced back to primitive times.

The thirty-third day of counting the *omer* is known as Lag b'Omer, "an ancient, heathen festival taken over by the folk religion of the Jews of old," which became the "Jewish counterpart of mid-lent ceremonies."[20] In later years, an effort was made to "Judaize this folk festival" by connecting it with a Jewish historical event.

In the first century C.E., a fatal plague struck down many disciples of the famous Rabbi Akiba; on Lag b'Omer, the plague suddenly ended. This plague became the "reason" for the penitential practices of the Jews, including a ban on marriages, during the *omer*-counting period. The marriage ban, still widely observed, was lifted for Lag b'Omer. One scholar says that the connection of Lag b'Omer with Rabbi Akiba is "forced and . . . baseless." Another commentator remarks that the reference to Akiba and his followers relates to their involvement in the Bar Kochba rebellion against the Romans. It is thus suggested that the observance of the *omer* days as a period of "semi-mourning" is related to Judea's last struggle for independence. Attacks on the Jews during the Crusades and in the 1648 Cossack invasion of Poland occurred during this period and may have reinforced the mourning practice.[21]

In any event, Lag b'Omer came to be celebrated with outdoor festivities for schoolchildren and Yeshiva students, and has become known as the students' festival. Whatever its origins, it is a worthy occasion for outdoor programs commemorating important events in Jewish history. Any group, religious or secular, may plan such an event according to its own interpretation.

Notes

1. Ausubel, *Book of Jewish Knowledge*, pp. 369—72.
2. Gaster, *Festivals*, pp. 31—32.
3. Waskow, *Seasons of our Joy*, p. 139.
4. Friedman, *How Was This Passover,"* p. 35.
5. Gaster, *Passover*, p. 29
6. Ausubel, *Book of Jewish Knowledge*, p. 324.
7. Gaster, *Festivals*, p. 35.
8. Ibid., p. 36.
9. Wine, *The Real Story of Passover*.
10. Morgenstern, *As a Mighty Stream*, p. 11.
11. Baron, *Treasury of Jewish Quotations*, p. 34
12. New Testament, Acts of the Apostles, Chapter 2:1—4.
13. Gaster, *Festivals*, p. 71.
14. Corners of fields were left partly unharvested and the right of gleaning was reserved for the poor and strangers. See Leviticus, 19:9, *Holy Scriptures*, p. 94.
15. *Holy Scriptures*, Exodus 32:1—35, pp. 68—69.
16. *Holy Scriptures*, p. 769, Numbers, pp. 116—17.
17. Greenstone, *Jewish Feasts*, p. 233.
18. *Holy Scriptures*, Genesis 8:21, 9:11, pp. 8—9.
19. Waskow, *Seasons of Our Joy*, p. 203.
20. Gaster, *Festivals*, p. 19.
21. Gaster, *Festivals*, ibid; Schauss, *Jewish Festivals*, p. 276; Greenstone, *Jewish Feasts*, p. 226.

CHAPTER NINE

The Sabbath
and Rites of Passage

The Oldest Jewish Holiday

The Jewish Sabbath (Shabbat) is celebrated weekly from sundown on Friday until the appearance of the stars after sundown on Saturday. Since it originates in the biblical story of Creation and is included in the Ten Commandments, the Sabbath is considered the oldest of all Jewish holidays. It did not become a regular observance, however, until the Babylonian exile, when it developed, simultaneously with the synagogue, into a major religious institution.[1] The true origin of Sabbath is uncertain. The biblical story that the Sabbath commemorates the day of rest taken by God after creating the world in six days is considered a "fanciful attempt to rationalize and explain a traditional institution."[2]

Practices similar to the Jewish sabbath are found in the folkways of other peoples. A regular day for abstention from work is a common phenomenon among some of the tribes in West Africa, for example. Each tribe has its own religion whose adherents are expected to desist from manual labour on the day set aside for the worship of their god. In many cases, the sabbath day arose for practical considerations and is observed as a market day; daily working practices are suspended so that people may gather at a central location to sell their wares. At least one tribe, however, the Yoruba of southern Nigeria, observe the sabbath more as a day of taboos based on superstitions rather than for utilitarian purposes.[3]

Jewish religious law proclaims thirty-nine actions that are prohibited on the Sabbath, including everything to do with working the fields, cooking, baking and other kinds of work, tying or untying, hunting, writing, lighting a fire, and transporting. Among devout Orthodox Jews, these prohibitions are interpreted to include speaking on the telephone, driving a car, turning on a light switch or any electrical appliance, tearing toilet paper, writing, and carrying anything, including a handkerchief. One biblical injunction[4] includes the death penalty for anyone who profanes the Sabbath, but the fourth commandment, to observe the Sabbath, omits the death penalty. It provides that the Sabbath shall also be observed by servants and even by beasts in the field.[5]

The Sabbath restrictions originally included not helping a person out who fell into a well. When the Jewish sages codified the sabbath rules, however, they recognized that the Sabbath was made for man, and not man for the Sabbath. Thus they provided that any Sabbath ban might be, and even should be, broken in case of life-and-death emergency, or of real danger to health.[6] One might assume that the Sabbath death penalty is a "life-and-death emergency" that could therefore be ignored; in any case it is one of the many biblical "laws" for which literal interpretation is unreasonable.

Many passages in the Talmud were written in defence of the bewildering number of sabbath laws, because they probably aroused much discontent even in ancient times.[7] But there was a more lofty purpose to the sabbath; it was the day when, in place of mundane activities, one took part in Torah study and sought mental and spiritual recreation. Before the first sabbath meal begins, on Friday evening, the day is consecrated, in family homes of the various Jewish denominations, with the blessing of the sabbath candles. This is the one ritual assigned to the woman of the household; it takes place just before sundown in observant homes. When the father returns from the Friday-evening synagogue service, he performs blessings over the wine and the sabbath *challah* (braided egg bread). The Saturday-morning service in the synagogue includes chanting the Torah portion of the week. The Bar Mitzvah ceremony for thirteen-year-old boys usually takes place at the Saturday service. The Bas Mitzvah ceremony for girls, introduced in many synagogues in the past several decades, usually takes place on Friday evening, though some synagogues grant girls equal rights with boys to the Saturday morning rites.

On Saturday evening after sundown, the Havdala service marks the separation of the Sabbath from the working week with blessings over symbolic items: a braided candle, a goblet of wine, and a spice-box. The main Havdala benediction makes a distinction between the holy and the profane, between light and darkness, between Israel and the nations, between the seventh day and the six working days. The braided candle is extinguished at the end of the service and used again a week later. The Havdala symbols are given universal meaning in the secular humanist tradition: the candle represents the many sources of the light of wisdom and beauty, the wine is the symbol of joy and fulfilment, and the spice-box fragrance recalls the good and the beautiful and the hope for happiness and peace in the week ahead.[8]

Perhaps the earliest secular humanist interpretation of the Sabbath comes from Moses Hess, a nineteenth-century theoretician on the Jewish question who is recognized as a "father" of modern Zionism. In his classic work, *Rome and Jerusalem* (1862), Hess wrote about the Sabbath through history:

> *The biblical story of Creation is told only for the sake of the Sabbath ideal.* It tells us, *in symbolic language,* that when the creation of the world of Nature was completed, with the calling into life of the highest organic being of the earth–man–and the Creator celebrated his natural Sabbath, there at once began the workdays of History. Then, also, began the history of creation of the

social world, which will celebrate its Sabbath, after the completion of the task of world history, by ushering in the messianic
epoch. Here, in this conception, you can see the high moral
value of *the Mosaic story of Creation, which is a symbolic story and
not, as narrow supernaturalists would have it, a system of science.*[9]

Hess also inspired the socialist ideal among Jews; other
thinkers have accepted his view that Sabbath symbolism represents the highest expression of social ethics. The Mosaic
approach suggests that the poorest and most downtrodden
person achieves dignity and moral stature on the Sabbath in
recognition that every person is endowed by nature with human rights that transcend property rights or social status. In the
religious view, God championed human rights and the Sabbath
asserts these rights.[10] However, when Hess wrote about the
"creation of the social world," he did so in the light of his views
about a Jewish liberation movement. It may thus be assumed
that he meant that people had to work to achieve their human
rights.

The observance of the Sabbath aroused anti-Jewish hostility
in ancient times, particularly in the pre-Christian era of the
Roman Empire, when some Romans were attracted by the
preaching of Jewish missionaries (later Jewish-Christians) of
the Sabbath ideal of a day of rest every seventh day. The
antipathy of the Roman elite for the Sabbath had an economic
base, since Roman prosperity was built on slave labour: the idea
that slaves or serfs might be entitled to rest one day out of seven
was regarded with horror as a potential loss of the labour from
which the Roman gentry profited.[11]

Despite the fact that other ancient people observed a form
of sabbath that may have preceded the introduction of the
Jewish practice, it is the Jewish Sabbath ideal which eventually
gained acceptance by other major religions. The idea of one
day a week off from work may also be seen as inspiring the

modern labour movement in its drive for the betterment of working conditions in the industrial age.

When the Jews, most of them devout Sabbath observers, began emigrating from Eastern Europe in the 1880s, they found that the Christian Sabbath, Sunday, was institutionalized as a legal day of rest in North America. Many Orthodox Jews were thus confronted with the problem of how to continue observing the Jewish Sabbath on Saturday, especially if they were legally obliged not to work on Sunday. In centres such as New York and Chicago, where Jews congregated in large numbers to form their own neighbourhoods, it was not difficult to keep the traditional Sabbath. But in smaller centres, where they depended on gentile trade, especially if they were storekeepers, they could not afford to keep their stores closed on both Saturday and Sunday.

In Canada in the early 1900s, a coalition of Protestant Christian groups known as the Lord's Day Alliance successfully lobbied the Canadian government to introduce the Lord's Day Act, making it illegal to keep stores open, do business, or even work a farm on Sunday. In 1906, Montreal's Baron de Hirsch Institute, the major Jewish welfare agency in the country, appealed to the government for an exemption for Jews from strict application of the Lord's Day Act. The Christian backers of the act would not countenance such an amendment; it was opposed by most MPs, except those from Quebec. A single concession was granted; each province could modify the regulations within its jurisdiction. Only Catholic Quebec took advantage of this provision and granted the exemption asked by the Jews. The Sunday Blue Law, as it became known, undoubtedly contributed to the weakening of the traditional sabbath observance among Jews in Canada. Even in Quebec, despite the exemption granted, many Jewish businesses felt they had to remain open on Saturday to keep up with non-Jewish competitors.

In the U.S., in the 1890s, a proposal was made to change the Jewish sabbath observance from Saturday to Sunday, but the main religious bodies rejected the idea. In practice, however, Sunday has become an important day in many synagogues, involving breakfast-club programs for adults and Sunday-school classes for children. Many synagogues also hold services late on Friday night; the main service of the week, on Saturday morning, usually gets a large attendance only for Bar Mitzvahs or the occasional Bat Mitzvah.

The historical importance of the Sabbath is widely recognized. The Christian Gospels record that "The Sabbath was made for man and not man for the Sabbath." Moreover, Achad ha-Am ("One of the People," pen name of Asher Ginsberg, 1856—1927), a leading exponent of Jewish cultural nationalism who was called "The Agnostic Rabbi,"[12] declared, "More than Jews have kept the Sabbath, the Sabbath has kept the Jews."[13]

Jewish cuisine was developed in honour of the Sabbath, including the *challah* (Sabbath bread), *gefilte* (stuffed) fish, chicken soup with *lockshen* (noodles), *tsimmes*, a sweet side-dish, usually carrots with honey, and *kugel*, noodle or bread pudding. Many of these traditional foods were borrowed and adapted from dishes eaten by non-Jewish neighbours. For example, the *challah*, called a *koiletch* in Yiddish, was borrowed from the Russian braided *kulitch*, served during Easter.[14] The *koiletch* gets its Jewish character because it is made with eggs and in accordance with Jewish dietary provisions. It is often placed on the table with an embroidered *challah* cover that is inscribed with the Hebrew blessing for bread. Other ceremonial objects, such as the kiddush-cup for the wine and the Havdala spice box, are similarly embellished.

The Sabbath dishes are always prepared with special care. In the days of the Second Temple, it was customary for the man of the house to take part in the shopping and cooking for the festive meal. He did this in honour of the "Sabbath Queen" who was about to enter his home. The Sabbath Queen was the inspiring spirit of the day of rest, greeted with *zmiros* (special hymns or songs), and maintained during the day with uplifting intellecual discourse. In the second century C.E., Rabbi Meir, of the Mishnah fathers, presented special lectures to the women on the Sabbath at a time when women were generally regarded as ineligble for Torah study. Rabbi Meir was married to Beruriah, one of the few recorded exceptional Jewish women scholars.

In the Greco-Roman era, Jews also found sustenance for the senses on the Sabbath by inhaling incense or the perfume of flowers. This was known as Oneg Shabbat, taking delight in the Sabbath. In more recent times an intellectual Oneg Shabbat custom was introduced by Chaim Nachman Bialik (1873—1934), the modern poet laureate of the Jewish people, in the form of social and cultural gatherings befitting the Sabbath spirit. Started in Palestine in the 1930s, the Oneg Shabbat custom spread to Jewish communities around the world with Friday-night or Saturday-afternoon programs in the synagogue. An Oneg Shabbat can also be secular; the Humanist Jewish movement has developed ways of celebrating the Sabbath as a day for families and community groups to come together for study and discussion to strengthen their Jewish identity without necessarily making it a day of worship.[15]

Brit Milah: Ritual Circumcision

Ancient tradition rates the Brit Milah, the ritual circumcision of a Jewish male baby, equal in importance to the observance of Sabbath as evidence of Jewish identity. In modern practice, many Jews who do not observe the Sabbath or follow other religious rites still have their infant sons circumcised. The Brit Milah may thus be the biblical law most widely observed by

Jews regardless of religious association. The Bible calls for the circumcision to be performed on the eighth day; this is strictly observed even if the eighth day falls on the Sabbath or on Yom Kippur. The penalty for not being ritually circumcised is ostracism; the soul of the uncircumcised male "shall be cut off from his people."[16] Apart from claimed health benefits, which have been challenged since the 1980s, the only justification for Brit Milah in modern times is its ancient religious significance.

There are several questionable aspects of the biblical provisions on circumcision. It is claimed that a non-Jewish man who wishes to marry a Jewish woman must first be circumcised.[17] The example given is of Dinah, Jacob's daughter, who was seduced by Shechem, the Hivite, who declared his love for her and asked to marry her.[18] Shechem agreed to her brothers' demand that he and all his men be circumcised. But Simeon and Levi, two of the brothers, killed Schechem and his men when they were at their weakest, after their circumcision.[19] This is hardly an advertisement for a non-Jew to undergo circumcision in order to be accepted into the Jewish fold.

Another issue is the Bible declaration that a visiting stranger who wishes to celebrate Passover with a Jewish family can only do so if he is circumcised![20] This ruling is in conflict with the opening Haggada recitation, which says, "Let anyone who is hungry come in and eat; let anyone who is needy come in and make Passover."

Circumcision may have been a way of appeasing the gods in primitive times, since it was done at puberty to protect the male and ensure his reproductive capacity. This was before the biblical Brit Milah was introduced. There is a grisly passage in the Bible that may be a reminder of the earlier practice. Moses, it is said, neglected to circumcise his first-born son. When he and his wife, Zipporah, and their sons were on their way back to Egypt from Midian, "the Lord met him and sought to kill him. . . . Then Zipporah took a flint, and cut off the foreskin of her son, and cast it at his feet. . . . So he let him alone." And Zipporah added, "A bridegroom of blood are thou to me . . . in regard of the circumcision."[21] Presumably, God was appeased by the bloody foreskin and allowed Moses to continue on to Egypt to deal with Pharaoh.

The Bible also speaks of another form of circumcision: the Israelites are admonished while they are in the desert, "Circumcise therefore the foreskin of your heart, and be no more stiffnecked."[22] This is in fact a warning to the people not to be hard-hearted; in the following verses, the Israelites are urged to deal justly with other people.[23] Later, in the time of the Prophets, Jeremiah warns the people of Israel that they will be punished equally with the uncircumcised nations because they are "uncircumcised in the heart."[24] This admonition urges that the wise man should not "glory in his wisdom," nor the "mighty man glory in his might," nor the rich man "in his riches." Men should rather glory "in justice and righteousness in the earth."[25] It is not unreasonable to suggest, therefore, that if someone insists on ostracizing a Jew who is physically uncircumcised that person may himself be "uncircumcised in the heart."

When Christianity was founded, Paul of Tarsus substituted the rite of baptism, immersion in water, for circumcision; this was borrowed from the Jewish Essene sect. The continued practice of circumcision brought hostility toward the Jews from early Christians, as it had from the Romans and Greeks, arising from the belief that the symbol of Jewish identity, stamped on the male body, strengthened the resistance of the Jews to assimilation. Antiochus Epiphanes, the Assyrian king, forbade circumcision and other Jewish practices on pain of death, thus helping to provoke the Maccabean revolt (168 B.C.E.). Later, circumcision was made a capital crime under the Roman Emperor Hadrian. His successor, Antonius Pius, said to be more enlightened, permitted circumcision for Jews born as Jews, but banned it for converts to Judaism. Under this law, Jewish missionary efforts in the Hellenistic era were curtailed. The field was thus open to the early Christians, who were still Jews, to proselytize the gentiles, since the rabbis were unyielding in the condition that a convert to Judaism had to undergo the rite of circumcision.[26] In fact, a male child who dies between the third and eighth day after birth must still be circumcised before burial. (It has been reported that in Israel this practice has been carried out on uncircumcised deceased Russian Jews before they were allowed burial in a Jewish cemetery.)

For those born of Jewish mothers, circumcision confirms adherence to the so-called covenant with God. But the Brit Milah does not have the same sacramental significance as does baptism for the Christians. The Shulchan Aruch, the codified manual of Jewish religious observance, makes it clear that even an uncircumcised Jew is still a full Jew by birth–though he might not be considered a "proper" Jew.[27] By the Middle Ages, the rite of circumcision impressed enlightened intellectual Jews as a throwback to tribal primitivism. Yehuda Halevi, the poet-philosopher of twelfth-century Spain, wrote of the Brit Milah, "This commandment is against nature," yet Abraham, at the age of one hundred, "subjected his person and that of his son to it" as the sign of the Covenant with "the Divine Power."[28]

In the Hellenistic era, Philo (c. 20 B.C.E.—after 40 C.E.), the philosopher-rabbi of Alexandria, argued that surgical removal of the foreskin was a benefit to health and personal hygiene.[29] Circumcision has been practiced by Muslims, but Christians continued to avoid it like the plague. Not until the twentieth century did Christians change their attitude, and then only when the medical profession concluded that the surgical procedure had therapeutic benefits. It thus gained wide acceptance, and eventually more than 85 percent of newborn males in the U.S. were being circumcised for secular medical reasons.

In 1971, however, the American Academy of Pediatrics announced that circumcision has no observable benefit. An anti-circumcision lobby then developed and the practice began to be abandoned. Until 1983, the A.A.P., supported by the American College of Obstetrics and Gynecology, continued to hold this view of circumcision.[30] But by 1988, new evidence led the Pediatrics Academy to a review of its critical decision. It was reported that out of fifty thousand known cases of penile cancer in North America, only nine had occurred in circumcised males. Urinary-tract infections occurred less often when the foreskin was removed, and uncircumcised males contracted aids far more often than circumcised males.

Civil libertarians have said that non-urgent elective surgery is being foisted on infants who cannot give their consent. As well, feminists have opposed the ritual because it is an initiation rite for boys only.[31] If the claims about circumcised males being less likely to contract certain diseases are true, parents may certainly make a decision for a child to have the operation. However, the feminist criticism of Brit Milah is valid as an example of unequal treatment of females because of the naming ceremony associated with it.

The humanist secular Jewish view suggests that the surgical circumcision practice be separated from the ceremonial birth celebration of a baby. Parents should be free to consider what weight they want to give to medical evidence on circumcision before deciding on a Brit Milah. Male children, circumcised or not, should be treated equally in the Jewish community. Birth celebrations, including baby-naming, can and are being devised to treat girls equally with boys.[32]

Bar/Bat Mitzvah: "Son–and Daughter?–of the Covenant"

Following his thirteenth birthday, a Jewish boy goes through the ceremony of Bar Mitzvah in the synagogue, by which he literally becomes a "son of the covenant." In the past half-century, a Bat Mitzvah ceremony has been introduced for girls in Reform and Conservative synagogues. The Bat Mitzvah is considered the equivalent of the Bar Mitzvah for boys, but it does not necessarily establish that girls are equal to boys in Jewish religious tradition.

A boy, on and after his Bar Mitzvah, is counted in the *minyan*, the traditional prayer quorum of ten men, and is expected to don *tefillin*, the phylactery prayer symbols, at morning prayers on weekdays. The Bar Mitzvah ceremony is, after circumcision, the most widely practiced ritual in Jewish life. Nevertheless, this synagogue ceremony is not prescribed in the Bible. The term "Bar Mitzvah" first appears in a Talmudic precept in the Mishnah; it declares that every male Jew be regarded as *bar mitzvah*, at the age of thirteen, based on a test of his knowledge of the Jewish faith, but no ceremony was prescribed.[33] The Talmud (*kiddushin* 16b) set thirteen, for boys, and twelve, for girls, as the age when they were to take responsibility and perform their respective halakhic rituals.[34]

The contemporary Bar Mitzvah can be traced back to the thirteenth century, when the synagogue-centred ceremony was started. At that time, a boy of thirteen was considered to be on the threshold of adulthood and even ready for marriage. In Europe and the Middle East, the Bar Mitzvah was an occasion for rejoicing in the religious educational achievement of the young man. The ceremony included reading of part of the Torah portion of the week, the reading of the *haftorah*, a chapter from the Prophets, and a *derasha*, a speech in the form of a miniature dissertation on a learned subject.

The modern Bar Mitzvah is not based on any religious law, but is a variation of the Middle Ages custom. It has become, in fact, something of an anachronism, insofar as recognition of adulthood is concerned. A thirteen-year-old boy today is just entering adolescence and is not considered an adult except for his acceptance as part of the synagogue *minyan*. Boys whose Bar Mitzvah preparation has been more than minimal may do all the prescribed recitations and lead other parts of the service, but a learned address is rare indeed. In past centuries, the party at the family home following the synagogue ritual had a folkloric quality, but in modern times the Bar Mitzvah party is often an elaborate formal event at a hotel or restaurant devoid of cultural or social content.

For family members who are active synagogue participants, the Bar Mitzvah may be a stage in the development of a thirteen-year-old as a member of the synagogue community. But for many families who are not regular synagogue members, the Bar Mitzvah is a pro forma celebration and, more often than not, mark's the end of the boy's formal Jewish education.

The Bat Mitzvah ceremony for girls, more or less the equivalent of the ceremony for boys, was introduced in the Conservative synagogue movement more than fifty years ago. The thirteen-year-old girl may perform all the same rituals as the boy, but in most synagogues the Bat Mitzvah takes place at a Friday-night service, rather than on Saturday morning. Moreover, the Bat Mitzvah girl does not become an equal member of the congregation except in synagogues that include women in the prayer quorum.

From the beginning of the Reform movement, the ceremony of group Confirmation was introduced in place of the individual Bar Mitzvah ceremony. The first Confirmation took place in the synagogue in Kassel, Germany, in 1810,[35] when that city was part of the Kingdom of Westphalia with Jerome Bonaparte as king. This experiment, which preceded the first

Reform Temple, founded in 1818, in Hamburg,[36] did not last; the Reform Confirmation program was for boys only when it first became a regular practice. It was introduced in the U.S. at New York's Temple Emanu-El in 1847, and only in later years were girls drawn into the ceremony. Confirmation is now a regular graduation-rite for students of Reform and Conservative religious schools and takes place annually during the feast of Shavuot, the festival commemorating the biblical legend of how the Jews received the Torah at Mount Sinai.

Reform Temples and Conservative synagogues also offer individual Bar/Bat Mitzvah programs for families who want it for their thirteen-year-old sons and daughters. It is even possible for an Orthodox family to have a Bat Mitzvah ceremony for a daughter, but not as part of the regular synagogue service. Some Orthodox rabbis have encouraged a form of bat mitzvah, but without a role for girls in the actual synagogue service.[37] Some Orthodox women have organized their own separate service in an auxiliary chapel of their synagogue, and a girl may have a Bat Mitzvah as part of this service.

There is, of course, another approach to Bar/Bat Mitzvah. Secular Humanistic Judaism recommends that the ceremony can be a celebration of the arrival of the thirteen-year-old boy or girl not into adulthood, but into adolescence, the beginning of the teenage years that are so important to every young person. It also proposes that the ceremony need not be called Bar Mitzvah (Bat Mitzvah), "where women always end up inside the parenthesis," but simply the Mitzvah ceremony. "Mitzvah" is a popular word in Hebrew and Yiddish that means not only "commandment" but also "good deed."[38] The ceremony can indeed be a good deed for the child, for the family, and for the community.[39] Nor need it be tied exclusively to the Torah: material is available on how to observe a secular Mitzvah ceremony: it may be built around the "Mitzvah" speech, an address based on study undertaken by the celebrant on a well-known figure in Jewish history,[40] ranging from the Prophets to Sholom Aleichem and Albert Einstein or from women in the Bible and the Talmud to Emma Lazarus, Henrietta Szold, and Golda Meir.

Notes

1. Ausubel, *Book of Jewish Knowledge*, p. 375.
2. Gaster, *Festivals*, p. 263.
3. Ibid., pp. 265—67.
4. Exodus 31:17.
5. Exodus 20.10; Deuteronomy 5:14.
6. Gaster, *Festivals*, pp. 270—71.
7. Ausubel, *Book of Jewish Knowledge*, p. 376.
8. *Guide to Humanistic Judaism*, p. 70.
9. Quoted in Hertzberg, *Zionist Idea*, pp. 131—32. Emphasis added.
10. Ausubel, *Book of Jewish Knowledge*, p. 374.
11. Ibid., 374.
12. Hertzberg, *Zionist Idea*, p. 247.
13. Ausubel, *Book of Jewish Knowledge*, p. 374.
14. Ibid., p. 378.
15. *Guide to Humanistic Judaism*, pp. 69-70.
16. Genesis 17:10—14.
17. Genesis 34: 14—15.
18. Genesis 34:2—4.
19. Genesis 34: 25—26.
20. Exodus 12:43—48
21. Exodus 4: 24—26.
22. Deuteronomy 10:16.
23. Deuteronomy 10:18—19.
24. Jeremiah 9: 24—25.
25. Jeremiah 9: 22—23.
26. Ausubel, *Book of Jewish Knowledge*, p. 116.
27. Ibid., p. 114.
28. Ibid., p. 116.
29. Ibid.
30. Wallerstein, "Circumcision and Anti-Semitism," pp. 43—44.
31. Wine, "Circumcision."
32. "Birth Celebrations," *Guide to Humanistic Judaism*, pp. 9—10.
33. Gaster, *Holy*, pp. 66—67.

34. Hertzberg, *Judaism*, p. 100.
35. Ausubel, *Book of Jewish Knowledge*, p. 122.
36. Ettinger, "The Modern Period," pp. 788, 834._
37. Hertzberg, *Judaism*, p. 103.
38. In Canada, CSJO affiliates in Toronto and Vancouver have introduced a B'nai Mitzvah program in which boys and girls participate equally.
39. Wine, *Judaism Beyond God*, pp. 183—84.
40. "Bar/Bat Mitsva and Confirmation," *Guide to Humanistic Judaism*, pp. 7—8.

Part Three

THE MODERN ERA

CHAPTER TEN

Anti-Semitism
and Human Rights

The term "anti-Semitism" was first used in 1879 by Wilhelm Marr, a German journalist who founded the Anti-Semitic League.[1] It is a misnomer, since Jews are not the only so-called Semitic people; nevertheless, it designates all manner of anti-Jewish prejudice and discrimination and is equated with Judaeophobia. Anti-Semitism has been the subject of countless treatises by Jews and non-Jews, but most historians, unless they are specially sensitive to the issue, avoid writing about it, even where it fits into the broader subject of a work of history or biography. [2]

Anti-Semitism has been called the greatest and longest hatred in human history. The term has been applied retroactively to ancient times, when hatred of the Jews was stirred among Christians over the death of Jesus Christ; the earliest anti-Jewish pogroms are said to have occurred in the city of Alexandria in the first two centuries C.E. Anti-Jewish ideas were introduced in the New Testament. The Book of Revelations (R. 21:2), for example, writes about the "Synagogue of Satan," a false concept that has influenced anti-Semitic propaganda even in recent times.

The early church fathers taught that the Jews had formerly belonged to the "chosen people" but that, in repudiating Jesus, they had forfeited their "chosenness," which was transferred to the Christians. "Jew" thus became a pejorative term. Early Christians absorbed some anti-Jewish ideas from the Roman aristocracy of the pagan empire.[3] When the New Testament was being written, the author of the Book of John continued the work of Paul to hide the fact that Christ was a Jew so that he could be accepted by the pagan world, "even the anti-Semitic World." (Fifty years before Jerusalem fell to the Romans, Strabo, a pagan Greek geographer, had complained "with anti-Semitic exaggeration" about Jews spreading everywhere on the "habitable earth."[4]) Anti-Jewish material was also produced by Apion, a first-century writer of Alexandria, and by the Roman historian Tacitus in the early second century C.E.[5]

James Parkes, a twentieth-century Anglican theologian, has written that "the evidence is inescapable" of the church's role in the "denigration of Judaism in the formative period of Christian history." He adds, "There is no break in the line from the exclusion of the Jews from civic equality in the period of the Church's first triumph in the fourth century, through the horrors of the Middle Ages, to the death camps of Hitler in our own day."[6]

"Hep Hep," the cry of anti-Jewish rioters in Germany in 1819, was an anti-Jewish slogan dating back to the Crusades and formed from the initials of *Heirosolyma est perdita*–Jerusalem is lost.[7] German Jews who wanted to get ahead professionally accepted baptism as Christians. Ludwig Börne (1786—1837), born Ludwig (Louis) Baruch, was one Jew who did so. He wrote, "What you call human rights, which it must be conceded you grant to Jews, are only animal rights. The right to seek food, to devour it, to sleep and to multiply are enjoyed also by the beasts of the field–until they are slain, and to the Jews you grant no more. But civic rights alone are human rights."[8] Appalled by the folly and cruelty of the "hep hep" year, Börne wrote an essay titled "For the Jews," explaining, "I should have said for right and liberty; but if these terms were understood, nothing need be said." Recalling that just as they were now storming against the Jews, Germans had stormed against Catholics twenty years earlier, he declared, "I love neither Jew as Jew, nor Christian as Christian; I love them because they are human beings and born to be free."[9]

In 1848, an Orthodox rabbi from Cracow, then part of Austrian Galicia, was elected to the first parliament of Austria. When he took his seat, the Speaker asked him why he sat with the Left. The rabbi is said to have replied, *"Juden haben keine Rechte"* (Jews have no rights). That rabbi was Dov Berush Meisels (1798—1870), who had joined with the Radicals.[10] Meisels knew that Jews suffered from a lack of human rights because of anti-Semitism. He supported Polish independence, in the belief that those who would repress the Poles were a greater threat to the Jews than were the Poles.

In 1856, Meisels became chief rabbi of Warsaw, where he again supported the Polish freedom movement. He once walked arm in arm with a Catholic bishop in a procession honouring victims of the insurrection. When the Russian government ordered the closing of Polish churches, charging that they were being misused for political purposes, Meisels ordered the synagogues to close, too. He was arrested and imprisoned in 1861, then compelled to leave Warsaw for his support of the Polish rebels. By the end of 1862, he was allowed to return to Warsaw. A new Polish governor, appointed by the czar, adopted a policy of reconciliation, revoked anti-Jewish laws, and granted Jews citizenship rights. Meisels was thus vindicated in his support of the Polish rebels. However, the Russians defeated a renewed rebellion and became undisputed masters of Poland. Russia's anti-Jewish laws were invoked and the Poles were provoked into hostile attacks on the Jews.[11]

Anti-Semitism certainly has ancient religious and social roots, but when the term was coined, in the nineteenth century, it was as part of the new political theory, racism, by which some "races" were held superior to others. One of its first

European propagandists was Count Joseph Arthur de Gobineau, a French diplomat and "orientalist" who published a
four-volume work, *Essay on the Inequality of Human Races* (Paris,
1853—55). It set out the notion of Aryan superiority, particularly over the "mongrel race" of the Jews: "Everything great,
noble and fruitful in the works of man . . . belongs to one family
[Aryan]."[12] English-born Houston Stewart Chamberlain, who
became a German citizen and the son-in-law of Richard Wag-
ner, the composer and anti-Semite, has been called the
"prophet" of De Gobineau for his libelous anti-Jewish work
with the misleading title *The Foundations of the Nineteenth Century* (1899).[13]

Then there was Sergei Nilus, Russian publisher of the
Protocols of the Elders of Zion, the infamous anti-Semitic forgery.
A *London Times* exposé by Philip Graves (1921) showed the
Protocols to be a plagiarized revision of an 1860 French pam-
phlet entitled *Dialogue aux enfers entre Machiavel et Montesquieu*
(Maurice Joly, Brussels, 1865) which attacked Napoleon III.
Nevertheless, the *Protocols* has been widely distributed around
the world in various languages and in different versions. One,
The International Jew, was published in the 1920s by Henry
Ford in his own newspaper, the *Dearborn Independent.*[14] An
attempt to sue Ford for libel failed, because accusations against
a whole people (group libel) were not actionable. But when
Ford's newspaper accused Aaron Sapiro, a Chicago lawyer, of
running several agricultural cooperatives for his own benefit,
Sapiro sued Ford for personal damages. The case went to trial
in Detroit in 1927, and the lies about the Jews in Ford's
newspaper were laid bare. In Europe, there were successful
legal actions against the Protocols, including one, in Berne,
Switzerland, in 1934. Notwithstanding these legal victories,
however, different versions of the Protocols are still in circula-
tion.[15]

The Socialism of Fools

As modern anti-Semitism took hold in the nineteenth century, some socialists also began to display anti-Jewish tendencies, because leading Jews were closely associated with capitalism. But when radical anti-Semitic parties began competing with the socialists for worker support, the Social Democratic parties dissociated themselves from anti-Semitism. It was recognized that "anti-Semitism is the socialism of fools."[16] Even Wilhelm Marr turned against the anti-Semitic movement in Germany, which he had helped to found. In 1891, Marr wrote, "Modern anti-Semitism . . . has become, for me, utterly futile. It deceives itself, only to deceive and swindle others."[17] But it was too late to put the evil genie of anti-Semitism back into the bottle of racist poison.

The French Revolution became a significant factor in the emancipation of the Jews, but it was followed by creation of the myth of a Jewish world conspiracy out of the demonology about the Jews inherited from the Middle Ages.[18] Thus modern Jewish stereotypes grew from the "evil Jew" image of medieval times based on fear of the integration and advancement of Jews in nineteenth-century society. Rothschild symbolized Jewish domination of finance; Disraeli became the symbol of Jewish political control; Karl Marx and Ferdinand Lassale (another German socialist) were the ogres of Jewish revolutionaries; Börne and Heine supposedly controlled radical literature and journalism, and Sarah Bernhardt "dominated" the theatre.[19]

In the late 1870s, German anti-Semites were blaming the Jews for all of Germany's problems. Adolph Stoecker, a preacher at the Imperial Court in Berlin, developed an anti-Semitic program for his Christian Social Workers Party. In 1880, a petition calling for Jewish immigrants to be barred from Germany, for Jews to be dismissed from administrative posts, and for separate registration of Jews in statistical surveys was circulated; it gathered 250,000 signatures in a year.[20]

In Russia, Czarist anti-Semitism spurred the exodus of Jews from that country in the 1880s. One Russian propagandist, in June 1881, welcomed the anti-Semitic alliance created in Germany "the country which leads European culture," and predicted that "the Western European Christian world will be faced in the future . . . with a life-and-death-struggle with Jewry." In 1882, the first "international" congress of anti-Semites, held in Dresden, published a "manifesto to the governments and peoples of the Christian countries in danger because of Jewry" and called for committees to combat the Jews in every town.[21] The new movement, while politically motivated, invoked memories of age-old Christian anti-Jewish practices.

One example of anti-Semitism with ancient Christian roots was the blood libel accusation used several times in the nineteenth and early twentieth centuries. When a Capuchin monk disappeared in Damascus in 1840, other monks claimed that Jews had murdered him as part of their religious ritual. Several Jews were arrested and tortured. One of them "confessed" and implicated others; more Jews were detained and tortured; there were more "confessions." One Jew died of injuries, and another converted. The French consul in Damascus, backed by his government, supported the anti-Jewish action to gain French influence in the Middle East. Isaac Adolph Cremieux (president of the Central Consistory of French Jews, 1843—45) questioned the French premier, Louis Thiers, about the Damascus case, but he got no answer.[22]

Heinrich Graetz gives a horrendous account of persecution of the Jews in the Damascus affair.[23] That episode marked a turning point in nineteenth-century Western European Jewish history. Jews learned that Catholic hostility toward them was so deep-rooted that the church would stoop to blood libel, and the French government, which had proclaimed Jewish equality, supported it. With the Damascus affair, there also emerged a "European Jewish opinion, which was ready to raise its voice against an attack on Jews anywhere."[24]

In England, for example, the Lord Mayor of London was prevailed upon to call a public meeting at the Mansion House, his official residence, to protest the Damascus case. Over two hundred people attended, leading Jews and non-Jews, merchants, bankers, members of Parliament, clergy, and "many ladies of rank." A member of Parliament, who moved the first resolution, called the Damascus charges against the Jews "as false as the natures of those who invented them are cruel and evil." Several resolutions passed unanimously, one of them deploring "that in this enlightened age a persecution of our Jewish brethren could be set on foot by ignorance and inflamed by bigotry." The Lord Mayor communicated the resolutions to the government, the ambassadors of all European powers, and the United States. The prime minister, Lord Palmerston, had earlier directed the Damascus consul to protest the anti-Jewish actions and seek remedial steps.

The Jews of London sent Sir Moses Montefiore to Egypt to seek redress for the Damascus Jews.[25] Montefiore went to Alexandria in a delegation with Cremieux and Solomon Munk, a Paris orientalist, to meet the ruler of Syria, Mohammed Ali. Their appeal, backed by European public opinion, led to the quashing of charges and the release of the remaining prisoners. Montefiore went on to Constantinople to meet the sultan and obtain from him a *firman* (pronouncement) condemning the ritual-murder libel and confirming Jewish rights.

The recognition of Jewish rights began in 1789 with the French Revolution and moved ahead in continental Europe under Napoleonic rule. The defeat of Napoleon contributed to the rise of modern anti-Semitism. At the Congress of Vienna (1814—15), called to reorganize post-Napoleonic Europe, the

Jewish question was on the agenda for the first time at an international gathering.[27] The proposed new German federation was supposed to grant Jews rights as citizens, but these rights were not to be easily acquired.

More than sixty years later, at the Congress of Berlin (1878) convened by Bismarck to deal with political issues in Eastern Europe, Jewish rights in the Balkan states were on the agenda. Disraeli, by then the Earl of Beaconsfield, was one of the dominant figures at the Congress, where the great powers supported equal rights for the Jews. With the Jews in mind, the Congress agreed to recognize Rumania's independence on condition that "absolute freedom of worship," full political rights, and "perfect equality" be granted to all people in that country. Rumania accepted the obligation but did not live up to it.[28] Indeed, in the 1880s and 1890s, anti-Semitism rose to new heights in Eastern Europe.

From 1492, when the Jews were expelled from Spain and Columbus set out to "discover" the New World, the persecution of the Jews in Europe influenced the migration of Jews to America. The expansion of anti-Jewish practices in Russia, in 1881, led to a sharp increase of emigration by Jews to the United States and Canada. Salo Baron argues against viewing 1881 as the turning point in East European Jewish migration,[29] but the Jews who began coming to Canada and United States in large numbers in the 1880s remembered that persecution, pogroms, and compulsory military service were what drove them out of the Russian Empire. This fact is substantiated by the numbers of public meetings to protest the Russian anti-Semitism, held in Western European capitals and in New York and other U.S. and Canadian cities.

One of the most significant of these meetings took place, once again, at London's Mansion House, the Lord Mayor's residence, on February 1, 1882. Many illustrious people attended, among them Charles Darwin, Matthew Arnold, Robert

Browning, and Alfred Tennyson, leading members of London's Jewish community, the Archbishop of Canterbury, Cardinal Edward Manning, and Sir Alexander Galt, the first Canadian High Commissioner to London.[30] This meeting led to the establishment of the Mansion House Committee and a fund to aid Jewish emigrants to Canada and the U.S.

Notable at the London meeting were the comments of Cardinal Manning, the Roman Catholic primate in England: "There are laws larger than any Russian legislation, laws which are equally binding in London, in St. Petersburg and in Moscow—the laws of humanity, of nature, and of God—which are the foundations of all other laws; and if in any legislation these are violated, all nations of Christian Europe, the whole commonwealth of civilized and Christian men, would instantly acquire a right to speak out loud." Cardinal Manning also spoke of the anti-Semitic movement in Germany over the previous year, which he looked upon "with abhorrence as tending to disintegrate the foundations of social life, and . . . with great fear lest it may tend to light up an animosity which has already taken fire in Russia and may spread elsewhere." [31]

A similar committee in aid of Russian Jews was set up in Paris under the chairmanship of Victor Hugo. It included Leon Gambettta and other noted Frenchmen; Baron Alphonse de Rothschild headed a Jewish committee.[32] The Paris group did not seem to be as broadly based as the one in London.

In fact, in France there was renewed anti-Semitism beginning in the early 1880s. For example, when the Catholic Union General Bank went bankrupt and many small Catholic investors lost their savings, the bank director blamed "Jewish capital" for the losses.[33] Some anti-Jewish papers began to appear and, in 1886, the demagogic Edouard Drumont published his violently anti-Jewish book *La France Juive*, which sold hundreds of thousands of copies. Drumont became the leader of a vociferous anti-Semitic movement, for which he founded the journal *La Libre Parole,* in 1892.[34] The lower echelons of the Roman Catholic clergy became active in the anti-Semitic movement and organized a "Christian-Democratic" movement.[35] These anti-Jewish activities helped to create the climate for the Dreyfus case, which burst forth in 1894.

Comparing the situation in England and France at this time, it may be concluded that the era of enlightenment in England made it possible for the Catholics to seek relief from the repression they had experienced since Henry VIII broke with Rome. Therefore, they were ready to take a more sympathetic view of the Jews, especially those in far-off Russia. In France, on the other hand, the enlightenment brought by the French revolution led to a repressive climate for the church; thus, Catholics joined in picking on the Jews as scapegoats. Anti-Jewish prejudice in the church was usually latent, but it was activated in countries where the clergy had reason to support anti-Semitism.

Anti-Semitism in Russia

Anti-Jewish sentiment was rising in Russia in the 1870s, among both the ruling classes and the masses, due to growing Jewish economic activity and an increased number of Jews in secondary schools and higher institutions. It was claimed that Russia was in danger of "Jewish domination," and agitation began to protect the Christian Russian population against "Jewish scheming." However, only with the murder of Czar Alexander II by revolutionaries in 1881 did conditions become worse for the Jews. The assassination provided excuse for the outbreak of violent anti-Jewish riots in the Ukrainian provinces of the Russian Empire; there were pogroms against Jews in Kiev, Odessa, and more than a hundred other centres.

The new czar, Alexander III, was said to approve of attacks on the Jews in revenge for the murder of his father. A clandestine group known as the Holy Brotherhood was believed to have instigated the pogroms. The Central Russian authorities were told, by a special emissary who investigated the pogroms, that they were an eruption of the people's anger at "Jewish exploitation." In August of 1881, the czar issued a decree establishing commissions to investigate the harm done to the population by Jewish economic activity in the territory where Jews lived. Since 1791, Jews had been restricted to living in western lands of the Russian empire designated as the Pale of Settlement. Some of the commissions recommended that Jews be permitted to settle anywhere in Russia to ease overcrowding in the Pale. Instead of easing restrictions, however, the czar issued certain "temporary rules" in early May, 1882, imposing new economic limitations against the Jews. These rules became known as the May Laws. Pogroms against the Jews were instigated in Warsaw at the end of 1881, but, unlike the czarists, Polish leaders condemned the pogroms.

The anti-Jewish agitation and outbreaks of 1881 led to a movement of Jews toward the eastern border seeking to leave the country. Early in 1882, meetings were called in major world centres, such as the one at London's Mansion House, to consider the plight of the Russian Jews. The exodus of Jews from the Russian empire had sharply increased the flow of immigrants to western Europe, England, and North America. and made it necessary to develop a planned aid program.

The departure of Jews from Eastern Europe began before the imposition of the May Laws, because of earlier economic restrictions that were part of the policy of anti-Jewish repression; pogroms exacerbated the situation in the 1880s and again in the 1890s, when they also spread to Rumania. The most infamous attack on the Jews was the Kishinev pogrom of 1903. Thus Jews came to the United States and Canada with the memory of European anti-Semitism sharply etched in their minds.[36]

Prior to 1881, when Jews in Canada numbered twenty-five hundred, anti-Semitism was a rare phenomenon. Under

French rule, prior to 1760, non-Catholics were not allowed to settle in Canada. From the beginning of Jewish settlement in Canada, after the British conquest, there were occasional expressions of prejudice against Jews, but they seemed to have little direct impact on the Jewish population of the time.[37] Then, in 1832, the Quebec Assembly enacted legislation providing political equality for the Jews. This enactment is legitimately celebrated by the Jews as their Canadian Magna Carta. Nevertheless, there were some manifestations of anti-Jewish prejudice before and after the 1832 law was enacted.[38]

One notable example of anti-Semitism occurred before Confederation. It involved taking the oath of office by swearing "on the true faith of a Christian," a vestige of anti-Jewish discrimination dating back to before the rise of feudalism. In England, Jews had been allowed, since 1667, to take the oath on the Old Testament in courts of law, but, for almost two centuries, this privilege did not extend to taking the oath in other situations, especially on being elected to public office. Thus Ezekiel Hart, twice elected to the Quebec Assembly, in 1807—09, was twice barred from taking his seat, on the ground that he could not take the Christian oath. The element of anti-Semitism in the political conflict of which Hart was a victim persisted even after the "Jewish Magna Carta" was adopted. English-language oath commissioners in Montreal would not allow two Jewish nominees for justice of the peace to take office without taking the Christian oath. Finally, in 1833, a French-language commissioner did grant Samuel Becancour Hart, Ezekiel's son, the right to take the oath in the Jewish custom in order to become a justice of the peace. S. B. Hart's experience was accepted as a precedent by a special committee appointed in 1834 to look into the alleged Jewish disability over the oath of office.[39]

In England, in 1858, Lionel de Rothschild, elected to the House of Commons several times, was finally allowed to swear allegiance in the Jewish custom and to sit in Parliament. Yet in

1860, when Selim Franklin, an English-born Jew, was elected to the Assembly of Vancouver Island, he was challenged on how he took the oath, but he was not barred from his seat. David Cameron, Vancouver Island's chief justice, issued a detailed report justifying the manner in which Franklin took the oath with precedents going back to 1740, but some members of the Assembly would not accept the judge's report. They had no real reason to exclude him, since, like him, they were all supporters of the government. So they passed their own resolution granting Franklin's right to his seat. The challenge to Franklin was "a farcical vestige of anti-Jewish feeling."[40]

The arrival in Canada of Jewish refugees from Russia was viewed sympathetically by enlightened elements among Canadian political and church leaders. However, the rapid growth in Jewish immigration to Canada also brought increased manifestations of anti-Jewish prejudice. Often, the Jews were not welcomed warmly or generously. The prime minister, Sir John A. Macdonald, set the tone in 1882, calling the plan to send Jews to the west "the old clo' move." "We are quite ready to assign the Jews lands," he declared, but the Jews who arrived in Winnipeg that spring were kept waiting for two years before land was found for them. In the meantime, immigration agents made disparaging remarks about the Jews from Russia. In 1887, when some Jews began to settle at Wapella, the local Liberal-Conservative Association protested the reserving of more land for the Jews and called them "a most undesirable class of settler." In 1892 when the government issued a handbill to attract new immigrants from the German agricultural population of Russia, it included the statement "No Jews will be brought out under this scheme."[41]

In pre-Confederation Canada there had been a "low level of inconsistent hostility" toward Jews, with "different emphases" in French and English Canada. The British North America Act sowed the seeds of future problems, since the Fathers of

Confederation conceived a state of Anglophones and Franco-phones, all of whom were Christians, whether Catholic or Protestant. They never imagined that any minority group would grow to such numbers that the cultural, linguistic, and religious character of the state would be affected. The Jews were the first to challenge the Confederation concept, and to stir up anti-immigrant sentiment, when they sought privileges in the Quebec denominational school system in the 1880s. In the 1890s and the early twentieth century, anti-Semitic senti-ment was stirred by renewed French Canadian nationalism, by the ultra-montane, anti-liberal movement in the Catholic Church, and by the Dreyfus case in France. By the turn of the century, some hard-core anti-Semitism had developed, though it was still a "fringe phenomenon."[43]

In the pre-World War One period, some anti-Semitic publi-cations began to appear in Quebec, partly influenced by the Dreyfus case. Most of them were short-lived. In fact, *La Presse,* the largest Quebec daily, was edited by a Jew, Jules Hellbron-ner, in the 1890s. In 1910, however, J.E. Plamondon, one of the anti-Semitic publishers, made a public anti-Jewish address in Quebec City, inciting some of his listeners to attack Jewish homes and the Quebec synagogue. The attackers were ar-rested and convicted of damaging the Jewish properties. Jew-ish leaders considered this insufficient; they wished to disprove Plamondon's libelous statements. Since Quebec City had just seventy-five Jewish families, it was decided to launch a civil libel action in the name of the synagogue's president and a synagogue member. After three years of litigation, the case was won on appeal, on the basis that each one of the Jewish families had been personally libelled by Plamondon.[44]

None of the anti-Semitic propagandists in French Canada at the turn of the century had more stature than one *English* Canadian. Goldwin Smith was an English-born, Oxford-edu-cated history professor, a political Liberal, and a member of the

Manchester school of laissez-faire economics, was one of the most prominent and outspoken Jew-haters of his day. Smith served as Oxford's Regius Professor of History, and before settling in Toronto in 1871 he was one of the founders of Cornell University in United States. His anti-Semitic outpourings started at Oxford. In Toronto, he began a career in journalism and his anti-Jewish articles were published in some of the most prestigious journals in the English-speaking world in addition to his own Canadian papers, *The Bystander*, *The Week*, and *The Weekly Sun*. Smith's name has been linked with the "international brotherhood" of anti-Semitic propagandists, including Wilhelm Marr and Adolph Stoecker in Germany.

In Canada, Smith was recognized as a leading intellectual; he influenced men like William Lyon Mackenzie King, a future prime minister, and Vincent Massey, who later served in Canada's external-affairs department and rose to be governor general. Massey was one of the bureaucrats who helped to keep Jews out of Canada before World War Two; Prime Minister King recalled, in his diary in 1946, that Goldwin Smith considered Jews "poison in the veins of a community."[45]

In the first half of the twentieth century, the rights of Canada's Jews were limited in a number of ways in different parts of the country. The first serious problem involved the education of Jewish children in Quebec. The granting of minority education rights to Jews was considered an infringement of the entrenched rights of Catholics and Protestants under the denominational school system. Negotiations went on for decades, until the 1920s, when Jews were finally granted rights in the Protestant school system.

In higher education in the 1920s and 1930s, anti-Jewish prejudice led to the introduction of a quota system for Jews at universities in different parts of the country. At McGill University in Montreal, for example, it was made mandatory for Jewish students to have higher marks than non-Jews to be accepted. In

Manitoba, quotas for university entrance were imposed on Jews and Ukrainians in the professional faculties such as medicine. Jews also faced discrimination in employment and were excluded from certain vacation resorts. "Gentlemen's agreements" excluding Jews existed, for example, at Victoria Beach on Manitoba's Lake Winnipeg, and in residential areas like Tuxedo, a Winnipeg suburb. Tuxedo had a Jewish mayor for many years, but no Jew could buy a home there. None of the banks employed Jews, even as tellers. The department-store chain Eaton's was notorious for not hiring Jews, and insurance companies that had Jewish salesmen had no Jews at the executive or managerial level or even as office help.

In the years before World War Two, there were pro-fascist and anti-Semitic activities in Montreal, Toronto, and Winnipeg. In Alberta, the Social Credit Party came to power in the 1930s with a definite anti-Semitic wing in its membership.

The nature of anti-Semitism in Canada has been documented in a number of books, including *Antisemitism in Canada*, edited by Alan Davies, *None Is Too Many*, by Irving Abella and Harold Troper, several essays in Brym et al.'s *The Jews in Canada*, and in Esther Delisle's *The Traitor and the Jew*. This list is not complete, nor do existing works represent a thorough documentation of anti-Semitism in Canada. A notable example is the anti-Semitism in the Social Credit party, which has not been fully exposed though that party formed the government for many years in British Columbia and Alberta.

In the 1980s and 1990s, the Canadian Jewish community has been much preoccupied with cases like that of James Keegstra, who taught anti-Semitism in the public school at Eckville, Alberta; Ernst Zundel, the Toronto neo-Nazi and anti-Semitic propagandist who promotes the theory of the Holocaust as a hoax; and Malcolm Ross, the New Brunswick teacher who wrote and spread anti-Semitic propaganda, though he apparently never taught it in the classroom. The cases of the first two men have been well documented in several books.[46] As well, B'nai Brith Canada publishes, through its League for Human Rights, an annual entitled *Review of Anti-Semitism in Canada,* which keeps tabs on anti-Jewish incidents across the country. From time to time, there are reports of vandalism attacks on synagogues. Nevertheless, it can be said that Jews in Canada live more and more with the memory and history of past anti-Semitism than with the living experience of anti-Jewish prejudice and discrimination.

Notes

1. Ausubel, *Book of Jewish Knowledge,* p. 6; Ettinger, "The Modern Period," p. 875; Elbogen, *Century of Jewish Life,* pp. 702—03.
2. Dawidowicz, *Holocaust,* p. 41; Tulchinsky, "Goldwin Smith," p. 69.
3. Safrai, "The Era of the Mishnah," p. 349.
4. Durant, *Story of Civilization,* vol. 3, *Caesar and Christ,* pp. 546, 549.
5. Baron, *History and Jewish Historians,* p. 7; Stern, "The Period of the Second Temple," p. 289; Roth and Wigoder, *New Standard Jewish Encyclopedia,* p. 128.
6. Parkes, *Antisemitism,* p. 60.
7. Roth and Wigoder, *New Standard Jewish Encyclopedia,* p. 890.
8. Graetz, *History of the Jews,* vol. 5, p. 543. See also Baron, *Treasury of Jewish Quotations,* p. 420.
9. Graetz, *History of the Jews,* pp. 542—44.
10. Wigoder, *Encyclopedia Judaica,* vol. 2, pp. 1264—65.
11. Elbogen, *Century of Jewish Life,* pp. 65—66.
12. Ausubel, *Book of Jewish Knowledge,* p. 8.
13. Ibid.; Elbogen, *Century of Jewish Life,* p. 514.
14. Ford, *The International Jew.*
15. For books dealing with the Protocols, see Curtis, *An Appraisal;* Pierre, *The Learned Elders;* Cohen, *Warrant for Genocide.*
16. Ettinger, "The Modern Period," p. 872.
17. Elbogen, *Century of Jewish Life,* p. 149.
18. See Trachtenberg, *The Devil and the Jews.*
19. Ettinger, "The Modern Period," p. 874. I would question Ettinger's comment that most of these people were "remote from Jewish problems, and even hostile towards Jews." Of the seven he names, at least four–Roth-

schild, Disraeli, Börne, and Heine–showed support or sympathy for the Jews.

20. Ibid., p. 875.

21. Ibid., p. 876.

22. Ibid., pp. 847—48.

23. Graetz, *History of the Jews*, vol. 5, chapter 17, pp. 634ff.

24. Ettinger, "The Modern Period," p. 872.

25. Graetz, *History of the Jews*, vol. 5, pp. 655—58.

26. Ettinger, "The Modern Period," p. 848; Roth and Wigoder, *New Standard Jewish Encyclopedia*, p. 519.

27. Roth and Wigoder, *New Standard Jewish Encyclopedia*, p. 474.

28. Elbogen, *Century of Jewish Life*, pp. 72—74; Roth and Wigoder, *New Standard Jewish Encyclopedia*, p. 474.

29. Baron, *Great Ages*, p. 398.

30. Elbogen, *Century of Jewish Life*, p. 226; Sack, *History*, pp. 192—93.

31. Sack, *History*, pp. 272—73.

32. Wischnitzer, *To Dwell in Safety*, p. 40.

33. Ettinger, "The Modern Period," p. 878.

34. James Parkes, *Antisemitism*, p. 36.

35. Ettinger, "The Modern Period," p. 878.

36. Ibid., pp. 881—88; Elbogen, *Century of Jewish Life*, pp. 200—30.

37. After the British conquest, in 1766, French seigneurs complained that "barbers, serving men–even Jews–have not hesitated to raise themselves above the new subjects" (Lower, *Canadians in the Making*, p. 108). And in 1858, when people began to arrive for the Fraser River gold rush, Alfred Waddington, himself a recent arrival in Victoria, wrote, "Victoria was assailed by an indescribable array of Polish Jews, Italian fishermen, French cooks, speculators of every kind" (Waddington, *Fraser River Mines Vindicated*).

38. Arnold, "Canada's Jewish Magna Carta."

39. Ibid.

40. Rome, *First Two Years*; Arnold, "Restrictive Christian Oath Retrieved for Final Fling," *Canadian Jewish News*, 1 Nov. 74.

41. Arnold, "Welcoming the Jews," pp, 93, 97—98, 100.

42. Menkis, "Pre-Confederation Canada," p. 29.

43. Brown, "Stereotype to Scapegoat," pp. 39—60.

44. Ibid., p 58; Arnold and Kurelek, *Jewish Life*, p. 77.

45. Tulchinsky, "Goldwin Smith," pp. 67—68, 84.

46. Bercuson and Wertheimer, "A Trust Betrayed:. . ."; Mertl and Ward, "Keegstra, The Trial..."; Weimann and Winn, "Hate on Trial...."

CHAPTER ELEVEN

The Holocaust:
Its Place in History

Yom Hashoah is the annual day of the commemoration of the Holocaust, the destruction of six million Jews in Europe under Nazi Germany's "Final Solution." The official date, the 27th day of Nissan on the Jewish lunar calendar, comes twelve days after the first day of Passover and was chosen by the Government of Israel. Controversy arose when a commemoration of the Nazi destruction of the Jews was first being considered; some Jews thought the observance should recall only the overwhelming tragedy of the six million who were slaughtered, while others saw it as a tribute to the heroic resistance of the ghetto fighters and Jewish partisans.

The term "Holocaust" was first used between 1957 and 1959 to describe the unique or unprecedented nature of what happened to the Jews.[1] One definition of the term implies a sacrificial burnt offering,[2] and some Orthodox Jewish leaders actually claimed that the six million died as a sacrifice to God for the sins of the Jews! The first reference to the burnt sacrifice of human beings in the Bible is in the story of Moloch, a "false god."[3] Later, human sacrifice was denounced and the burning of children was called an abomination.[4] There is also a nonspecific definition of "holocaust" as a bolt from the blue–like an earthquake or a flood–which does not imply a deliberate criminal act.[5] The Hebrew term *Shoah,* meaning "total destruction," is thus more appropriate. But, whether appropriate or not, "Holocaust" has come to mean the mass murder of the Jews under the Nazi regime.[6]

Before the official day for Yom Hashoah was chosen, an addition to the Passover Haggada was introduced to commemorate the Warsaw Ghetto Uprising, which began on the first night of Passover, April 19, 1943, in response to an all-out attack by the German army. Some secular groups, especially those wishing to emphasize the resistance theme, observe the Warsaw Ghetto uprising each year on April 19. Since the 1960s, many communities have observed Holocaust Memorial Week, beginning on Nissan 27; the observances include Jewish resistance stories and secular themes as well as religious services.

In 1977, Israel's then prime minister, Menachem Begin, proposed that Yom Hashoah be incorporated with Tisha b'Av, the midsummer fast day for the destruction of the Jerusalem Temples, as "one day of national mourning and remembrance." This idea was backed by Israel's then chief rabbis, Shlomo Goren and O. Yosef, and by a leading U.S. rabbi, J. B. Soloveitchik. The *Jerusalem Post* also endorsed it, suggesting that the combination would not lessen the importance of either memorial.

Other tragic events in Jewish history have already been combined with Tisha b'Av, including the expulsion of the Jews from England (July 18, 1290) and the expulsion of the Jews from Spain, for which the ninth of Av (1492) was said to be the deadline. Despite the linking of these events with Tisha b'Av, the English expulsion is hardly remembered, while the Spanish expulsion is remembered more because it sparked a revival of interest in Jewish history. Few people are usually in the synagogue when the *kinot*, Tisha b'Av day of memorial dirges, are recited. Moreover, according to Theodor Gaster, the original selection of the ninth day of Av to commemorate the destruction of the First Temple was more influenced by the customs of the people among whom the Jews lived during the Babylonian exile than by the actual events in Jerusalem in 568 B.C.E.[7]

The Holocaust destruction of six million Jews was a cataclysmic experience in Jewish and world history, exceeding by far all earlier catastrophes endured by the Jews. Nevertheless, it may be placed in context with other catastrophes, as David Roskies has shown in *Against the Apocalypse*. And it is right that Yom Hashoah be linked with events associated with Passover. If the legendary liberation of the Israelites from slavery in Egypt has been an example for other peoples, the resistance of the Ghetto fighters and Jewish partisans is a worthy example of the struggle of humankind against tyranny, repression, slavery, and annihilation.

After the war, many people asked why so many Jews had gone to the slaughter without protest, and why they hadn't fought back. Raul Hilberg, in both editions of his book *The Destruction of European Jews*, states that the reaction of the Jews to the Nazi onslaught "is characterized by almost complete lack of resistance,"[8] although he enlarges on actual Jewish resistance in his second edition. Alexander Donat, a Holocaust survivor activist, charged Hilberg with "desecrating the memory of our martyrs," and set out the conditions under which ghetto resistance took place.[9]

Yuri Suhl charged that Hilberg based himself entirely on official German documents, in which he found no sign of Jewish resistance. German officers would not tell their superiors of Jewish heroism in resistance because they were taught to believe that Jews were subhuman,[10] but the only source Hilberg cites on Jewish resistance is the SS officer who was the chief of Germany's anti-partisan activities.[11]

Hilberg's assertions have also been challenged by Lucy Dawidowicz: "The depiction of the Jews as suffering martyrs under the Nazis was soon challenged by a segment of survivors: those who had participated in the resistance movements in the ghettos and had fought with the partisans." She confirms what others have said: the Jewish fighters came largely from the left-wing political parties and youth movements, Zionist and non-Zionist, and she explains that before the Second World War, and even before the First World War, "the young Jews who streamed into the secular radical movements that transformed traditional Jewish society in Eastern Europe had committed themselves to changing the status of the Jews as a pariah people."[12] Socialist and socialist-Zionist ideals permeated East European Jewish youth between the wars. These were the people who not only "fantasized" about Jewish resistance to the Germans, as Dawidowicz suggests, but mounted such resistance in the ghettos.

The story of Jewish resistance in Nazi-dominated Europe was recorded as early as 1946 in *The Black Book: The Nazi Crime Against the Jewish People*, a 560-page volume published by the Jewish Black Book Committee, composed of an international group of Jewish organizations: World Jewish Congress, New York; Jewish Anti-Fascist Committee, Moscow; Vaad Leumi (Jewish National Council of Palestine), Jerusalem; and the American Committee of Jewish Writers, Artists and Scientists, New York.[13]

The *Black Book* relates that trained "shock troops" from Tel Aviv were sent into Nazi Europe to organize Jewish resistance. Thousands of Jews refused the "proffered opportunity" to get out of Europe; they stayed because "there was much work to be done."[14] An outstanding example of such an individual was Emmanuel Ringelblum, a Warsaw Jewish community worker, who was in Geneva at a Zionist Congress when war broke out in September, 1939. Some Polish delegates did not go home, but Ringelblum decided to return to Warsaw and became the ghetto archivist.[15]

In a sixty-page account of Jewish resistance throughout Europe,[16] the *Black Book* relates that inside Europe Jews formed their own relief and resistance groups. As forced labourers, they sabotaged and hindered the deportation of comrades. In ghettoes, they organized armed uprisings, and in the forests they joined partisan and guerrilla bands.[17] Ringelblum said that "the Jews in the ghetto were in a struggle between a fly and an elephant. But our national dignity dictated . . . that the Jews must offer resistance and not allow themselves to be led wantonly to the slaughter." [18]

The uprising in the Warsaw Ghetto became the exemplar of Jewish resistance. The Nazi German army launched its attack to destroy the Ghetto on Passover night for two reasons: they hoped to do it in one night as a present for Hitler's birthday the next day; it was also considered important symbolically to destroy the ghetto as the Jews celebrated their liberation from slavery in Egypt. The ghetto fighters battled their attackers for six weeks. Resistance also occurred in ghettos in Vilna, Bialystok, Minsk, Lodz, and throughout Eastern Europe, though the other struggles are less well documented.

In 1992, Raul Hilberg published a one-volume work on the Holocaust that includes several passages on Jewish resistance. He describes the "salient characteristic" of the Jews under Nazi rule as "step-by-step adjustment to step-by-step destruction." There were some Jews, he adds, who would not make adjustments to their fate. "The principal manifestations of such non-conformist behavior were suicide, hiding, escape and resistance."[19] Hilberg discusses aspects of Jewish resistance in the ghettos of Vilnius (Vilna), Lithuania, and at Lublin and Warsaw. In his account of Vilnius, the leading character is Jacob Gens, the German-appointed ghetto police chief, described as "a Lithuanian patriot who made anti-Soviet speeches . . . [and] a conscious Jew who followed the right-wing militant Zionist movement"–the Revisionists, led by Vladimir Jabotinsky. Hilberg adds that Gens "tolerated" the ghetto resistance movement, "with which he was in competition."[20]

Auschwitz was located at the Polish city of Oswiecim, which had a Jewish community of some four thousand before the war. In 1940, the German army expelled or annihilated all the Jews in the town and built the death camp. There is little other information about the Jews of Oswiecim before the Germans made it Auschwitz.[21] S. L. Shneiderman, a Polish-born and -educated Jewish journalist and author who escaped from occupied France in 1940, has said that Oswiecim "should be remembered for its place in the development of Yiddish culture." Oswiecim, he said, "was the first larger community along the Vistula River where the Yiddish culture began to develop in the thirteenth century." It was part of a Czech duchy annexed by the Polish king in the fourteenth century.[22]

Shneiderman wrote a book telling the story of the Jewish communities on the Vistula, including his home town of Kazimierz. The Vistula, he noted, is to Poland what the Volga is to Russia and the Mississippi to the United States.[23] For centuries, the Jews lived on the banks of the Vistula, where they developed their own civilization; they perished in the most ghastly way ever recorded.[24]

He was critical of Western countries, including Canada, for refusing to allow the entry of German Jewish refugees before the war. He recalled the case of the S.S. *St. Louis*, which left Hamburg in May 1939 with over nine hundred German Jewish refugees carrying visas for Cuba. When they arrived in Havana, the Cuban government refused to accept them. Appeals to numerous other American countries to take in the *St. Louis* passengers all failed. Shneiderman accused American Jewry of indifference for its failure to pressure President Roosevelt to change the immigrant quota schedule to allow the Jews on the *St. Louis* to enter the U.S. Over seven hundred of them had American quota permits that would have allowed them in within three months to three years. For its part, the Canadian government refused the plea of "leading Christians" to allow some of the *St. Louis* refugees to enter Canada, even temporarily.[25] They were forced to return to Europe, where most found sanctuary in England, Belgium, Holland, and France.

Except for those in England this was only a temporary reprieve from the death camps. A few months later, war came and the German armies overran all of continental Europe.[26]

Shneiderman also criticized the Orthodox concept of the Holocaust as a sacrificial offering: "It was nothing like that. It was simply the worst example of man-made destruction. There was no theology about it. Hitler took over the slogans of Martin Luther, who had been a friend of the Jews, but later turned against them and said: 'Drive them to Jerusalem.' Hitler tried the same thing at first, but the 'civilized world' refused to let them into Jerusalem or anywhere else."[27]

Other sources confirm the view that Hitler's plan to destroy the Jews was based on the anti-Semitic program advocated by Martin Luther, founder of Christian Protestantism in Germany. Hilberg points out that the Nazis "had little to add" to the propaganda picture of the Jews drawn by Luther.[28] Nora Levin comments that the words of Hitler's *Mein Kampf* "are merely latter-day racist versions of age-old views of Christian leaders," like Martin Luther and others, "all of whom fatally influenced German thinking about Jews."[29] Nathan Ausubel wrote that Luther took the Catholic church to task for twenty years for its "cruel" and "un-Christian" treatment of the Jews. But when he failed to win the Jews over to his brand of Christianity, he produced a manifesto, "Concerning the Jews and Their Lies," which became a blueprint for Hitler's genocidal program. Luther advocated setting fire to synagogues, destroying Jewish homes, and putting the Jews "under one roof, or in a stable, like gypsies [and] miserable captives."[30]

In 1980, Prof. Stephen Berk of Union College, New York, speaking at a Holocaust Education Day program in Winnipeg, cited the industrial revolution as another contributing factor in setting the stage for the destruction of European Jewry. Speaking of "things we were afraid to say before," Berk commented, "The most sordid aspect is the inescapable link of nineteen hundred years of Christian anti-Semitism with the unfolding of the Holocaust. . . . The nineteenth century was most significant to the development of the Holocaust due to the triumph of the liberal capitalist order and the industrial revolution." Religious anti-Semitism, regarding the Jews as a "rejected people" and maintaining the charge of deicide, contributed to the development of "secular anti-Semitism as a response to the negative economic effects of industrialization," Berk stated. The nineteenth century also produced a situation in which "the different races of people became locked in mortal combat." One result was the concoction of the fraudulent "Protocols of the Wise Men of Zion," directed against the Jews at a time when "anti-Semitic impulses were already ingrained in the European psyche." Berk called World War One the "seminal event" setting the stage for the "lunatic right" to enter the political mainstream in Europe.[31]

For a number of years, the Holocaust memorial committee in Winnipeg had been seeking the participation of Christian clergy. It was not until 1980 that a sensitive public statement on the Holocaust was made by an Anglican priest, Rev. Harold MacDonald, chaplain at the University of Manitoba. MacDonald said many Christians were so deeply shocked at learning of "the horror of the Holocaust" that they began to question the "efficacy" of the church. The Holocaust had shattered the pre-World War Two "belief in the church as an instrument of divine action and power to create new life although the whole church did not come into a state of trauma as a result." MacDonald, also a member of the Winnipeg City Council at that time, did not accept the claim of those who said that the Holocaust had been forecast in the Christian Gospels. He added, "I recognized to my astonishment that the church did help to set the preconditions for the Holocaust. The church must come to a new understanding of this because if the German people belonged to anybody, they belonged to the church. If the outcome of the witness of the church is Holocaust we have experienced the kind of quantum leap in human experience that makes it necessary to reformulate our views." Christians have to turn back to "God's people–the Jews, who rejected Christ–to find Christ again for themselves," MacDonald declared. He spoke of efforts to change Christian theology to win "fresh acceptance for the idea of universal grace" by understanding that "God works in traditions outside our own" and that "active pluralism" in religion is possible:

> Rabbis have wondered how God could permit the Holocaust. Priests must also wonder. We must come to a new understanding of power and powerlessness. If God was powerless in the face of Holocaust then we must act with power to prevent such things from happening again. We must forsake our triumphalist approach to faith and recast our beliefs in terms of better understanding of human suffering.[32]

There is a vast and growing array of Jewish literature, art, and film on the Holocaust and the experience of the Jews under Nazi rule. This creativity, which arose out of destruction, began with the victims themselves and has continued with the survivors and their heirs. "The life of the Jews during the time of the worst persecution never lacked an element of hope, of spirit, of creativity."[33]

David Roskies has sensitively demonstrated the creativity of the Jews under Nazi repression in his unusual book, *Against the Apocalypse*. In a chapter entitled "Scribes of the Ghetto," Roskies quotes Zelig Kalmanovich, a noted Jewish scholar in the Vilna ghetto. In 1942, a year before being deported to a death camp, Kalmanovich wrote, "History will revere your memory, people of the ghetto. Your least utterance will be studied, your struggle for human dignity will inspire poems, your scum and moral degradation will summon and awaken morality."[34]

The poems, diaries, and archival records left by the ghetto victims in Warsaw, Vilna, Lodz, and other centres have been studied, recited, and dramatized by survivors, such as Abraham Sutzkever, the Yiddish poet who celebrated his eightieth birthday in Israel in 1993, and by post-Holocaust heirs, such as Dawidowicz and Roskies. Sutskever himself was a creator of Jewish culture in the Vilna ghetto, where he belonged to the United Partisan Organization. He joined a partisan unit in the forests in September of 1943, was flown to Moscow with his wife six months later, served on the Jewish Anti-Fascist Committee, testified at the Nuremburg trials of Nazi war criminals in 1946, and reached Palestine in 1947, with the help of Golda Meir. Two years later, he founded *Di Goldene Keit* (The Golden Chain) a Yiddish literary journal, which he has since edited.

Roskies, an alumnus of Montreal's Jewish secular schools, reviews more than a thousand years of Jewish responses to catastrophe; only in the second half of his book does he deal directly with the Holocaust. He never descends to the lachrymose school of Jewish history; he brings cultural responses to earlier catastrophes into a continuum that helps to make clear Jewish resistance and the struggle to survive Hitler's hell.

Other Jews, probably well intentioned, invoke the Holocaust and the memory of six million dead to ensure a successful appeal for any Jewish cause, whether a fund-raising campaign for Israel, an appeal for Jewish "community relations," or for any other worthy purpose. This approach involves calling up tearful recollections of the Jewish past that Baron warned against: "[The] lachrymose conception of Jewish history has served as an eminent means of social control from the days of the ancient rabbis, and its repudiation . . . might help further to weaken the authority and control of Jewish communal leadership."[35] Mourning over past tragedies cannot be a primary element in building the Jewish future. Such an approach more likely fosters indifference among Jews and an unsympathetic perception among non-Jews.

A half-century after the end of World War Two, it is still necessary to explain the destruction of the Jews as the most extreme case of genocide; the enormity of the Shoah is still difficult for people to comprehend. There are Holocaust museums in Jerusalem and Washington; monuments in Warsaw, in London's High Park, and in Winnipeg; documentary and fiction films, from the "Holocaust" TV series of 1976 to Lanzmann's "Shoah" of 1989, to Spielberg's "Schindler's List" of 1993; and exhibitions of Holocaust art and artifacts; as well as many books. Above all, the Holocaust must be related to the insidious racism that still has a negative effect on the lives of millions of people.

Notes

1. Bauer, *Holocaust in Historical Perspective*, p. 31 .

2. Marrus, *Holocaust in History*, pp. 3—4.

3. Leviticus 18:21, 20:2—5.

4. Jeremiah 19:1—5; Chronicles 2—28:3.

5. Marrus, *Holocaust in History*. See also Fackenheim, "Holocaust," in Cohen and Mendes-Flohr, *Contemporary Jewish Religious Thought*, p. 399.

6. Bauer, *Holocaust in Historical Perspective*, p. 30.

7. Gaster, *Festivals*, pp. 192—93.

8. Hilberg, *Destruction of European Jews*, 1st ed., p. 662, 2nd ed. p. 1030.

9. Donat, "Jewish Resistance."

10. Suhl, *They Fought Back*, pp. 3—4.

11. Hilberg, *Destruction of European Jews*, 1st ed., p. 662.

12. Dawidowicz, *Holocaust and the Historians*, pp. 130—31.

13. The entire *Black Book* manuscript went to the U.N. War Crimes Commission at Nuremberg, as evidence of Nazi crimes against the Jewish people. The authors and editors are unnamed on the title page, though some names appear in the text. The book begins with a quote from Itzik Fefer, of the Jewish Anti-Fascist Committee: "The globe is too small to hold both mankind and fascism." Fefer was later murdered by order of Joseph Stalin.

14. *Black Book*, pp. 414—15.

15. Jacob Sloan, "Introduction," p. xiii, in Ringelblum, *Notes from the Warsaw Ghetto*, p. xiii.

16. *Black Book* (1946), pp 414—64.

17. *Black Book* (1946), p. 415. Another "Black Book," on the destruction of Soviet Jews, based on a material at the Yad Vashem Holocaust Memorial Centre in Israel, was published in 1981 (New York: Holocaust Library). This latter volume was initiated by the Jewish Anti-Fascist Committee in Moscow and lists Ilya Ehrenburg and Vasily Grossman, as editors. It was to be published in Russian and Yiddish (U.S.S.R.), in English (U.S.), and in Hebrew (Palestine). Publication of the Russian version was suspended, and it never appeared. Ehrenburg sent copies of his documentation to New York. The 1946 English edition contains large excerpts on Soviet Jews from the original source. Lucy Dawidowicz explains how the original *Black Book* in English was published, but she does not mention the second edition, which appeared a year before her book *The Holocaust and the Historians*. See Dawidowicz, *Holocaust and the Historians*, pp. 81—82, 164 fn1.

18. Suhl, *They Fought Back*, p. 6.

19. Hilberg, *Perpetrators, Victims, Bystanders*, p. 170.

20. Ibid., pp. 110—11.

21. "Auschwitz," in Roth and Widoger, *New Standard Jewish Encyclopedia*, pp. 195—96. See also "Oswiecim," in Roth and Widoger, *Encyclopedia Judaica*, p. 1520.

22. Interview with the author, 1978, in *Western Jewish News*, 2 Sept. 1978.

23. Shneiderman, *The River Remembers*, p. 11.

24. On a visit to the University of Manitoba, Shneiderman also presented "The Last Chapter," a documentary film on the thousand-year history of the Jews of Poland. He and his wife, Eileen, spent ten years making this documentary and did research on three continents.

25. Abella and Troper, *None is Too Many*, pp. 63—64.

26. Morse, *While Six Million Died*, pp. 270—88.

27. Arnold, *Western Jewish News*, 2. Sept. 1978.

28. Hilberg, *Destruction of European Jews*, 1st ed., p. 8.

29. Levin, *Holocaust*, p. 10.

30. Ausubel, *Book of Jewish Knowledge*, p. 313.

31. Arnold, *Western Jewish News*, 24 May 1980.

32. Arnold, *Canadian Jewish News*, 5 May 1980; *Western Jewish News* 24 Apr. 1980.

33. Gilbert, "The Holocaust," pp. 41—42.

34. Roskies, *Against the Apocalypse*, p. 197. Lucy Dawidowicz used part of the same quotation in *Holocaust Reader*, ending it with "inspire poems." Roskies and Dawidowicz each did their own translation of this quotation. I have used the Roskies translation, except that I have used Dawidowicz's term, "human dignity," rather than Roskies's, "man's dignity."

35. Baron, *History and Jewish Historians*, p. 88.

CHAPTER TWELVE

Israel:
From Biblical "Promise" to Modern Reality

The name *Israel* has its origin in the story of Jacob, the legendary third patriarch of the Jews. By the Jabok River, Jacob supposedly wrestled all night with an angel of God, whom he finally bested. When his adversary tried to leave in the morning, Jacob said that he would not let him go, "except thou bless me." The angel gave Jacob a new name, Israel, because he had "striven with God and with men and had prevailed." Jacob is said to have been so blessed because he was strong spiritually and physically.[1]

This story is a Jewish version of an ancient legend some aspects of which were "slurred over by the compilers of Genesis because they savored of heathendom."[2] Jacob's adversary, it is suggested, was the river god with whom Jacob allegedly arranged an encounter to obtain his blessing. This legend is shared with the ancient Greeks and Persians, and with the Zulus and other African tribes.[3] Its universal meaning appears to be clear: men and women must struggle to survive.

Jacob's progeny thus became known as the children of Israel. The modern Jewish state is appropriately named Israel, because it was certainly born through struggle. Historically, there is more to the naming of the Jewish state than the legend behind Jacob's second name. Modern scholars suggest that the tribal history began before the exodus from Egypt and that the tradition of the patriarchs came from different tribal groups. Abraham, Isaac, and Jacob were thus tribal chiefs,[4] and Jacob and Israel may have been two separate figures.[5] The original tribes that later became the Israelites probably entered the land of Canaan at different times. Some of them went to Egypt and returned later, after the exodus. Over more than seven hundred years, the tribes eventually came together as the Biblical people of Israel.

The forebears of the Israelites were known as Habiru, corresponding to the biblical Hebrews. The three generations of patriarchs seem to reflect three stages of Habiru clans. Abraham and the Terahites, living in caravans, wandered into Canaan between 1950 and 1700 B.C.E.; the followers of Isaac tried to settle in the northern Negev Desert about 1700—1620 B.C.E.; and Jacob and his descendants started a pastoral, semi-nomadic way of life and began mixing with the native population from 1620 to 1580. Eventually, many, but not all, of the Habiru clans went to Egypt, where they became slaves. The first group of Israelite families, who returned to Canaan by the early 1300s, were from the tribes of Asher and Naphtali. The second group, which followed some time later, were the Leah tribes (Reuben, Simeon, Levi, Judah, and so on). The third group, the Rachel tribes (Ephraim, Manasseh and Benjamin), came after 1285. By 1220 B.C.E., the "Israelite conquest of Canaan is said to have been completed." [6]

Canaan had been "promised" to Abraham "[7]from the river of Egypt to the great river, the river Euphrates."[8] This was the origin of the so-called Promised Land. It was later interpreted as extending over 58,000 square miles, from the Nile delta in Egypt, and the Gulf of Elath to the Euphrates River opposite Aleppo, and from the Mediterranean Sea through most of Syria and Transjordan. Only under David and Solomon did the biblical Israelites occupy this entire area. Some groups in modern Israel believe that they have a right to a "greater Israel" based on the Biblical "promise." But other people, particularly the Syrians, have claimed the "promise" for themselves based on their own legendary tradition; thus, they have harbored the ambition for a "Greater Syria."

The Israelite tribes did not enter the land of Canaan as a single group. David brought them together in a united kingdom after he captured the stronghold of Zion in Jerusalem, which became known as the City of David. The united kingdom lasted from 1040 to 937 B.C.E., the end of Solomon's reign. Some ten tribes then formed the northern kingdom of Israel, with Samaria as its capital. The kingdom of Judah comprised the remaining tribes, clustered around Jerusalem. The northern kingdom was eventually completely overrun by the Assyrians and the legend of the ten lost tribes developed. The people of Judah, later Judaea, became the Jews and claimed the heritage of all of Israel.

After the destruction of the First Temple (586 B.C.E.), when the people of Judah were exiled to Babylonia, the hope for a return to Zion became a national goal. Zion became identified with all of Jerusalem and was inscribed in Psalms:

By the rivers of Babylon,
There we sat down, yea, we wept.
When we remembered Zion. . . .
If I forget thee, O Jerusalem,
Let my right hand forget her cunning.
Let my tongue cleave to the roof of my mouth,
If I remember thee not;
If I set not Jerusalem
Above my chiefest joy. [9]

The hope of a return to Zion inspired the modern movement for a Jewish homeland in Palestine and the founding of a Jewish state. The hope was translated into conflicting territorial goals, ranging from minimalist to maximalist. A maximalist Jewish state existed for a relatively short time in the Biblical era and again for a short time under the Maccabees. But one of the primary lessons of history is that the boundaries of states, city-states, and countries have always been subject to change brought about by war and conquest. For modern Israel, territorial maximalism based on the biblical "Promised Land" is unrealistic and unjust, as we shall see.

Palestine was originally the name of the land of the Philistines, the invaders from the sea who had to be defeated in war by Saul and David, before the independence of the biblical Jewish state could be secured. In ancient times, most of the territory of Israel and Judah became known as Palestine, and later as Judaea. The Romans are said to have renamed Judaea Syrian Palestine. Palestine never became an independent country under that name. In fact, Palestine was known as Southern Syria until the end of World War One.

A more realistic view of the development of the modern Jewish state is a comparison with the tribal movements of biblical times. Since the Zionist movement was founded, more than a century ago, the modern tribes of Jews also moved into the country in stages but over a far shorter period of time. Some twenty thousand pious Jews moved to Palestine between 1850 and 1880, to engage in Torah study and in the hope of hastening the coming of the Messiah; as well, to die there and be buried in the sacred soil of the Holy Land.

In 1882, the Hibbat Zion (Lovers of Zion) started the Bilu pioneer group, in response to Russian pogroms, to settle Jews in Palestine. Land was purchased for settlements with financial support from the Rothschilds. In the summer of 1882, a Committee of Pioneers was formed in Jaffa to set up a central body for aid to the settlers. The twenty-five thousand Bilu settlers of 1882—1903 were the first organized Aliyah (immigration to Israel); hundreds of families came from Russia and Rumania and several dozen from Yemen. Thus the two major religious-geographic "tribes" of the Jews, European Ashkenazim and Middle East Sephardim, began to enter the country. They had to contend with the hostility of the Turkish rulers, who actually banned Jewish settlement from 1882 to 1890. During this period, immigrants continued to enter the country secretly. Conflict also developed between the secular and religious elements of the settler leadership. The Second Aliyah (1904—14) brought some forty thousand immigrants, also mainly from Russia, sparked by the the pogroms and the failure of the 1905 revolution. This Aliyah included many imbued with socialism from Eastern Europe, and again some from Middle East countries; the latter did not share modern European ideologies.[11]

When Britain issued the Balfour Declaration in 1917, promising a national homeland for the Jews, the Arabs immediately opposed it. They claimed that Britain had promised independence for a federation of Arab states, which would include Palestine as South Syria. This promise was assumed from the 1915—16 correspondence between Ali Hussein, Sherif of Mecca, and Sir Henry McMahon, the British High Commissioner in Egypt. Some parts of Syria were to be excluded from the Arab Federation, and a dispute arose between British and Arab representatives as to whether Palestine was part of the excluded area.[12]

The Balfour Declaration inspired the Third Aliyah (1919—23), in which members of youth pioneer groups such as He-Halutz were prominent. In the Fourth Aliyah (1924—31), most of the newcomers were from Poland, where economic restrictions had been imposed on the Jews. The Jewish population of Palestine rose to 190,000 by 1931.[13]

After the Balfour Declaration was issued, Chaim Weizmann, then president of the Zionist Organization, began discussions with Emir Feisal of Damascus, the son of Sherif Hussein, who was closely involved in planning the Arab Federation. Feisal had led an Arab revolt against Turkey in 1916 and had aided British General Allenby's Allied forces in liberating Syria and Palestine from Turkish rule. The Weizmann-Feisal talks led to an agreement, in January 1919, calling for close co-operation between the Arab national movement, represented by the "Arab State," and the Jewish national movement, represented by the Zionists, for Palestine. The Zionists would give aid and advice to the Arabs on economic development, and large-scale Jewish immigration and settlement in Palestine would be encouraged. Other Zionist leaders were also involved in the talks with Emir Feisal. In March 1919 Feisal wrote to Felix Frankfurter, a leading U.S. Zionist, saying, "We wish the Jews a hearty welcome home. . . . The Jewish Movement is national and not imperialistic. Our movement is national and not impe-rialistic, and there is room in Syria for us both. Indeed, I think that neither can be a real success without the other." [14]

In signing the agreement with the Zionists, however, Feisal stipulated that it would be void if Arab independence plans were not satisfied. In March of 1919, a Syrian Arab Congress objected to the idea of a "Jewish Commonwealth in the south-ern part of Syria, known as Palestine." In March of 1920, the same Arab Congress crowned Feisal king of Syria, but he was ousted by the French. He later became king of Iraq, but the Arab Federation never came into being. Zionist contacts with Arab leaders continued into the early 1920s, but extreme nationalism came to determine the Arab attitude toward Zion-ism; the Arabs began to demonstrate against the Jews in Pal-estine. [15]

When the hope for a greater Syrian kingdom came to an end, the Arabs of Palestine became a separate political entity. They began to struggle against the Jews for the future control of the country, and also against Britain, which had been granted a mandate over Palestine by the League of Nations. Under the terms of the mandate, Palestine, including Transjordan, would become a political unit. However, the British requested, and received, League of Nations approval to remove Transjordan from the mandate provisions for a Jewish national home. In 1922, Britain set up the territory east of the Jordan as an emirate, under Abdullah Hussein; Transjordan eventually became the kingdom of Jordan, with Abdullah as king.[16]

The mandate also provided for setting up a Jewish agency for Palestine. The British suggested forming an Arab agency, similar to the Jewish one, but the Arabs refused. Instead, they elected a Supreme Muslim Council with Hajj Amin al-Husseini, the Mufti of Jerusalem, as president; the British recognized the Muslim Council as the Arab authority. But an internal Arab controversy developed in the Council between supporters and opponents of the Mufti, who still favoured Syrian unity. The Mufti instigated anti-Jewish riots in 1929 and was later a Nazi supporter; he also became head of a body called the Arab Higher Committee (AHC), which led the struggle against the British and the Jews. In 1937, the British dissolved the elected Muslim Council, replaced it with an appointed council, and outlawed the AHC.[17]

There were two waves in the Fifth Aliyah (1932—40). First, from 1932 to 1935, at the beginning of the Nazi persecution, 144,000 Jews arrived, most of them from Germany; the Youth Aliyah movement was started to bring young people to Israel, and there was economic prosperity. Then, from 1936 to 1940, there were Arab riots and an economic depression, and Britain began to restrict immigration. Yet another 89,000 Jews arrived, including 15,000 "illegal" immigrants without government permits. The Sixth Aliyah (1941—47), extending beyond World War Two, was a period of struggle against immigration restrictions, when tragic incidents occurred on refugee ships from Europe and would-be immigrants were interned on Cyprus.[18]

After World War Two, in November 1947, the United Nations adopted a resolution for the establishment of separate Jewish and Arab states in Palestine. The plan was rejected by Arab leaders inside and outside Palestine, who were not prepared to grant the Jews more than minority status in an Arab

Palestine. After Israel was established, in 1948, Jordan's King Abdullah annexed the West Bank, which would have been the main territory of the Arab Palestine state. The other Arab leaders objected to the annexation, but accepted it on condition that Abdullah would not enter into a separate non-aggression pact with Israel, a pact that had actually been negotiated. The annexation was called "temporary," until all of Palestine was liberated. In 1949, however, the use of the name Palestine was eliminated from official documents and "West Bank" was substituted for it. Jordan granted citizenship and the right to vote to the Palestinian Arabs, and they held positions at all levels of the Jordanian government.

At the time, there was no demand for a state of Palestine, or for secession from or autonomy within Jordan, but this condition was temporary. The view that the Palestine Arabs formed a separate ethnic and national group had won acceptance in the 1920s and was recognized in the 1947 UN resolution providing for a separate Arab state. But Arab leaders put the idea of a Palestine Arab entity in mothballs when they rejected the UN resolution and went to war against Israel.

In the late 1950s, the idea of an Arab Palestine entity was revived, at first as an anti-Jordan movement. By the early 1960s, the demand for recognition of a Palestine Arab nation with its own territory was raised by the younger generation of Arabs. This element had started anti-Israel *fedayin*, terrorist gangs. (The name *fedayin* came from medieval Islamic Shi'ite concepts, among them the *hashashyin*, the "assassins," a name dating from the time of the Crusades.) A number of Palestine Arab groups grew out of the *fedayin*, notably al-Fatah, all of which originally wanted to eliminate Israel and replace it with an Arab state. Fatah became the main component of the Palestine Liberation Organization when it was established as an umbrella organization in 1964.[19]

Another reality demonstrated by the evolving place of Palestine in the Middle East is that national groups are born out of social and political conditions of the times. In the early decades of the twentieth century, the Jews were called Palestinians and the Arabs were still Syrians. Politics turned many Syrian Arabs into Jordanians; only later did the remaining "South Syria" Arabs become Palestinians. In Israel, Jews became Israelis, but they are not a monolithic group. Jews have come to Israel from many parts of the world, bringing customs and traditions from the countries where they lived. There are Russians, Rumanians, Poles, and others from Europe; Yemenites, Iraqis, and Iranians from "Arabia" and "Persia"; Bene Israel from India; Egyptian, Morrocan, Algerian, Tunisian, and Ethiopian Jews (Falashas) from Africa; and smaller groups from other continents.

The most significant group to settle in Israel is the Shearit Hapletah, the remnant of survivors of the Nazi Holocaust. Many among the European Ashkenzi groups were motivated by Zionism and other modern ideologies; other groups, from the Sephardic communities of Asia and African, remained closer to Biblical and Middle Ages traditions. The Zionist movement has popularized the term "ingathering of exiles" to describe Jewish immigration to Israel. This concept goes back to the idea of kibbutz Galuyyot, pingathering of exiled communities," which originated during the Babylonian exile.[20] I prefer to think of the modern immigration as an ingathering of Jewish tribes, who may be considered ethnic groups in Israel.

Zionism, Religion, and Secularism

Zionism, which sparked the establishment of a national Jewish homeland in Palestine and led to the founding of the modern state of Israel, grew out of the philosophies of nineteenth-century European nationalism. It was spurred by growing Western influence on the Jews following their emancipation after the French Revolution and by the disappointment of many Jews who sought to become accepted by and assimilated with the people among whom they lived. And, of course, it was motivated by the persistence and intensification of anti-Semitism in the nineteenth and twentieth centuries. Zionism is an essentially secular movement, even though it invoked the biblical memory of the hope for a return to Zion.

While the goal of Zionism was to seek a homeland and a state for the Jews, there were always differing views on how to achieve it, as demonstrated from the beginning by the "fathers" of Zionism, among them Hirsch Kalischer (1795—1874) an Orthodox rabbi; Moses Hess (1812—75), a socialist-internationalist; Leo Pinsker (1821—91), a physician and advocate of Haskalah; and Theodore Herzl (1860—1904), who began as an assimilationist.

Kalischer, born in Posen, Prussian Poland, concluded that it was not inconsistent with the belief in messianic redemption to undertake practical work for the restoration of Israel in Palestine. In 1836 he wrote to the Rothschilds in Berlin, "The beginning of the Redemption will come through natural causes by human effort and by the will of the governments to gather the scattered of Israel into the Holy Land."[21] Most other religious Jews considered Kalischer's plan blasphemous, but there were some exceptions. One contemporary, Rabbi Yehuda Alkelai (1798—1878), born in Sarajevo and a Kabbalist, shared Kalischer's view, arguing that self-redemption was justified by "proof texts" from the tradition and that natural precedes supernatural redemption.[22] Kalischer and Alkelai inspired the formation of the Mizrachi religious Zionist Organization.

Moses Hess was born to an Orthodox family in Bonn, Germany. He was an early collaborator with Karl Marx, but he broke with the Marxist approach. Part of the Heinrich Heine generation, Hess embraced the philosophy of Spinoza. He was influenced by the European nineteenth-century national-liberation movements, particularly the one led by Mazzini and Garibaldi in Italy. His views were expressed in his book Rome and Jerusalem (1862), in which he advocated a Jewish liberation movement and conceived the idea of a world order as a "harmonious symphony of national cultures," each expressing "ethical socialism" in its own way.[23] Hess was the inspiration for the Labour Zionist movement.

Leo Pinsker was born in Tomashov, Russian Poland. He was an assimilated Russian Jew who became a Zionist as a result of the anti-Jewish events of 1881. Concluding that the Haskalah was not enough to solve the Jewish question, he founded the Hibbat Zion (Love of Zion), a forerunner of the World Zionist Organization. Pinsker also concluded that the Jews could become emancipated through their own efforts, and he wrote a pamphlet called Auto-Emancipation; this became the platform of Hovevay Zion (Lovers of Zion), a society that established more than fifty branches in Europe, the United States, and Canada before the World Zionist Organization was founded.[24]

Theodor Herzl, born in Vienna, became involved with the Jewish question after witnessing the anti-Semitism in France attendant to the Dreyfus case. He concluded that a political movement was needed after failing in his efforts to win support for a Jewish homeland or state from courtiers and statesmen, princes and kings, and decided to start a "society of Jews." This was the origin of the World Zionist Organization, whose first constituent groups were most of the branches of Hovevay Zion. After the first World Zionist Congress, in Basle in 1897, he wrote in his diary, "In Basle I created the Jewish State. Were I to say this aloud I would be greeted by universal laughter. But perhaps five years hence . . . certainly fifty years hence, everyone will perceive it."[25] Pinsker and Herzl may be said to have fathered the middle-of-the-road group that became known as General Zionists.

At the first World Zionist Congress, no Zionist parties had yet been formed, although socialist and religious Zionists were present, along with many middle-of-the-roaders. The Socialist Zionists established the Poale Zion (Workers of Zion) party in 1900. A year later, the religious Zionists started the Mizrachi. The General Zionist Party was formed as a centrist group in response to the establishment of the socialist and religious parties. In 1921, some religious Zionists formed the Hapoel Hamizrachi, which became the religious labour party. A right-wing group broke away from the General Zionist Party; in 1925, this element formed the Revisionist Party, under Vladimir Jabotinsky, advocating a Jewish state on both sides of the Jordan. There have been continual new groupings and re-groupings in the Zionist movement; these have been reflected in the Israeli political parties since the founding of the state. All the parties have support groups in Jewish communities throughout the world.[26]

In the first general election in Israel, in January of 1949, Mapai, the main-line Israel Labour Party, received a plurality of votes, though it did not enjoy an outright majority. With forty-six of the total of one hundred and twenty seats, Mapai could have formed a majority Labour government with the left-wing Mapam, which had nineteen seats, but relations between the two groups were not conducive to such an arrangement. David Ben Gurion, the leader of Mapai, turned to the religious parties, with sixteen seats, and some smaller right-of-centre groups for a governing majority. In the first Knesset, the extreme-right Herut party, organized by Menachem Begin, had sixteen members; there were also four communist members.[27] The religious parties, whether the number of their Knesset seats rose or fell, played a key role in Mapai-led governments, which ruled until 1977. Proportional representation, the basis on which Knesset members were elected from party lists until 1992, made coalition governments a necessity.

On June 5, 1967, Israel launched the Six-Day-War, after open provocation by the Arab states, particularly Egypt, and captured all of the West Bank, the Gaza Strip, the Golan Heights, and the Sinai. This war brought the Labour-led government to its high point in popularity. Six years later, on October 6, 1973, Egypt and Syria launched a simultaneous attack on Israel from the south and the north, which came as a complete surprise to the Israeli government.[28] This became known as the Yom Kippur War; it ended in military victory for Israel after nearly three weeks of fierce combat and serious losses on the Israeli side. The political damage was even more serious, since the Yom Kippur War occurred during the election campaign for the eighth Knesset. The charge of military unpreparedness became an election issue. The Labour coalition suffered losses in the December 31, 1973, election, but held its dominant position in the Knesset with fifty seats. However, a stronger right-wing bloc, known as Likud, led by Menachem Begin, emerged with thirty-eight seats.[29]

Controversy over the occupied Arab lands had begun immediately after the Six-Day War. The problems intensified after the Yom Kippur War and led to the defeat of the Labour-led coalition in 1977. Likud emerged as the strongest group and built a new right-wing coalition government. The religious parties shifted their support from Labour to Likud.

Israel's first peace agreement with Egypt was made under the leadership of Begin, inspired by the 1977 surprise visit to Jerusalem of Egyptian President Anwar Sadat, who later fell victim to a fundamentalist assassin. After giving up the Sinai, Begin developed the hard-line policy of no withdrawal from the other occupied territories, which he called by their biblical names, Judea and Samaria. This approach led to the policy of annexation under the aegis of a "Greater Israel," which was maintained by Yitshak Shamir, Begin's successor.

To appreciate the period of Likud rule, it should be noted that Begin and Shamir came from the right wing of the Zionist movement. Begin was a disciple of Vladimir Jabotinsky, the founder of the Zionist Revisionist Party, and opposed the kibbutz collective approach in agriculture. In the British mandate period, the Revisionists were aggressively militant toward the British and the Arabs; in 1937, they founded an underground military group comprising some three to five thousand members, the Irgun Zvai Leumi, which broke with the Haganah, the established Jewish defence organization, over its moderate policies in defending the Yishuv, the Palestine Jewish community. During World War Two, the Irgun declared a truce in its fight against the British and supported the war effort. Begin became commander of the Irgun in 1943, after its first leader, David Raziel, was killed on a British mission in Iraq. After the war, the Irgun resorted to terrorist attacks on the British and on Arabs. When Israel's independence was proclaimed, serious tensions developed between the Irgun and the new government. But after a short period, the Irgun disbanded and its members joined the Hagana, which was transformed into the Israel Defense Force (IDF), the Israeli army.

Yitshak Shamir was part of a splinter group from the Irgun, known as the Stern Gang, which rejected the wartime truce and continued to fight the British. Shamir was the operations commander of the Stern Gang, which never had more than three hundred members. In January, 1941, before the Nazi policy of total destruction of the Jews became known, some Stern members tried to contact the Nazi Axis powers, particularly Italy, to develop a common struggle against Britain and thus achieve Zionist political objectives.[30]

Shamir's move toward the Nazis was foolhardy. A more recent example of Shamir's foolhardiness was his policy of no compromise on the occupied territories. In the light of warnings that Arabs in a "Greater Israel" would eventually become a majority or near-majority, this approach was highly unrealistic. The long-term existence of the Jewish state could not be taken for granted if half, or more, of the population were Arab.

When Baruch Goldstein, in February of 1994, walked into a Hebron Mosque on the West Bank armed with a machine gun and killed twenty-nine Arabs at prayer, the whole world was shocked. How could this be explained? Goldstein may have been mentally disturbed, but his criminal act has to be seen in terms of Arab and Jewish/Israeli perceptions about each other. Yehoshefat Harkabi, a former director of military intelligence for the State of Israel, has written a cogent interpretation of Arab-Jewish relations that may also be applied to Baruch Goldstein.

Harkabi explains how the policy of some Arabs changed from absolute opposition to the existence of the Jewish state to the moderate position that led to peace with Egypt. After Begin and Sadat signed the Camp David accords (1978—79), Jordan and the PLO began to plan a policy favouring a political accommodation. But it took longer than it might have for the moderating Arab position to lead to the peace negotiations between Israel, the PLO, and the other Arab states that began in 1993.

On Israel-Arab relations, Harkabi draws an important distinction: he explains that the Arabs gradually let go of the policy based on their "grand design" to eliminate Israel, in favour of the policy of political accommodation. However, "There is no way of extinguishing a people's vicious dreams, which are liable to persist even after political accommodations. A political settlement eventually uproots the vicious dreams and cancels them out, while lack of political accommodation establishes and reinforces them."[31]

The Arab "grand design" of getting rid of Israel, still strongly held among Muslim fundamentalists, has been countered by a Jewish "grand design," held primarily by Israeli political extremists and fundamentalists, to establish a "Greater Israel" and expel all the Arabs. Both the Jewish and the Arab grand designs have been transformed into the "vicious dreams" that, among Arabs, motivate groups like Hezbolah and Hamas and, among Jews, the disciples of Meir Kahane, who founded Kach, the Israeli racist party. Baruch Goldstein was a Kach follower.

Goldstein's massacre of the Hebron Palestinians not only threatened the Arab-Israel peace process, it also caused an internal crisis among all those who oppose giving up land for peace. Most Israelis immediately and overwhelmingly condemned Goldstein's brutal act, and forty-four Orthodox rabbis from the National Religious camp, including leading rabbis in "Judea and Samaria" (the occupied territories) condemned the massacre. Their statement, posted through the country, said in part, "We rabbis in Israel express our shock and condemn in the harshest terms the brutal murder carried out by a Jew on innocent people."[32]

The Israeli government quickly outlawed Kach and Kahane Chai, another right-wing radical group, and branded them as terrorist organizations. The antiterrorist laws, used for years only against Arabs, were used for the first time against Jews. The declaration outlawing Kach and Kahane Chai labelled as terrorists any group seeking "the establishment of a theocracy in the biblical land of Israel and the violent expulsion of Arabs from that land."[33]

As Jordan and the PLO moved away from their commitment to the grand design, Jordan's King Hussein and Yasser Arafat agreed, in 1985, to offer Israel a political accommodation based on the principle of "land for peace." This offer was considered revolutionary in the Arab-Israel dispute, according to Harkabi. Israel could have made an agreement with Jordan alone earlier, he maintained, but the Israeli government had refused. Hussein was therefore compelled to include the PLO and, later, the Syrians. Israel's failure to respond to the offer contributed to the Arab uprising, the Intifada, which began in December of 1987, in the occupied West Bank and Gaza Strip. These disturbances should not have come as a surprise, Harkabi asserted. He had warned against them in his lectures and in his 1986 book.[35]

Harkabi had predicted that "reality" would force Israel to withdraw from its political stance of no negotiations with the PLO and no withdrawal from the occupied territories. This reality came about at long last with the end of the Cold War and the result of the 1991 Gulf War against Iraq. The changed political conditions at the world level and in the Middle East persuaded the Likud prime minister, Yitshak Shamir, to agree to a Middle East conference in Madrid. For the same reasons, Syria agreed to a meeting for peace, making it possible for Jordan and Lebanon to join the conference, which led to the opening of bilateral negotiations in Washington between Israel and the Palestinians, and to negotiations between Israel and each of the front-line Arab states.

By the time of the June, 1992, election, a majority of the Israeli electorate realized that it would take a change in government to achieve positive results in the peace talks. Mapai, the Israel Labour Party, had begun to advocate land for peace; for this and several other reasons, it won the largest number of Knesset seats and was able to form a coalition government dedicated to speeding up the peace process. In September, 1993, little more than a year later, the Israeli-PLO peace accord was signed in the White House garden in Washington. As I am writing, certain political elements on both the Israeli side and the Arab side, continue to seek to derail the peace process. In Israel, the right is aligned with the religious extremists. On the

Arab side, the Muslim fundamentalists are the main right-wing force.

Jews who identify themselves as religious, originally almost all of them Orthodox, have always been a minority in Israel. Yet, as part of the government, the Orthodox have been able to secure control of key areas of Jewish life, including marriage and divorce, dietary laws, Sabbath observance, and the question of who may be considered a Jew. Ben Gurion, himself a secularist, originally yielded to the Orthodox demands not only for their political support but to avoid a *kulturkampf*, a struggle between religious Jews and secular Jews.[36] But the struggle over religious freedom has become a major domestic issue.

Yehuda Bauer told the 1988 Secular Humanist World Conference in Brussels that there are "hair-splitting divisions" between religious and non-religious Jews. The split is such, however, that "if we do not come to an understanding of ourselves that goes beyond religious definitions we are endangering the existence of the Jewish people."[37] Ze'ev Gries, another Hebrew University professor, criticized the political surrender to the Orthodox in Israel on so-called "small" religious issues: "The consequence of that surrender may well prove extremely harmful to the State of Israel and the Jewish people at large."[38] Moreover, Gershom Scholem, the great twentieth-century scholar of Kabbalah and Jewish mysticism, had predicted, a few years before he died, that "Jewish theology may undergo radical changes in the State of Israel because secularism is a powerful reality, the meaning of which has to be lived out and confronted squarely." New forms of Judaism, Scholem added, will devolve from all of Jewish history, and from the struggle to create a just society.[39]

The struggle over religious freedom has been waged more vigorously since the Reform, Conservative, and Secular Humanist movements have established themselves in Israel. The non-Orthodox groups are in conflict with the municipal religious councils, the bastion of Orthodox control. In 1993, the Supreme Court ruled that the religious councils could not reject Conservative and Reform candidates for the councils because of their religious orientation. In defiance of the court, Israel's two chief rabbis (Ashkenazi and Sephardic) adopted a resolution that non-Orthodox Jews should not serve on the councils.

The Supreme Court also directed the religious councils to apply civil law, rather than halacha (religious law), to property settlements in divorce cases. Again, the chief rabbis voted not to comply with the court's ruling. This decision was made after consultation with other Orthodox rabbis, rabbinical court judges, and heads of the religious councils; the chief rabbis recognize only one side in the dispute. The rabbis also asked the Knesset to pass legislation preventing non-Orthodox delegates from sitting on the religious councils. At the time of writing, the Knesset has not yet responded.

There has also been a scandalous situation over Orthodox control of burial of the dead. In one case, the body of a non-Jew found buried in a Jewish cemetery was removed and interred elsewhere. In another case, Orthodox authorities protested the burial of a Jewish soldier in a military cemetery next to a Bedouin war hero of the Israel Defence Force. It has also been reported that bodies of uncircumcised Jews have been subject to circumcision before burial in a Jewish cemetery was permitted.

The Orthodox monopoly over burials was challenged in the courts some years ago, and the Supreme Court ruled that the Ministry of Religious Affairs must grant a license to a burial society regardless of its religious affiliation. A new burial society, Menucha Nechona (Society for Eternal Rest), which was a party to the court action, was granted more than ten acres of land in 1994 in a new cemetery on the outskirts of Haifa. Those using the new cemetery may choose an Orthodox or a non-Orthodox service, and a husband and wife may be buried side by side even if one was not Jewish. In a poll of Haifa residents on the alternative burial service, 70 per cent approved of it in principle, though only 44 per cent said that they would themselves use it. The new burial service also allows the use of coffins, rather than shrouds alone, which are traditional in Orthodox burials in Israel. There has been little demand for cremation, especially among families with a memory of the Holocaust, and it is taboo under Orthodox law.[40]

One of the concessions made to the Orthodox minority many years ago was to prohibit Jews from raising pigs (Christian Arabs are permitted to produce pork). A new concession was made to Orthodoxy early in 1994 when the Knesset approved a bill to ban imports of all non-kosher meat and seafood. This prohibition was the price then demanded by the Orthodox Shas Party for rejoining the government. Shas had been part of Rabin's coalition until late 1993; it left when its leader, Aryeh Deri, who had been in the Cabinet, resigned because he was indicted for bribery, fraud, and breach of public trust. The ban on non-kosher imports was achieved by amending Israel's basic law, freedom of occupation, thus causing a restriction of economic freedom based on religious values that are supported by a minority.

As I write, Shas is still not satisfied. It has demanded that the government pledge to adopt a law "nullifying any Supreme Court ruling that challenges the status quo on religious affairs." Rabbi Alexander Schindler, president of the Union of American Hebrew Congregations (Reform), has written to Prime Minister Rabin, warning him that "caving in to Shas demands would bring 'lasting damage to Israel-Diaspora relations.'" Rabin had earlier agreed to the Shas demands, but he ran into opposition in his own party, and the left-wing Meretz bloc, his main coalition partner, refused to accept the deal. Shas is now making its demands a condition of support for Rabin's efforts to achieve peace with Syria.[41]

Meretz, an alliance between Mapam, the left-labour party, and the Civil Rights group, led by Shulamit Aloni. Aloni, a leader of the Israeli secular movement, served as minister of education until she offended the religious element and was moved to the communications portfolio. The Rabin government probably had a stronger secular component than any previous Israeli government. However, Meretz went along with the ban on non-kosher food imports, despite its goal of introducing American-style civil liberties in Israel. Secularists outside the government have expressed the concern that Israel may become the only Western-type state in which the law dictates what its citizens may or may not eat, based on ancient taboos observed by a minority of the population.[42]

In addition to the ongoing Orthodox rabbinical efforts to control the personal status of all Israeli Jews, some elements among the religious parties played a leading part in developing the "Greater Israel" movement after the six-day war in 1967. Orthodox groups were active in founding settlements in the occupied territories and in opposing proposals to return territory to Arab control, because the Holy Land was "divinely promised" to the Jews. Some rabbinical authorities, however, did not accept this view and declared that the "holiness of human life" was endangered by staying in the territories; this fact outweighed the holiness of the land. But after the Likud took power, in 1977, it was joined by ultra-Orthodox elements that supported the building of more settlements in the occupied territories.[43]

Shalom Achshav, the Peace Now movement in Israel, was started by retired officers of the IDF in 1978 to mobilize public support for peace with Egypt after President Sadat's visit to Jerusalem. An open letter signed by 350 reserve officers urged then Premier Begin to exchange territories for peace. In 1982,

Peace Now rallied mass support opposing Israel's war against Lebanon. Peace Now and other Israeli peace groups, such as N'tivot Shalom, "a dovish religious faction"; Yesh G'vul, Soldiers Against Silence; Parents Against Silence; and Hamizrach l'Shalom, East for Peace play a significant role in Israel.[44] Hamizrachi l'Shalom members come from Israel's non-European communities and it was formed "to counter the Orientals' image as indiscriminate Arab haters." Hours after the Hebron massacre, Peace Now youths organized prayer vigils in Jerusalem, Tel Aviv, Beer Sheva, and Haifa. The next day, the organization brought more than five thousand people to the prime minister's residence to express their grief and to support peace as an alternative to violence and hatred. A week later, Peace Now demonstrated in Tel Aviv, twenty-five thousand strong, against the Hebron massacre and demanded the removal of Israeli settlers from the heart of Hebron and Gaza.

The Hebron incident further stimulated a movement that had started among Jewish settlers in the occupied territories seeking compensation for moving back within Israel's pre-1967 borders. About 60 per cent of Jewish settlers in the West Bank were non-Orthodox, living there for cheaper and better housing, not for ideology.

At this writing, Jordan's King Hussein, who earlier would not move to an accommodation with Israel without the PLO and Syria, has now signed a "warm peace" with the Rabin government. Israel and the PLO, now the Palestinian Authority, are moving ahead with their peace process; this, despite the Hamas fundamentalists turning their vicious dreams into deadly nightmares. There is movement toward peace between Israel and Syria, and the Rabin government is building political accommodations with other Arab states. Despite the needless casualties perpetrated by vicious dreamers, the banner of peace in the Middle East is still flying.

Notes

1. Genesis 32:28—30; *Holy Scriptures*, "Encyclopedic Dictionary," p. 847.
2. Gaster, *Myth, Legend and Custom*, pp. 205—10.
3. Ibid.
4. Malamat, *History of the Jewish People*, p. 30.
5. "Jacob," *Encyclopedia of Religion*, vol. 7, p. 503.
6. Mazar, Davis, and Ben Sasson, *Illustrated History*, pp. 23—37.
7. Genesis 17:8.
8. Genesis 15:18.
9. Psalms 137:1, 5—6.
10. Ettinger, "The Modern Period," pp. 918—19; Roth and Wigoder, *New Standard Jewish Encyclopedia*, 902—03; Ausabel, *Book of Jewish Knowledge*, p. 530.
11. Ettinger, "The Modern Period," pp. 921—22.
12. Levine and Shimoni, *Political Dictionary*, p. 250.
13. Roth and Wigoder, *New Standard Jewish Encyclopedia*, p. 73.
14. Ettinger, "The Modern Period," pp. 994—95.
15. Levine and Shimoni, *Political Dictionary*, pp. 131—32, 292—93.
16. Ibid., pp. 247, 300—01.
17. Ibid., pp. 163—64.
18. Roth and Wigoder, *New Standard Jewish Encyclopedia*, p. 73.
19. Levine and Shimoni, *Political Dictionary*, pp. 129—30, 292—309.
20. Roth and Wigoder, *New Standard Jewish Encyclopedia*, pp. 1134—35.
21. Quoted in Hertzberg, *The Zionist Idea*, pp. 109—10.
22. Ibid., pp. 103-07.
23. Ibid., p. 118.
24. Ibid., pp. 178—98.
25. Herzl, *Jewish State*, pp. 52—53. See also Ausubel, *Book of Jewish Knowledge*, p. 532; Ettinger, "The Modern Period," pp. 898—900.
26. Ausubel, *Book of Jewish Knowledge*, p. 533.
27. Ettinger, "The Modern Period," pp. 1089—93.
28. Malamat, "Origins and Formative Period," pp. 1082—83, 1086—88.
29. Ibid., p. 1093.
30. Ettinger, "The Modern Period," p. 1044. In a 1989 article, Yehuda Bauer disclosed that he has documentary evidence linking Shamir to the Stern Gang's attempt to negotiate with the Nazis. See Bauer, "Our Stake," p. 29.
31. Harkabi, "A Policy for the Moment," p. 21. See also: "Israel's Fateful Hour." Harkabi, recently deceased, was a professor of international relations

at Hebrew University; he participated in the 1988 conference of the International Federation of Secular Humanistic Jews.

32. Herb Keinon in the *Jerusalem Post*, International Ed., 12 Mar. 1994, quoted in *Jewish Currents*, May 1994

33. Clyde Haberman, New York *Times*, 14 Mar. 1994, quoted in *Jewish Currents*, May 1994, p. 13.

34. Harkabi, "A Policy for the Moment," pp. 21—22.

35. Harkabi, "Israel's Fateful Hour," pp. xii-xiv. See also Beilin, *Israel*, pp. 46—51.

36. Wigoder, *Encyclopedia of Judaism*, p. 374.

37. Bauer, "Our Stake," p. 7.

38. Quoted in Cohen and Mendes-Flohr, *Contemporary Jewish Religious Thought*, p. 351.

39. Quoted in ibid., p. 508.

40. Carl Alpert, CJN, 3 Mar. 1994.

41. Jewish Telegraphic Agency dispatch in *Canadian Jewish News*, 6 Oct. 1994.

42. Bauer, "Future of the Jewish People," p. 9.

43. Wigoder, *Encyclopedia of Judaism*, p. 375.

44. Sachar, *History of Israel*, vol. 2, *From the Aftermath*, pp. 58, 198, 205, 242.

CHAPTER 13

Final Thoughts . . . for Now

There are some writers from whom both secular humanists and religionists draw inspiration. One of these is Chaim Nachman Bialik (1873—1934), a contemporary of Sholom Aleichem and Peretz, who achieved rare acclaim as a Hebrew poet. I first encountered the name "Bialik" at the first Hebrew school I attended in Montreal. We didn't really learn who Bialik was, however, and for a time I assumed him to be a religious Hebrew icon. Eventually, I learned about the real Bialik, whose essence is revealed in his poem *My Spark:*

> I have not won the light from freedom's courses,
>   Nor from my father's part
> Came it to me; 'tis hewn from crags of mine,
>   I carved it from my heart.
>
> One spark is hid in the fortress of my heart,
>   So small, but mine alone;
> I asked it of no man, I stole it not,
>   'Tis in me, and my own.[1]

In saying that he did not gain the light from his father, Bialik demonstrated his conscious break with his Orthodox background, which was confirmed when he was sixteen and studying at the Volozhin Yeshiva in Lithuania. There, he began reading Haskalah literature in Hebrew and became a *maskil*, a dissenter from religious practice. In addition to his poetry, he produced many works based on traditional Jewish sources from the Bible onward. Thus did he kindle his own light from his personal spark. During his lifetime, he was known as the poet laureate of the Jewish people, and his works inspired Jews of various ideologies and beliefs.

In a later poem, *Al Hashechita (On the Slaughter)*, on the Kishinev pogrom, Bialik inveighed against the killing of innocent people: "If you have a God, and he can be reached . . . pray for me–but I've not found him."[2] In a second poem, *The City of Slaughter*, Bialik urged an end to the Jewish custom of looking at calamity as a punishment for sins:

> Let them against me raise their outraged hand–
> Let them demand!
> Demand the retribution for the shamed
> Of all the centuries, and every age!
> Let fists be flung like stone
> Against the heavens and the heavenly throne![3]

Bialik became a Zionist in the 1920s and he moved to Tel Aviv. There, he introduced the modern Oneg Shabbat (Sabbath Delight) custom of presenting lectures or cultural programs on Saturday afternoons to interest Jews in the cultural values of Judaism. In 1925, speaking at the inauguration of the Hebrew University in Jerusalem, he declared, "In the consciousness of the nation the comprehensive human concept of 'culture' . . . has taken the place of the theological one of 'Torah.'"[4] He also acknowledged that "our people in its 'diasporas' is creating a culture," but he felt that Jewish culture in the Diaspora was being "absorbed in the culture of others . . . and never accounted to the credit of the Jews." In this respect, Bialik has been proven wrong. For example, his Oneg Shabbat concept has been adopted by Jewish communities throughout the world, from the religious to the secular.

In particular, the organized movement of secular humanistic Jews in Canada, the United States, and other countries seeks to follow the Bialik concept of culture replacing Torah theology. In North America, this movement has given rise to the

Society for Humanistic Judaism, which celebrated its twenty-fifth anniversary in 1994, and the Congress of Secular Jewish Organizations. The SHJ and the CSJO have joined together in the North American Federation of Secular Humanistic Jews.[5] Under this umbrella, the two organizations meet at conferences and sponsor the Institute for Secular Humanistic Judaism. The institute conducts education and training courses, including an innovative *madrikh/vegvayser* leadership program, which trains people to be secular-humanistic family counsellors and officiators at alternative life-cycle events. The *madrikhim/vegvaysers,* described as quasi-rabbis, are legally empowered to perform marriages in a number of American states, including California.

There are certain differences in approach between the SHJ and the CSJO arising from the origins of each group. The SHJ, a relatively new departure for secular Jews, seeks to address the needs of Jewish middle-class professionals, and seems more concerned with personal and spiritual enrichment and community building than with social action. The CSJO is apparently more social-action oriented, since it was founded by elements of the left-wing Yiddishist-labour-socialist movement that flourished in the U.S. and Canada in the first half of the twentieth century.

The SHJ is also said to owe more to humanist thinkers, such as Corliss Lamont, John Dewey, and Bertrand Russell, than to Simon Dubnow, Ahad Ha'am, and Chaim Zhitlowsky, according to one writer.[6] This may be true of some of the initiators of the SHJ, but in the pages of *Humanistic Judaism*, which I have been reading for close to a decade, Jewish secular humanists of the past century are clearly among the Society's main influences.

The SHJ comprises societies, congregations, and one temple, with many members coming from a synagogue background; thus, there is an emphasis on creating and practising nontheistic rituals and life-cycle ceremonies. Its goal is to establish a secular humanistic alternative to other Jewish denominations. The CSJO comprises societies, clubs, and *shules* (schools); many of its members come from a Yiddish culture and school background. The Congress is devoted to the development of a secular Jewish cultural community. The SHJ has influenced the CSJO to consider the personal and spiritual needs of secular Jews, while the CSJO has moved the SHJ to recognize the importance of Yiddish culture to secular Jewish identity.[7]

The leaders of the SHJ and the CSJO share the belief that humanism is at the core of Jewish experience, and they both stress the importance of social action in the secular Jewish milieu. They differ, however, on the earliest source of Jewish humanism. Neil Salzman, of the CSJO, traces Jewish humanism to the biblical prophets, as well as to Spinoza and the Haskalah. Rabbi Sherwin Wine, the SHJ leader, rejects the prophetic tradition for its primary concern with suppression of "rival religious beliefs and only marginally with peace and social justice." Wine disapproves of the authoritarianism of the prophets and their threats of divine reprisal, instead of using reason to convince people to lead moral lives. In a keynote address to the SHJ, Salzman said that the prophets were radicals for their time who should be recognized for placing ethical behaviour ahead of religious ritual observance.[8]

There is also an active secular humanist movement in Israel, where the struggle between Orthodox and secular Judaism is most intense. In his book *This Year in Jerusalem,* Mordecai Richler recounts his meetings in Israel in 1992 with friends of his youth who had made *aliyah* (settled in Israel) in the 1950s. One of them disclosed that he was a secular humanist and that he worked with a support group for children of *haredim* (strict religionists) who had broken with Orthodox observances.[9]

"Jewish continuity" has been taken up as a major issue by many communities outside Israel. In April of 1994, the Canadian Jewish Congress sponsored a national education conference in Winnipeg devoted largely to "continuity" question. As CJC president, Irving Abella, stated, "Jewish survival is at risk in tolerant and multicultural societies."[10] This conference came up with very few new answers; it emphasized a return to "tradition" and the synagogue and the need for the home to play a role in ensuring Jewish continuity. When I raised the need to recognize the secular trend in Jewish life at a conference workshop entitled "Building Bridges between Organizations," I was told that this was passé by a long-ago graduate of a once-thriving Yiddish secular school. I was also urged to return to *davening* (reciting the Jewish prayers).

In Toronto, a task force on Jewish continuity has devoted two years to producing a report, which was recently discussed at a meeting of a new organization, the Association for Jewish Continuity. The report, as summarized in the Anglo-Jewish press, advocates an "inclusive approach . . . embracing synagogues, young people and those who feel alienated from the mainstream community." It identifies "three priority areas: urging Jewish families to live Jewish lives in the home; Jewish education; addressing 'singles issues.'" In the discussion following presesntation of the report, a number of pertinent points were made: secular Jews, non-Zionists, Israelis, and Jews of non-European descent were not addressed by the task force; people need to have somewhere to go in a nonreligious environment and "still feel connected"; there is a reluctance to accept couples in which one party was not born Jewish, even when the non-Jewish spouse wants to participate in community activities. A call was made for greater community tolerance.[11] These concerns are not new, but there is still an overemphasis on bringing disaffected Jews into the "mainstream" of synagogue, Bible studies, and the prayer book.

Recognition of the diversity of Jewish culture beyond the Torah and the Siddur is given little credence.

Some Jews, who are consciously secular, have moved beyond the canonized Torah and the Siddur, but the path should be opened to many more. The organized Jewish community also has a responsibility in this regard. In 1966, Judah Shapiro, then the secretary of the National Foundation for Jewish Culture in New York, addressed the World Jewish Congress in a speech entitled "The Challenge to the Jewish Community." Relating the nature of the Jewish communities to the level of modernization of the societies that host them, Shapiro said, "Modernization is not merely an industrial process but a crucial challenge to tradition. To the extent that 'tradition' [is] a commitment to doing what one's ancestors had always done in the past, it [is] an inhibition to progress, experimentation, new knowledge." Among the "non-modernized" general societies of nineteenth-century eastern Europe, Shapiro continued, Jewish communities could remain traditional. But it is an "almost perverse misunderstanding" of historical reality that "today . . . we permit the traditional patterns of non-modernized eastern European Jewish communities to be the yardsticks of what is good and bad in contemporary Jewish communities." He concluded, "The Jewish community has been deteriorating through failure to make active forms of being Jewish intellectually and emotionally [its] *raison d'être.* Knowing and reinterpreting the Jewish heritage is really the only business of the Jewish community for the time to come."[12] Almost three decades later, the organized Jewish community has yet to acknowledge that there are ways of being Jewish beyond the observance of *kashrut* and the reciting of *birkat hamazon,* the traditional grace after meals.

Sholom Aleichem, the humanist Yiddish writer, suggested an alternative to prayer in his will, which the *New York Times* called "one of the great ethical wills in history." He said that if his sons and sons-in-law were not inclined to say *Kaddish* (the traditional prayer for the dead)–if it was against their religious conviction–they could be "absolved therefrom" if, on the anniversary of his death, all his family and friends would "foregather" and read his will, and also select "one of my stories, of the very merry ones, and recite it in whatever language is more intelligible . . . and let my name be recalled with laughter rather than not be remembered at all." For more than half a century, Sholom Aleichem's children carried out his last wish.[13] It is not necessary to wait for a beloved relative to die to adopt Sholom Aleichem's suggestion to his children. Jewish holidays may be observed by following non-theistic rituals if one is so inclined, or one may choose from the vast array of Jewish literature relating to each Jewish traditional observance or celebration. With the exercise of some intellectual effort, the Jewish heritage may be reinterpreted to be meaningful for today and tomorrow.

While writing this book, I was asked from time to time when it would be finished; I didn't really have a definitive answer. With this final chapter I am completing this book, but I cannot say that the work is finished. My active involvement with this subject will contine to the end of my days, and the meaning of Judaism will continue to be debated as long as there are Jews.

Notes

1. Quoted in *Poems from the Hebrew*, p. 42. The Hebrew title of the poem is *Lo Zakhiti ba-or min ha-hefker (I Did Not Gain the Light from Nothing)*.

2. Quoted in Aberbach, *Bialik: Jewish Thinkers*, p. 61.

3. Quoted in Frank, "Hayyim Nahman Bialik," p. 186; poem trans. A.M. Klein.

4. Quoted in Hertzberg, *The Zionist Idea*, p. 284.

5. The North American Federation (SHJ and CSJO) is affiliated with the Internation Federation of Secular Humanistic Jews which sponsors the International Institute for Secular Humanistic Judaism. SHJ has 19 affiliates (see *Humanistic Judaism*, Spring/94). CSJO has 22 affiliates including four

in Canada. The International Federation has affiliates in Israel, Argentina, Australia, France, and Belgium, and offices in the United States and Israel (See Secular Humanistic Judaism, November/91).

6. Bennett Muraskin, "Secular Humanistic Judaism Today," *Jewish Currents* (September 1994): 4—7, 34.

7. Ibid., p. 4.

8. Ibid., p. 6.

9. Richler, *This Year in Jerusalem*, p. 91.

10. "Review of Conference Sessions," CJC National Education Conference, Winnipeg, 16—18 April 1994, p. 7.

11. Paul Lungen, *Canadian Jewish News*, 6 Nov. 1994, p. 2.

12. Article in *World Jewry: The Review of the World Jewish Congress*, November/December 1966, pp. 14, 16.

13. Waife-Goldberg, *My Father Sholom Aleichem*, pp. 316—17.

Bibliography

Abella, Irving, and Harold Troper. *None Is Too Many.* Toronto: Lester & Orpen Dennys, 1983.

Aberbach, David. *Bialik: Jewish Thinkers.* New York: Grove Press, 1988.

Abrahams, Israel. *Jewish Life in the Middle Ages.* London: Edward Goldston, 1932. Rev. by Cecil Roth. New York: Jewish Publication Society, 1958.

Adler, Rachel. "Tumah and Tahara." *The Jewish Woman An Anthology,* special ed. of *Response, A Contemporary Jewish Review* (Summer 1973): 126.

Aleichem, Sholom. *The Old Country.* New York: Crown, 1946.

Alpert, Carl, "New Israeli Burial Society offers Alternatives," *Canadian Jewish News,* 3 Mar. 1994, p. 13.

American Heritage Dictionary of the English Language, William Morris, ed. New York, Houghton Mifflin, 1970.

Arnold, Abraham J. "Welcoming the Jews." In B.G. Smillie, ed., *Visions of The New Jerusalem: Religious Settlement on the Prairies,* pp. 91—107. Edmonton: NeWest Press, 1983.

–. "Canada's Jewish Magna Carta." *Jewish Life and Times,* vol. 5 (1988): 69-78.

–. Various articles in *Canadian Jewish News,* Toronto, and *Western Jewish News,* Winnipeg. On Yom Hashoah and Tisha b'Av, 1977; on S.L. Shneiderman, 1978; on Irving Howe, 1978—79; on Berl Frymer and Itche Goldberg, 1979; on Stephen Berk, 1980; on Rev. Harold MacDonald, 1980.

Arnold, Abraham, with William Kurelek. *Jewish Life in Canada.* Edmonton: Hurtig, 1976.

Ausubel, Nathan. *Book of Jewish Knowledge.* New York City: Crown, 1964.

–. *A Treasury of Jewish Folklore.* New York City: Crown, 1948.

Baron, J.L., ed. *Treasury of Jewish Quotations.* London: Thomas Yoseloff and New York: A.S. Barnes, 1965.

Baron, Salo W. "Work Among Our Youth." *Proceedings,* Canadian Jewish Congress Plenary Assembly, Montreal, 1947.

–. "The Modern Age." In Leo W. Schwartz, ed., *Great Ages & Ideas of the Jewish People,* pp. 315—484.

–. *History and Jewish Historians: Essays and Addresses.* Comp. Arthur Hertzberg with Leon A. Feldman. Philadelphia: Jewish Publication Society, 1964.

Barr, Robert. "Hannuka: Its Origin and Development." *Humanistic Judaism* (Autumn 1983): 10—13.

Bauer, Yehuda. *The Holocaust in Historical Perspective*. Seattle: University of Washington Press, 1978.

—. "Who is a Jew? Why a New Definition?" *Humanistic Judaism* (Spring 1988): 6—9.

—. "Our Stake in the Palestine Issue." *Humanistic Judaism* (Winter 1991): 7—10.

—. "The Future of the Jewish People." *Humanistic Judaism* (Winter 1991): 29—30.

Bauman, Batya. *On Being a Jewish Feminist: A Reader*. New York: Schocken.

Beilin, Yossi. *Israel: A Concise Political History*. London: Weidenfeld & Nicolson, 1992.

Ben-Sasson, H.H., ed. *A History of the Jewish People*. Cambridge: Harvard University Press, 1976.

Bentwich, Norman. *Hellenism*. Philadelphia: Jewish Publication Society, 1919.

Bercuson, David, and Douglas Wertheimer. *A Trust Betrayed: The Keegstra Affair*. Toronto: Seal/McClelland-Bantam, 1987.

Berman, Saul. "The Status of Women in Halakhic Judaism." In Elizabeth Koltun, ed., *The Jewish Woman: New Perspectives*, pp. 116—20. New York: Schocken Books, 1976.

Bialik, Chaim Nachman. *Poems from the Hebrew*. Ed. L.V. Snowman. London: Hasefer, 1924.

Bickerman, Elias. "The Maccabean Uprising: An Interpretation." In J. Goldin, ed., *The Jewish Expression*, pp. 67—86. Princeton: Yale University Press, 1976.

The Black Book: The Nazi Crime Against the Jewish People. New York: World Jewish Congress; Moscow, Vaad Leumi, Palestine: Jewish Anti-Fascist Committee; New York: Committee of Jewish Writers, Artists and Scientists, 1946.

Brown, Michael. "Stereotype to Scapegoat." In Alan Davies, ed., *Antisemitism in Canada*, pp. 39—60. Waterloo, ON: Wilfrid Laurier University Press, 1992.

Brym, Robert J., William Shaffir, and Morton Weinfeld, eds. *The Jews in Canada*. Toronto: Oxford University Press, 1993.

Buber, Martin. *Tales of Chassidim: Later Masters*. New York: Schocken, 1948.

BIBLIOGRAPHY

Chiel, A.A. *The Jews in Manitoba.* Toronto: University of Toronto Press.

Cohen, Arthur A., and Paul Mendes-Flohr (eds.). *Contemporary Jewish Religious Thought: Original Essays on Critical Concepts, Movements, and Beliefs.* New York: Charles Scribner's Sons, 1987.

Cohen, Gerson D. "The Talmudic Age." In Leo W. Schwartz, ed., *Great Ages and Ideas of the Jewish People,* pp. 143—212.

—. "Conservative Judaism," in A.A. Cohen and P. Mendes-Flohr, *Contemporary Jewish Religious Thought.*

Cohen, Norman. *Warrant for Genocide: The Myth of the Jewish World Conspiracy.* London: Eyre & Spottiswoode, 1967.

Cohen, Stephen M. "An Overview of the Canadian Jewish Community" in Brym, Robert J., William Shaffir, and Morton Weinfeld, eds. *The Jews in Canada.* Toronto: Oxford University Press, 1993.

Curtis, John S. *An Appraisal of the Protocols of Zion.* New York: Columbia University Press, 1942.

Davies, Allan, ed. *Anti-semitism in Canada.* Waterloo, On: Wilfred Laurier University Press 1992.

Dawidowicz, Lucy S., ed. *A Holocaust Reader.* New York: Beherman House.

–. *The Holocaust and the Historians.* Cambridge: Harvard University Press.

Delisle, Esther. *The Traitor and the Jew.* Trans. Madeleine Hébert, Claire Rothman, and Käthe Roth. Montreal: Robert Davies Publishing, 1993.

Dewey, John. *A Common Faith.* Princeton: Yale University Press, 1934.

Donat, Alexander. "Jewish Resistance." In Albert H. Friedlander, ed., *Out of the Whirlwind: A Reader of Holocaust Literature.*

Dubnow, Simon. *Nationalism and History.* Ed. and intro. by Koppel S. Pinson. Philadelphia: Jewish Publication Society of America, 1958.

–. *Velt Geschichte fun Yiddishen Folk.* 10 vols. Republished in English as *History of the Jews.* 5 vols. New York/London: Thomas Yoseloff, 1967—73.

Durant, Will. *The Story of Civilization.* Vol. 1, *Our Oriental Heritage.* Vol. 2, *The Life of Greece.* Vol. 3, *Caesar and Christ.*

Ehrenburg, Ilya, and Vasily Grossman, eds. *The Black Book: Documents the Nazis' destruction of 1.5 Million Soviet Jews.* Trans. John Glad and James S. Levine. New York: Holocaust Library, 1980.

Einstein, Albert. *Out of My Later Years.* New York: Philosophical Library.

–. *Ideas and Opinions.* New York: Crown, 1954.

Elbogen, Ismar. *A Century of Jewish Life*. Philadelphia: Jewish Publication Society, 1966.

Encyclopedia of Religion. New York: Macmillan, 1987.

Encyclopedia of Social Sciences. New York: Macmillan, 1948.

Ettinger, S. "The Modern Period." In H.H. Ben-Sasson, Ed., *A History of the Jewish People*, pp. 727—1096.

Finkelstein, Louis. *The Pharisees: The Sociological Background of their Faith*. 2 vols. Philadelphia: Jewish Publication Society, 1946.

Ford, Henry. *The International Jew: The World's Foremost Problem*. Dearborn, MI: Dearborn Publishing Co., 1920.

Frank, M.Z. "Hayyim Nahman Bialik." in Simon Noveck, ed., *Great Personalities in Modern Times*. B'nai Brith Great Book Series, 1960.

Friedlander, Albert H., ed. *Out of the Whirlwind: A Reader of Holocaust Literature*. New York: Schocken, 1976.

Friedman, Reena, ed. "How Was This Passover Different from All Other Passovers. *Lilith, The Jewish Women's Magazine* (Spring/Summer 1977): 35.

Gaster, Theodor H. *Passover: Its History and Tradition*. New York: Henry Schuman, 1949.

—. *Festivals of the Jewish Year*. New York: Commentary/Morrow, 1953.

—. *The Holy and the Profane*. New York: Morrow, 1955.

—. *Myth, Legend and Custom in the Old Testament*. New York: Harper and Row.

Gendler, Esther. "The Restoration of Vashti." In Elizabeth Koltun, ed., *The Jewish Woman: New Perspectives*, pp. 241—47. New York: Schocken Books.

Gilbert, Martin. "The Holocaust: Unfinished Business." *Humanistic Judaism* (Spring, 1991): 41—42.

Ginzberg, Louis. *Legends of the Jews*. Trans. Henrietta Szold. 7 vols. Philadelphia: Jewish Publication Society, 1968.

Goldberg, I. "Secularism and Jewish Tradition." *Jewish Spectator* (Summer, 1981): 29—31.

Goldenberg, Naomi R. "Judaism: Where does the Feminist Go?" *Humanistic Judaism* (Winter, 1981): 14—18.

Goodman, Philip. *The Purim Anthology*. Philadelphia: Jewish Publication Society, 1949.

—. *Rejoice in Thy Festival*. New York: Bloch, 1956.

—. *The Hannukah Anthology*. Philadelphia: Jewish Publication Society, 1976.

Goodman, Saul, ed. *The Faith of Secular Jews*. New York: Ktav, 1976.

BIBLIOGRAPHY

Graetz, H. *History of the Jews*. 6 vols. Philadelphia: Jewish Publication Society of America, 1891—98.

Greenstone, Julius H. *Jewish Feasts and Fasts*. New York: Bloch, 1946.

Gries Ze'ev, "Heresy," in Cohen, Arthur A., and Paul Mendes-Flohr (eds.). *Contemporary Jewish Religious Thought*.

Guide to Humanistic Judaism. Special issue of Humanistic Judaism . Myrna Bonnie Cousens and Ruth Duskin Feldmen, eds. Summer/Autumn 1993.

Halkin, Abraham S. "The Judeo-Islamic Age." In Leo W. Schwartz, ed., *Great Ages and Ideas of the Jewish People*, pp. 213—63.

Harkabi, Y. *Israel's Fateful Hour*. Harper & Row, 1988.

—. "A Policy for the Moment of Truth," *Humanistic Judaism*, Spring 1989.

Henry, Sondra, and Emily Taitz. *Written out of History: A Hidden Legacy of Jewish Women*. New York: Bloch Publishing, 1978.

Hertz, Joseph H. *Authorized Daily Prayer Book*. New York: Bloch, 1952.

Hertzberg, Arthur, ed. *The Zionist Idea*. Garden City, NY: Doubleday & Herzl Press, 1959.

–. *Judaism: The Key Spiritual Writings of the Jewish Tradition*. New York: Simon & Schuster/Touchstone, 1991.

Hertzberg, Arthur, and Leon Feldman. *History and Jewish Historians: Essays and Addresses by Salo W. Baron*. Philadelphia: Jewish Publication Society.

Herzl, Theodor. *The Jewish State*. New York: American Zionist Emergency Council, 1946.

Hess, Moses. "Rome and Jerusalem." In Arthur Hertzberg, ed., *The Zionist Idea*, pp. 117—39. Gardon City, NY: Doubleday and Herzl Press, 1959.

Hilberg, Raul. *The Destruction of the European Jews*. 1st ed. Chicago: Quadrangle Books, 1961. 2nd ed. 3 vols. Holmes & Meier, 1985.

–. *Perpetrators, Victims, Bystanders: The Jewish Catastrophe 1933—45*. New York: HarperCollins, 1992.

The Holy Bible, authorized King James Version. Cleveland and New York: World Publishing Company, 1945.

The Holy Scriptures: A Jewish Family Bible, According to the Masoretic Text. With encyclopedic dictionary. Chicago: Menorah Press, 1957.

Howe, Irving, and Eliezer Greenberg. *A Treasury of Yiddish Stories*. New York: Viking Press, 1954.

–. *A Treasury of Yiddish Poetry*. New York: Shocken, 1976.

–. *Ashes out of Hope: Fiction by Soviet-Yiddish Writers*. New York: Schocken.

Howe, Irving, and Ruth R. Wisse. *The Best of Sholom Aleichem*. New York: Washington Square Press, 1982.

The Jewish Encyclopedia. 13 vols. New York and London: Funk & Wagnalls, 1910.

Jewish Life and Times. Vol. 5. Winnipeg: Jewish Historical Society of Western Canada, 1988.

Kallen, Horace M. *Judaism at Bay: Essays Toward the Adjustment of Judaism to Modernity*. New York: Bloch, 1932.

–. "American Jews: What Now." *Jewish Social Services Quarterly* (Fall 1955): 12—29.

–. "Is There a Jewish View of Life." In Judah Pilch, ed., *Of Them Which Say They Are Jews*, pp., 104—06. New York: Bloch, 1932.

–. *Secularism Is the Will of God: An Essay in the Social Philosophy of Democracy and Religion*. New York: Twayne Publishers, 1954.

Kalmar, Ivan. *The Trotskys, the Freuds, and the Woody Allens*. Penguin Books Canada, 1993.

Kaplan, Mordecai M. *A New Zionism*. New York: Theodor Herzl Foundation, 1955.

–. *Questions Jews Ask*. New York: Reconstructionist Press, 1956.

–. *Judaism Without Supernaturalism: The Only Alternative to Orthodoxy and Secularism*. New York: Reconstructionist Press, 1958.

Kaufmann, Y. "The Biblical Age." In Leo W. Schwartz, ed., *Great Ages and Ideas of the Jewish People*, pp. 1—92.

Klein, Isaac, trans. *The Code of Maimonides, Book Four: The Book of Women*. Princeton: Yale University Press, 1972.

Kravitz, Nathaniel. *3000 Years of Hebrew Literature*. Chicago: Swallow Press, 1972.

Lacks, Roslyn. *Women and Judaism: Myth, History and Struggle*. New York: Doubleday, 1980.

Landman, Nathan M. "The Book of Esther as Delicious Dramatic Farce. *Humanistic Judaism* (Winter 1992): 17—18.

Levin, Nora. *The Holocaust*. New York: Thomas Crowell, 1973.

Lower, A.R.M. *Canadians in the Making*. Longmans Canada Ltd. 1766.

Lowin, Joseph. "Sukkot: A Traditional View." *Humanistic Judaism* (Summer 1990): 6—9.

BIBLIOGRAPHY

Lungen, Paul . "'Bureaucratic Roadblocks' Hinder Implementation of Continuity Report," *Canadian Jewish News*, 6 Nov. 1994, p. 2.

Maimonides, Moses. *The Guide for the Perplexed*. Trans. M. Friedlander. Pardes Publishing House, 1881. Chicago: University of Chicago Press, 1963.

Malamat, A. "Origins and Formative Period." In H.H. Ben-Sasson, ed., *A History of the Jewish People*, pp. 3—87.

Marcus, Jacob R. *Jews in the Medieval World*. New York: Atheneum/Jewish Publication Society, 1973.

–. *The American Jewish Woman*, 1654—1980. Cincinnati: Ktav, 1981.

Marcus, Ralph. "The Hellenistic Age." In Leo W. Schwartz, ed., *Great Ages and Ideas of the Jewish People*, 93—129. New York: Random House/Commentary, 1956.

Marrus, Michael R. *The Holocaust in History*. Markham, ON: Penguin Books.

Mazar, Benjamin, Moshe Davis, and Ch. H. Ben Sasson, eds. *Illustrated History of the Jews*. Israeli Publishing Institute, 1963.

Menkis, Richard. "Pre-Confederation Canada. In Alan Davies, ed., *Antisemitism in Canada*, pp. 11—38.

Mertl, Steve, and John Ward. *Keegstra: The Issues, the Trial, the Consquences*. Saskatoon: Western Producer Prairie Books, 1985.

Montefiore, C.G., and H. Loewe, eds. *A Rabbinic Anthology*. London: Macmillan, 1938.

Morgenstern, Julian. *As a Mighty Stream: The Progress of Judaism through History*. Philadelphia: Jewish Publication Society, 1949.

Morse, Arthur D. *While Six Million Died*. New York: Random House, 1967.

New Catholic Encyclopedia. New York: McGraw-Hill, 1967.

Parkes, James. *Antisemitism*. London: Valentine Mitchell, 1963.

Peltz, Rakhmiel. *Mama-Loshen–A History of Yiddish Culture*. New York: Columbia University Press/Congress of Secular Jewish Organizations.

Peretz, I.L. *In This World and the Next: Selected Writings of I. L. Peretz*. Trans. Moshe Spiegel. London: Thomas Yoseloff, 1958.

–. "What is this Jewish Heritage?" In Saul Goodman, ed., *The Faith of Secular Jews*, pp. 127—40. New York: Ktav, 1976.

Pilch, Judah, ed. *Of Them Which Say They Are Jews*. New York: Bloch, 1932.

Plaskow, Judith. "The Jewish Feminist: Conflict in Identities." In Elizabeth Koltun, *The Jewish Woman: New Perspectives*, pp. 3—10. New York: Schocken Books, 1976.

–. *Standing Again at Sinai*. San Francisco: HarperCollins, 1990.

Plaut, W. Gunther. *The Rise of Reform Judaism: A Sourcebook of its European Origins*. Preface by Solomon B. Freehof. New York: World Union for Progressive Judaism, 1963.

–. *Your Neighbour Is a Jew*. Toronto: McClelland and Stewart, 1965.

Richler, Mordecai. *This Year in Jerusalem*. Toronto: Knopf Canada, 1994.

Ringelblum, Emmanuel. *Notes from the Warsaw Ghetto*. Ed. and trans. by Jacob Sloan. New York: McGraw-Hill, 1958.

Rivkin, Ellis. *The Shaping of Jewish History*. New York: Scribner, 1971.

Rome, David. *The First Two Years: A Record of Jewish Pioneers on Canada's Pacific Coast*. Montreal: H.M. Caiserman, 1942.

Roskies, David G. *Against the Apocalypse: Responses to Catastrophe in Modern Jewish Culture*. Cambridge: Harvard University Press, 1984.

Roth, Cecil. *The History of the Jews of Italy*. Philadelphia: Jewish Publication Society, 1946.

–. *The Jews in the Renaissance*. New York: Harper Torchbooks, 1965.

–. *A Short History of the Jewish People*. Rev. ed. London: Hartmore House.

Roth, C., and Wigoder, G., eds. *New Standard Jewish Encyclopedia*. 4th ed. Garden City, NY: Doubleday, 1970. 5th ed. 1992, Wigoder, ed.

–. *Encyclopedia Judaica*. 16 vols. and 8 yearbooks. Jerusalem: Keter Publications, 1972.

Sachar, Howard M. History of Israel. Vol. 2, *From the Aftermath of the Yom Kippor War*. New York: Oxford 1987.

Sack, B.G. *History of the Jews in Canada*. Montreal: Harvest House, 1965.

Safrai, S. "The Era of the Mishnah and Talmud (70—640)." In H.H. Ben-Sasson, ed., *A History of the Jews*.

Sandrow, Nahma. *Vagabond Stars: A World History of Yiddish Theatre*. New York: Harper & Row/JPS, 1977.

Schauss, Hayyim. *The Jewish Festivals: History and Observance*. New York: Schocken Books, 1962.

Schneider, Susan Weidman. *Jewish and Female*. New York: Simon & Schuster, 1984.

"A Seder for Tu Bi-Shavet." *Humanistic Judaism* (Winter 1993): 39—43.

BIBLIOGRAPHY

Scholem, G. *Sabbetai Sevi, the Mystical Messiah*. Princeton University Press.

Schwartz, Leo W., ed. Great Ages and Ideas of the Jewish People. New York: Commentary/Random House, 1956.

Seforim, Mendele Mocher. *Travels of Benjamin III*. Trans. Moshe Spiegel. New York: Schocken, 1949.

Seltzer, Robert M. "Graetz, Dubnow, Baron: A Commemorative Essay." *Jewish Book Annual* 48 (1990—91): 169—82.

–. "History, Jewish Views." In *Encyclopedia of Religion*, vol. 6, pp. 390—94.

Shapiro, Judah J. "Zionism in America since the Establishment of the State." *Jewish Frontier* (May 1969): 13—17.

–. "Zionist Heresy and Secularity." *Insight, Official Publication of the Labor Zionist Movement of Canada*, Montreal, (September 1974): 7—8.

Shimoni, Y., and E. Levine, eds. *Political Dictionary of the Middle East.* Jerusalem: Jerusalem Publishing House, 1972.

Shneiderman, S.L. *The River Remembers*. New York: Horizon Press, 1978.

Sleeper, J.A., and A.L. Mintz (eds.). *The New Jews*. New York: Vintage Books.

Smillie, B.G., ed. *Visions of the New Jerusalem: Religious Settlement on the Prairies*. Edmonton: NeWest Publishers, 1983.

Steinberg, Milton. *As a Driven Leaf.* Indianapolis: Bobbs-Merrill, 1939; Northvale, NJ: Jason Aronson, 1987.

Stern, M. "The Period of the Second Temple." In H.H. Ben-Sasson, ed., *A History of the Jewish People*, pp. 185—303.

Suhl, Yuri, ed. and trans. *They Fought Back*. New York: Crown, 1967.

Sutzkever, Abraham. "Outlandish Words." In *The Fiddle Rose Poems 1970— 1972*. Trans. Ruth Whitman. Intro. by Ruth R. Wisse. Detroit: Wayne State University Press, 1990.

Swidler, Leonard. *Women in Judaism: The Status of Women in Formative Judaism*. Metuchin, NJ: Scarecrow Press, 1976.

Tadmor, H. "The Period of the First Temple: The Babylonian Exile and the Restoration. In H.H. Ben-Sasson, ed., *A History of the Jewish People*, 91—182. Cambridge: Harvard University Press, 1976.

Teubal, Savina J. *Sarah the Priestess*. Athens, OH: Swallow Press, 1984.

Trachtenberg, Josha. *The Devil and the Jews–The Medieval Conception of the Jews and Its Relation to Modern Anti-Semitism*. New York: Harper Torchbooks, 1943.

Trattner, Ernest R. *Understanding the Talmud*. New York: Nelson, 1955.

Tulchinsky, Gerald. "Goldwin Smith: Victorian Canadian Anti-Semite." In Alan Davies (ed.), *Antisemitism in Canada*, pp. 67—91.

Waddington, Alfred. *Fraser River Mines Vindicated*. Victoria, 1860.

Waife-Goldberg, Marie. *My Father Sholom Aleichem* New York: Simon and Shuster, 1960.

Wallerstein, E. "Circumcision and Anti-Semitism: An Update." *Humanistic Judaism* (Summer 1988): 43—44.

Ward, Barbara. *Faith and Freedom*. Garden City: Image Books, 1954.

–. *Spaceship Earth*. New York: Columbia University Press, 1966.

Waskow, Arthur. *Seasons of Our Joy*. Toronto: Bantam Books, 1982.

Weinmann, Gabriel, and Conrad Winn, *Hate on Trial: The Zundel Affair, the Media, and Public Opinion in Canada*, Mosaic Press, Oakville, ON; New York; London, 1986.

Weinreich, U. *Modern English-Yiddish Dictionary*. New York: YIVO/McGraw-Hill, 1968.

Wigoder, Geoffrey, ed. *Encyclopedia of Judaism*. New York: Macmillan, 1989.

Wine, Sherwin T. *The Real History of the Jews. Part 1. A History of the Jewish People from Early Times to the Maccabees*. Farmington Hills, MI: Society for Humanistic Judaism, undated.

–. *The Real Story of Passover*. Farmington Hills, MI: Society for Humanistic Judaism, *A Passover Manual*, undated.

—. Perspective, *Humanistic Judaism* (Winter 1981): pp. 22-25.

–. "Hannuka: How It Happened." *Humanistic Judaism* (Autumn 1983): 3—9.

–. "National Liberation: The Hannuka Question." *Humanistic Judaism* (Autumn 1993): 20—24.

–. "Symposium: Humanistic Judaism and God," *Humanistic Judaism* (Winter 1983): 26—30.

–. *Judaism Beyond God*. Farmington Hills, MI: Society for Humanistic Judaism, 1985.

–. "A Short Humanistic History of the High Holidays," *Humanistic Judaism* (Summer 1986):2—6.

–. "Circumcision." *Humanistic Judaism* (Summer 1988): 4—8.

–. "Tu-Bi-Shevat, Eart Day and Environmentalism." *Humanistic Judaism* (Winter 1993): 5—9.

Wirth, Louis. *The Ghetto*. Chicago: University of Chicago Press, 1962.

BIBLIOGRAPHY

Wischnitzer, Mark. *To Dwell in Safety: The Story of Jewish Migration Since 1800.* Philadelphia: Jewish Publication Society, 1948.

Yerushalmi, Yosef Hayim. *Zakhor: Jewish History and Jewish Memory.* Seattle and London: University of Washington Press, 1982.

Zborowski, M., and E. Herzog. *Life Is with People: The Culture of the Shtetl.* New York: Schocken, 1952.

Zirndorf, H. *Some Jewish Women.* Philadelphia: Jewish Publication Society, 1892.

Zuckoff, Aviva Cantor. "The Lilith Question." *Lilith Magazine,* vol. 1, no. 1 (Fall 1976): 5, 7, 9—10, 38.

INDEX

INDEX

T

INDEX

Tishri - seventh month on lunar calendar 143

Titus, Arch of 56

Torah, 182, 188-189,191, 206, 208, 268; canonized 49, 157; Scroll 58-59, 155; the Pentateuch, 68; authorship 156-157

Trattner, Ernest 98, 101

Turkish, Turkey, Constantinople, 219, 246-247

Tzedaka - justice 24

U

United Nations 249

United States, 38, 74, 220, 223

V

Vashti 173-174, 177

Vilna, Vilnius 134, 135, 235, 239-240

Vistula River 236

W

Ward, Barbara 147

Warsaw 215; Ghetto fighters, 181-182; ghetto uprising 232, 235, 239

Wasserman, Dora 82

Weizmann, Chaim 247

West Bank 250 255, 257, 259

Who is a Jew, 36-41, priests ruled on 113-114

Wigoder, Geoffrey 138

Wine, Rabbi Sherwin, 63, 108-109, 153, 172, 270

Wisse, Ruth 115

Wolf, Immanuel 30

Women, 86-109, 191, 196

Workmen's Circle, (Arbeiter Ring) 127

World War Two 181, 249, 256

World War One 246

Y

Yahveh 49-50, 52, 166, 176; Yahvistic period 86

Yavneh 28

Yerushalmi, Yosef Hayim 32-33 (see bibliography)

Yeshiva bocher (seminary student) 114, 194

Yiddish Scientific Institute (YIVO) 135

Yiddish, culture 236; first books 71; language 76, 78, 79-80; theatre 82; Irving Howe on 116-117; in Israel 119-120; secularism 124, 128; prayers for women 129; Yiddishism 83

Yishuv, Palestine Jewish Community 256

Yizkor (memorial prayer) 152

YMHA 13-16

Yom Kippur - Day of Atonement 13, 143, 149-154, 202; Yom Kippur War 255

Z

Zadokite priests 155, 164-166, 169

Zelophedad, five daughters of 98

Zeus 53, 166

Zhitlowsky, Chaim 124-125, 128-129, 269